1942

WILLIAM DWIGHT WHITNEY
LINGUISTIC SERIES

EDITED BY

FRANKLIN EDGERTON   ALBRECHT GOETZE
EDGAR H. STURTEVANT
of the Department of Linguistics in Yale University

❧

THE PRONUNCIATION

OF

GREEK AND LATIN

BY

EDGAR H. STURTEVANT

Second Edition

❧

PUBLISHED FOR
YALE UNIVERSITY
BY THE
LINGUISTIC SOCIETY OF AMERICA

SPECIAL PUBLICATIONS

OF THE

LINGUISTIC SOCIETY OF AMERICA

EDITED BY

BERNARD BLOCH
Brown University

HANS KURATH
Brown University

M. B. EMENEAU
University of California

URBAN T. HOLMES JR.
University of North Carolina

THE PRONUNCIATION

OF

GREEK AND LATIN

BY

EDGAR H. STURTEVANT

Professor of Linguistics in Yale University

SECOND EDITION

WILLIAM DWIGHT WHITNEY
LINGUISTIC SERIES

LINGUISTIC SOCIETY OF AMERICA

UNIVERSITY OF PENNSYLVANIA

PHILADELPHIA

1940

COMPOSED AND PRINTED BY THE
WAVERLY PRESS, INC.
BALTIMORE, MARYLAND

PREFACE

PREFACE

This new edition retains the general character of the original edition of my book on Greek and Latin pronunciation. The treatment has been kept as concise as possible. Evidence that appears to me to be inconclusive is usually not even mentioned. Rejected theories that have been refuted in print are ignored unless they are either of recent origin or appear to me to contain a part of the truth.

Nevertheless the revision has been very thorough. There are considerable changes on almost every page and many parts of the book have been completely rewritten, notably the chapters on accent and the treatment of the mutes, both Greek and Latin.

Much more use than before has been made of phonetic symbols, and a table of these is now included.

Paragraph numbers have been added, and cross references [in square brackets] are to these.

Greek loans from other languages are cited without accent marks, except a few common words.

I have tried to take account of suggestions made by reviewers of the first edition; but not all of these could be adopted. For example, several of my critics have thought that the material on the speech sounds should be grouped according to the phonetic (nowadays they would probably say phonemic) system of the languages, rather than according to the letters of the alphabet. They have not realized that the problem before us is precisely the interpretation of alphabetic symbols; our documents are recorded only by this means, and all our evidence is presented to us from the point of view of the written word. Our partial knowledge of Greek and Latin phonetics and phonemics consists of a tissue of inferences. It would not be desirable to take this for granted at the beginning of the argument.

Professor George Bechtel has been closely associated with me during the two years devoted to the task of revision. He wrote the first draft of several sections of the Latin chapters and of the introduction; and he has studied and discussed with me most of the problems that have arisen in connection with all parts of the book. I have profited at many points from his knowledge not only of Greek and Latin but also of the other languages that have been brought into the discussion. In particular his keen acumen in interpreting the ancient grammarians has been of service. Nevertheless the final wording is usually mine, and in case of disagreement I have made the final decision and must accept full responsibility.

The entire manuscript has been read by Professors Bernard Bloch, Franklin Edgerton, and Albrecht Goetze, and by Dr. George L. Trager, who have made many important suggestions and corrections. I am under obligations also to Professor Hans Kurath and Dr. Murray B. Emeneau for advice on matters of phonetics. Professor E. Adelaide Hahn has read the proof and has prevented a number of serious errors.

TABLE OF CONTENTS

INDEX OF ANCIENT AUTHORS

ABBREVIATIONS

1. BOOKS AND PERIODICALS

AJP = American Journal of Philology, founded by B. L. Gildersleeve. Baltimore.

ALL = Archiv für lateinische Lexikographie und Grammatik. 15 vols. Leipzig.

Ath. Mitt. = Archaeologisches Institut des Deutschen Reichs, Athenische Zweiganstalt. Mitteilungen. Berlin.

BCH = Bulletin de correspondance hellénique. Paris.

Blass = Friedrich Blass, Ueber die Aussprache des Griechischen. 3rd edition. Berlin. 1888.

Brugmann-Thumb = Karl Brugmann, Griechische Grammatik. 4th edition. Revised by Albert Thumb. Munich. 1913.

Buck = Carl D. Buck, Introduction to the Study of the Greek Dialects. Revised edition. Boston. 1928.

Buck, Gramm. = Carl D. Buck, A Grammar of Oscan and Umbrian. Boston. 1904. Additions and Corrections (pp. 353–71). 1928.

ByzZ = Byzantinische Zeitschrift. Leipzig.

CGL = Corpus Glossariorum Latinorum. 7 vols. Leipzig. 1888–1923.

CIG = Corpus Inscriptionum Graecarum. 4 vols. Berlin. 1827–77.

CIL = Corpus Inscriptionum Latinarum. Berlin.

Comp. Verb. = Dion. Hal., q.v.

CJ = The Classical Journal. Menasha, Wis.

CP = Classical Philology. Chicago.

CQ = Classical Quarterly. London.

CR = Classical Review. London.

Curt. Stud. = Georg Curtius, Studien zur griechischen und lateinischen Grammatik. 10 vols. Leipzig. 1868–78.

Dion. Hal. = Dionysius Halicarnassensis, De Compositione Verborum. Edd. Usener et Radermacher in Dionysii Halicarnasei Opusculis 2.1.1–143. Leipzig. 1894.

Dion. Hal., Ant. Rom. = Dionysius Halicarnassensis, Antiquitates Romanae.

Dion. Thr. = Dionysius Thrax, Ars Grammatica. Ed. G. Uhlig. Leipzig. 1883.

Dittenberger, Sylloge³ = Wilhelm Dittenberger, Sylloge Inscriptionum Graecarum. 3rd edition. Leipzig. 1915–24.

Edict. Diocl. = Edictum Diocletiani de Pretiis Rerum Venalium, CIL 3 Suppl. 1. pp. 1909–53.

Eph. Arch. = Ἐφημερὶς Ἀρχαιολογική. Athens.

Eph. Ep. = Ephemeris Epigraphica, Corporis Inscriptionum Latinarum Supplementum. Berlin.

Gardner, Indian Coins = Percy Gardner, The Coins of the Greek and Scythic Kings of Bactria and India in the British Museum. London. 1886.

Gött. Nachr. = Nachrichten von der kgl. Gesellschaft der Wissenschaften zu Göttingen, Philologisch-historische Klasse.

Grandgent = C. H. Grandgent, An Introduction to Vulgar Latin. Boston. 1907.

GS = M. Terenti Varronis de Lingua Latina quae Supersunt. Edd. Georg. Goetz et Friedric. Schoell. Leipzig. 1910.

Hammer, Roman. Lautwandlungen = Hammer, Die lokale Verbreitung frühester romanischer Lautwandlungen im alten Italien. Halle. 1894.

Hatzidakis, Ἀναγνώσματα = Hatzidakis, Ἀκαδημεϊκὰ ἀναγνώσματα εἰς τὴν Ἑλληνικὴν, Λατινικὴν, καὶ μικρὸν εἰς τὴν Ἰνδικὴν γραμματικήν. 2 vols. Athens. 1902. (I have not seen the second edition, published 1924–30.)

ICUR = Giovanni de Rossi, Inscriptiones Christianae Urbis Romae Septimo Saeculo Antiquiores; Vol. 1. Rome. 1861.

IF = Indogermanische Forschungen. Berlin and Leipzig.

IG = Inscriptiones Graecae. Berlin. IG 1², 2² = Inscriptiones Graecae, editio minor.

IGRRP = Inscriptiones Graecae ad Res Romanas Pertinentes. Paris.

J of Ph. = Journal of Philology. London.

K = Grammatici Latini. Ed. Heinrich Keil. 7 vols. Leipzig. 1857–88.

Krauss, Lehnwörter = Samuel Krauss, Griechische und lateinische Lehnwörter im Talmud, Midrasch, und Targum. 2 vols. Berlin. 1898–9.

Kretschmer, Einl. = Paul Kretschmer, Einleitung in die Geschichte der griechischen Sprache. Göttingen. 1896.

Kretschmer, Vaseninschriften = Paul Kretschmer, Die griechischen

Vaseninschriften ihrer Sprache nach untersucht. Gütersloh. 1894.

KZ = Zeitschrift für vergleichende Sprachforschung. Göttingen.

Lang. = Language, journal of the Linguistic Society of America. Philadelphia and Baltimore.

Laum, Al. Akzent. = Bernhard Laum, Das alexandrinische Akzentuations-system unter Zugrundelegung der theoretischen Lehren der Grammatiker und Heranziehung der praktischen Verwendung der Papyri. Paderborn. 1928.

Leumann = Stolz-Schmalz, Lateinische Grammatik in fünfter Auflage völlig neu gearbeitet von Manu Leumann und J. B. Hofmann; Laut- und Formenlehre, pp. 1–344. Munich. 1928.

Lindsay = Wallace M. Lindsay, The Latin Language. Oxford. 1894.

M = C. Lucilii Carminum Reliquiae. Recensuit enarravit Fridericus Marx. Leipzig. 1904–5.

Mayser = Edwin Mayser, Grammatik der griechischen Papyri aus der Ptolemäerzeit; Lautlehre, Vol. 1, pp. 1–248. Leipzig. 1906.

Meinersmann = Bernhard Meinersmann, Die lateinischen Wörter und Namen in den griechischen Papyri = Studien zur Epigraphik und Papyruskunde 1.1. Leipzig. 1927.

Meisterhans-Schwyzer = K. Meisterhans, Grammatik der attischen Inschriften. 3rd edition by Eduard Schwyzer. Berlin. 1900.

MSL = Mémoires de la Société de Linguistique de Paris. Paris.

Niedermann = Max Niedermann, Précis de phonétique historique du latin. Paris. 1931.

PAPA = Proceedings of the American Philological Association. Swarthmore, Pa.

P. Berl. = Aegyptische Urkunden aus den königlichen Museen zu Berlin; griechische Urkunden. Berlin.

P. Eud. = Eudoxi Ars Astronomica, qualis in charta Aegyptiaca superest. Ed. Friedrich Blass. Kiel. 1887.

P. Grenf. 1 = P. B. Grenfell, An Alexandrian Erotic Fragment and Other Greek Papyri Chiefly Ptolemaic. Oxford. 1896.

P. Grenf. 2 = Grenfell and Arthur S. Hunt, New Classical Fragments and Other Greek and Latin Papyri. Oxford. 1897.

P. Leid. = C. Leemans, Papyri Graeci Musei Antiquarii Publici Lugduni-Batavi, vol. 1. Leiden. 1843.

P. Lond. = F. G. Kenyon, Greek Papyri in the British Museum. London.

P. Oxy. = The Oxyrhynchos Papyri. London.

P. Petr. = John P. Mahaffy, The Flinders Petrie Papyri with Transcriptions, Commentaries, etc. Two parts and appendix. Dublin. 1891–4.

P. Petr.[2] = Mahaffy and J. Gilbart Smyly, On the Flinders Petrie Papyri with Transcriptions, Commentaries, and Index. Dublin. 1905.

P. Rev. L. = Grenfell, Revenue Laws of Ptolemy Philadelphus. Oxford. 1896.

P. Tebt. = The Tebtunis Papyri. London.

P. Weil = Henri Weil, Un papyrus inédit de la bibliothèque de M. Ambroise Firmin-Didot = Monuments grecs publiés par l'association pour l'encouragement des études grecques en France, 8 (1879).

Phil. = Philologus, Zeitschrift für das klassische Altertum. Göttingen and Leipzig.

Priene = Hiller von Gaertringen, Inschriften von Priene. Berlin. 1906.

Prinz = Otto Prinz, De o et u Vocalibus inter se Permutatis in Lingua Latina Quaestiones Epigraphicae, Halis Saxonum. 1932.

R = O. Ribbeck, Scaenicae Romanorum Poesis Fragmenta. Ed. 2. Leipzig. 1871–3.

REL = Revue des études latines. Paris.

RhM = Rheinisches Museum für Philologie. Bonn.

RLR = Revue des langues romanes. Montpellier.

Rom. Forsch. = Romanische Forschungen. Erlangen.

Schol. Dion. Thr. = Scholia in Dionysii Thracis Artem Grammaticam. Rec. Alfredus Hilgard. Leipzig. 1901.

Schuchardt = Hugo Schuchardt, Der Vokalismus des Vulgärlateins. 3 vols. Leipzig. 1866–8.

Seelmann = Emil Seelmann, Die Aussprache des Latein nach physiologisch-historischen Grundsätzen. Heilbronn. 1885.

SGDI = Hermann Collitz und Fritz Bechtel, Sammlung der griechischen Dialektinschriften. 4 vols. Göttingen. 1883–1915.

Sommer = Ferdinand Sommer, Handbuch der lateinischen Laut- und Formenlehre. 2nd edition. Heidelberg. 1914.

Sturtevant, Contraction = E. H. Sturtevant, Contraction in the Caseforms of the Latin io- and iā-stems and of deus, is, and īdem. Chicago. 1902.

TAPA = Transactions of the American Philological Association. Philadelphia.

TPhS = Transactions of the Philological Society. London.

Thumb, Hellenismus = Albert Thumb, Die griechische Sprache im Zeitalter des Hellenismus. Strassburg. 1901.

UPZ = Urkunden der Ptolemäerzeit (ältere Funde) herausgegeben von U. Wilcken. Berlin and Leipzig.

V = J. Vahlen, Ennianae Poesis Reliquiae. 2nd edition. Leipzig. 1903.

Väänänen = Veikko Väänänen, Le latin vulgaire des inscriptions pompéiennes. Helsinki. 1937.

Varro, LL = M. Terentius Varro, De Lingua Latina. Quotations from Books 5–10 are given according to Kent (Varro on the Latin Language with an English Translation, 2 vols., Cambridge, Mass., 1938).

Vendryes = J. Vendryes, Recherches sur l'histoire et les effets de l'intensité initiale en latin. Paris. 1902.

Walde = Alois Walde, Lateinisches etymologisches Wörterbuch. 2nd edition. Heidelberg. 1910.

Walde-Hofmann = Alois Walde, Lateinisches etymologisches Wörterbuch. 3rd edition by J. B. Hofmann. Vol. 1. Heidelberg. 1938.

2. LANGUAGES AND DIALECTS

Arm. = Armenian	Lat. = Latin
Att. = Attic	Lith. = Lithuanian
Av. = Avestan	Log. = Logudorian
Dor. = Doric	OE = Old English
Eng. = English	OFr. = Old French
Fr. = French	OIr. = Old Irish
Germ. = German(ic)	ON = Old Norse
Gk. = Greek	OP = Old Persian
Goth. = Gothic	Osc. = Oscan
Hitt. = Hittite	Port. = Portuguese
IE = Primitive Indo-European	Rum. = Rumanian
IH = Primitive Indo-Hittite	Skt. = Sanskrit
It. = Italian	Sp. = Spanish

Umbr. = Umbrian

PHONETIC SYMBOLS[1]

	Similar to	Written in[2] Greek	Latin
ɑ	Eng. *f*ather		a
a	Fr. *patte*	α	
b	Eng. *b*ase	β	b
β	Sp. aca*b*ar, S. Germ. *w*as	β	b, v
ç	Germ. i*ch*		
d	Fr. *d*ent	δ	d
ε	Fr. *tê*te	η	e
e	Fr. *été*	ε, ει	e
ẹ	fn. 3		e, ei
f	Fr. *f*in	φ	f
φ	fn. 4	φ	f
g	Eng. *g*o	γ	g
ǥ	North Germ. Wa*g*en	γ	
h	Eng. *h*and	η, ʼ, θ, φ, χ	h
ʽ	fn. 5	β, γ, δ	
ɪ	fn. 6		i
i	Fr. f*i*ni	ι, ει, η, etc.	i, ei
j	Eng. *y*ou	γ	i, g
k	Fr. *c*ou	κ, ϙ, ξ	c, k, q, x
l	Fr. *l*a	λ	l
ḷ	Fr. peup*l*e	λh	

[1] Since our knowledge of ancient pronunciation is at best only approximate, these symbols, as used in this book, must not be given as precise an interpretation as is usual in books on the pronunciation of a modern language.

[2] I have included here not only an outline of standard ancient orthography but also an indication of variant spellings that have been current for longer or shorter periods. Details can be found by consulting the paragraphs dealing with the various letters.

[3] See [120].

[4] The voiceless bilabial fricative [φ] is rarely heard in Western Europe. Jespersen, Lehrbuch der Phonetik[2] 132, cites it as a variant for [β] in Germ. *Qual*, etc.

[5] A weaker puff of breath than that denoted by [h].

[6] In this book [ɪ] is used for a relatively open *i*, which may or may not have been laxly articulated, as *i* in Eng. *pin*.

ł	Eng. bulk	λ	l
λ	Sp. villa		
m	Eng. mix	μ	m
m̥	fn. 7	μh	
n	Fr. nous	ν	n
ŋ	Eng. sing	γ, ν	n
ɔ	Germ. Gott	ω	o
o	Fr. rose, Germ. Rose	o, ου	o
p	Fr. peau	π	p
q	fn. 8		qu
r	It. re	ρ	r
ŗ	Rural Fr. quatre	ρ̇	
s	Fr. sel	σ	s, ti, z
š	Eng. shoe		
t	Fr. tort	τ	t
θ	Eng. thin	θ	
ʊ	Germ. dumm		u
u	Fr. route, Germ. du	υ, ου, αυ, ευ	u
v	Fr. vin	β	b, v
w	Eng. we	ϝ	u
w̥	fn. 9	ϝh	
x	Germ. ach	η, χ	
y	Fr. pur	υ	y
z	Fr. zone	σ, ζ	s, z, di
ž	Eng. pleasure		

Vowel length is indicated by a raised dot after the symbol, e.g. [a·].

[7] A voiceless m; cf. [ŗ], [ļ], [w̥].
[8] See [193 d].
[9] A voiceless w; cf. [m̥], [ŗ], [ļ].

CHAPTER I

THE NATURE AND VALUE OF THE EVIDENCE

1. The original clue to the speech-sounds of Greek and Latin—the starting-point of our knowledge of the subject—is tradition. Both languages have been in use constantly from ancient times to the present, and each generation of scholars has passed on to the next, without intentional change (except in modern times), the pronunciation which it received from its predecessors. In spite of numerous divergences, the tradition of scholars in all parts of the world is harmonious in regard to a majority of the features of Greek and Latin pronunciation. For example, Latin *s* and Greek *σ* are traditionally pronounced as sibilants everywhere; and Greek *κ* and Latin *c* are voiceless sounds in the speech of all scholars. This tradition of the schools, then, forms the historical basis of our knowledge.

Yet the very fact that scholars in different lands pronounce Greek and Latin differently proves that the tradition of the schools is fallible. Except for some wholly inadequate reforms in modern times, scholars everywhere usually follow their native articulation habits in speaking these languages. In fact the pronunciation of Greek and Latin has in each country tended to change along with changes in vernacular pronunciation, except as the former has been held in check by the unchanging orthography.

2 a. Again, Latin after the Classical period never ceased to be spoken by the great mass of the people. It gradually underwent such changes, however, (differing in different parts of the Roman world) that it came eventually to be no longer considered the same language, but a group of new languages. Now even if there were no remains of ancient Latin whatever, it would still be possible to work back from the various Romance dialects by the comparative method, and so to determine what the parent language was like just before the separation of the dialects. This reconstruction of "Vulgar Latin" has been done, and while the result is by no means identical with Classical Latin, it is appreciably closer to it than even the oldest recorded forms of the Romance languages. It remains to bridge, by other evidence, the comparatively small gap between reconstructed late popular Latin and the Latin of the Classical period.

21

For example, the word for 'time', French *temps*, Spanish *tiempo*, Italian and Portuguese *tempo*, Rumanian *timp*, has as its initial sound an unvoiced dental stop [t] in every case.   Hence we reconstruct the word with initial *t*, and this agrees exactly with the traditionally preserved Latin *tempus*.   Latin *t*, then, was probably an unvoiced dental stop.   Further, the Romance languages agree in making the sound unaspirated; hence this was probably the value of the Latin phoneme.

2 b. The same methods that enable us to reconstruct the ancestor of the Romance languages enable us also to go backward from all the languages of the Indo-European family, of which Latin is one, and reconstruct their prehistoric ancestor.   We cannot always say with certainty just what the phonetic value of a given Primitive Indo-European phoneme was, but we can often approximate it, and this gives us a chance to approach the sounds of Latin from the opposite direction.   For example, the sound written in Latin as *t* is etymologically equivalent to a sound which in most of the cognate languages is a voiceless dental stop, and which we reconstruct as Primitive Indo-European *t*.   This is the same sound which persisted into the Romance languages, and in the absence of evidence to the contrary we infer that it remained the same throughout the Latin period.

3 a. The Romans borrowed their alphabet either directly or indirectly from the Greeks.   It is reasonable to assume that they represented each of their native phonemes by the letter that stood for the most similar phoneme in the language from which they borrowed the alphabet.   We can thus employ our knowledge of how the letters were pronounced in Greek, to infer approximately what their values were in Latin.   Thus Greek τ is an unvoiced dental stop.   This value agrees with the other evidence we have cited for Latin *t*.

3 b. Words are frequently borrowed from one language into another, and in such cases they naturally assume a phonetic form in the new language as near to the original as the speech habits permit.   By a study of such borrowings we can often, from our knowledge of the sounds of one of the languages concerned, derive information as to those of the other.   For example, if a sound x in a given language A is regularly represented in another language B by a sound y, this does not necessarily mean that x and y are identical, but it does mean that y is more nearly like x than any other phoneme in language B, and this information may be useful.   On the other hand, if a phoneme x in A is represented in B sometimes by a sound y, sometimes by a sound z, we may assume that x was somewhere between y and z, so that to the speakers of B it sounded sometimes like the one, sometimes like the other; we may thus infer the approximate value of x.   It must not be forgotten, however, that, with certain exceptions (e.g. [127–129]), new phonemes are not introduced into a language by borrowing.   English loans from German do not introduce the German umlauted vowels into the language; and consequently a scholar who knew English but not German could never learn the value of German *ü* from any one American pronunciation of the name *Kühner*.   Just so we cannot learn the value of Lat. *v* from its early transliteration by Greek *β*; the truth is simply that prior to the second century A.D. Attic and Hellenistic Greek had no sound similar to Lat. *v* [95].

3 c. A very large number of Latin words have been taken over into every language of modern Europe, but as most of these are medieval or modern borrowings, they reflect only the medieval or modern pronunciation of Latin and are valueless for our present purposes.   There are a few words, however, which were taken over into the Celtic or Germanic languages at a very early date, and these sometimes tell us a great deal.   For example, the English word *street*, Old English *strǣt*, is from Latin (*via*) *strāta*, and goes back at least to the Roman occupation of Britain.   Now, except for the vowels, the English sounds correspond rather closely to what we assume on other grounds was the ancient pronunciation; in the case of the second *t*, English has preserved the ancient sound better than most of the Romance languages, since even Italian *strada* has voiced it to *d* (though Sicilian has *strata*).   More important is the evidence for the vowel, since comparison of the Germanic languages shows that OE *ǣ* is from long *ā*, and neither the popular tradition of the Romance languages nor the scholarly tradition would tell us anything as to the quantity of the vowel.

The most abundant evidence from borrowed words is, of course, presented by those borrowed from Latin into Greek and from Greek into Latin.   These occur, not only in literary texts, but also in great numbers in inscriptions and papyri.   It is important to distinguish between popular and learned borrowings.   Since the former are based on sound, the latter to a large extent on spelling, we are in danger of being misled by precisely the most common and regular method of transcription.

4. While it is tradition which enables us to translate into sound the written documents of antiquity, ancient orthography itself frequently corrects or supplements the tradition.   The substitution of Greek *φ* for *π* before a rough breathing (ἐφ᾽ ᾧ, ἀφ᾽ οὗ) is one of several proofs that Greek *φ* really denoted *π* followed by a puff of breath [90 i].

A change in the approved orthography indicates a change in pronunciation, although the change in pronunciation may have occurred long before the change in orthography. The Latin diphthong *ai* began to be written *ae* about 200 B.C. [130]; early Latin *quoius, quoi, quom* became *cuius, cui, cum* [124, 143, 144 a]. Such changes of spelling occur only when the old spelling has ceased to be phonetic.

In case a change in pronunciation is not reflected in standard orthography, it is often betrayed by mistakes in spelling. The confusion of Latin *ae* and *e* in carelessly written inscriptions of the first century A.D. indicates that *ae* had ceased to be a diphthong in the poorer quarters of Rome and Pompeii [132].

5. The Greeks and Romans have left us a large body of grammatical literature, in which pronunciation is a frequent topic, and there are besides many chance references to pronunciation in the ancient literatures. A very few of the ancient descriptions of sounds are quite clear and satisfactory. Marius Victorinus says: "Putting the lower lip against the upper teeth, with the tongue bent back toward the top of the palate, we will pronounce *f* with a smooth breath." A modern phonetician could add little of real importance to this [188 a].

As an example of unsatisfactory phonetic description, from which, nevertheless, something may be learned, we may take this from Varro: "One should know that the voice, like every body, has three dimensions, height, thickness, and length. We measure length by time and syllables; for it is important to distinguish how much time is taken in pronouncing words, and how many and what sort of syllables each word has. Accent marks the distinction of height, when a part of a word is lowered to the grave accent or raised to the acute. Thickness, however, depends upon the breath (whence the Greeks call breathings rough and smooth); for we make all words either thicker by pronouncing them with aspiration or thinner by pronouncing them without aspiration." Absurd as the comparison is, we learn that Latin accent was, in part, a matter of pitch [212], and that by "long syllables" the Romans meant syllables that require a relatively long time to pronounce them.

Sometimes a grammatical discussion which is not primarily devoted to pronunciation yields valuable information. That Latin *eu* was a true diphthong appears from Agroecius' semantic distinctions between *eo, eho, heu,* and *eu*; he evidently regards them as homonyms [140].

Catullus' famous epigram on Arrius proves that *h* initial and *h* after mutes were similar, and that in both positions the sound was used by the educated, neglected by the uneducated, and incorrectly used by the half-educated [183].

5 a. The direct testimony of the ancient writers has two serious defects.   There were no trained phoneticians in antiquity, and consequently there was no altogether trustworthy observation and scarcely any exact description of speech-sounds.   Only an untrained observer would have failed to detect, or an unscientific writer to record, the element of stress in the Latin accent [207–10].   The difference in place of articulation between Latin *d* and *t*, which Terentianus Maurus and Marius Victorinus imply, must be illusory [195].   Furthermore, the professional grammarians were so fond of constructing systems that the requirements of a theory were likely to blind them to the data of observation.   Varro, 200.12 GS, allowed theoretic considerations (combined with Greek tradition) to convince him that *h* was not a letter!

Ancient, even more than modern, scholars were prone to repeat the statements of their predecessors without sufficient criticism.   Thus many a description of sound was reproduced in the grammars and taught in the schools long after it had ceased to correspond with actual usage. The Greek grammarians continued to ascribe breath to the rough breathing after the total loss of the sound, much as contemporary French grammarians speak of "*h* aspirée."   The same fault sometimes led the Roman grammarians falsely to ascribe to Latin features which their Greek predecessors had observed in the pronunciation of Greek. Thus Priscian, 2.20.9–14 K, tells us that Latin *b*, *d*, and *g* had more aspiration than *p*, *t*, and *c*.

It follows that statements which are inconsistent with grammatical tradition are in general more reliable than those which may be purely imitative.   We cannot doubt Sextus Empiricus' assertion that the sound of $\alpha\iota$ was not diphthongal [49]; and the description by Roman grammarians of Latin $\bar{o}$ as a close *o* gains in credibility from the fact that Greek ω was an open *o* [46].

5 b. The testimony of the ancients is usually of value in proportion as the phenomena reported are concrete and easy to observe.   No scholar would doubt that *ss* after long vowels and diphthongs was simplified, at least in spelling, between the time of Vergil and Quintilian, even if we had no evidence but the following:

Quintilian 1.7.20:[1] Quid quod Ciceronis temporibus paulumque infra, fere quotiens *s* littera media vocalium longarum vel subiecta longis esset, geminabatur, ut *caussae, cassus, divissiones*; quomodo et ipsum et Vergilium quoque scripsisse manus eorum docent.

---

[1] 'Besides, in Cicero's time and a little later, when *s* stood between or after long vowels it was usually doubled, e.g., *caussae, cāssus, dīvīssiōnēs*; that Cicero himself and Vergil also wrote this way, their autograph manuscripts show.'

Of equal value is Cicero's testimony in regard to aspiration after mutes in Latin [183].   On the other hand, the various attempts to give acoustic descriptions of speech-sounds can scarcely be understood, and they probably meant very little even to their authors; such terms as *pinguis* and *tenuis*, as applied to Latin vowels, may have served no higher purpose than to conceal ignorance.

5 c. Certain of the ancient writers are very much better witnesses than others.   In general we should prefer those who had high ability, good education, and an interest in language, but no motive for reducing language to a system.   Probably Cicero, Quintilian, and Dionysius of Halicarnassus are our best witnesses, while in the second rank may be placed Aristotle, Dionysius of Thrace, and Varro.   For late Latin we have one witness who may fairly be called a phonetician, Terentianus Maurus, who probably wrote during the second half of the second century A.D.

6. Ancient etymologies are sometimes instructive although almost always foolish.   When Priscian, 2.18.9 f. K, derived *caelebs* from *caelestium vītam dūcēns*, he must have pronounced *b* and *v* alike.   Plato derives ἡμέρα from ἵμερος, and says that η was substituted for ι because it was a more impressive sound; it follows that η and ι differed in sound [25].

7. Occasionally cries of animals are represented by speech-sounds. The Greek comic poets spelled the cry of a sheep βῆ βῆ.   This cannot be read in the modern Greek fashion [vi·vi·], nor yet with a close *e*-sound [be·be·]; it might be read with the vowel either of English *far* or of English *care* [23].

8. Verse often furnishes evidence concerning pronunciation, particularly in regard to syllabification and quantity.   Latin versification shows that in *nunciam* consonantal *i* became a vowel, while in Ennius' quadrisyllabic *īnsidiantēs* and Vergil's trisyllabic *fluviōrum* vocalic *i* became a consonant.   These and similar forms are evidence that the two sounds were fairly close together; that is, consonantal *i* was a semivowel rather than a spirant [158].   A final vowel before *huic* is elided in verse; therefore the digraph *ui* does not begin with a consonant; the Romans certainly did not say [hwi·k] [144 d].   In Greek verse αυ and ευ are scanned long even before vowels; therefore we cannot read them in the modern Greek fashion as [αv, εv] [55, 56].

9. Our scanty knowledge of Greek music has contributed one or two scraps of evidence in regard to the nature of the Greek accent.   In the Delphic hymns that have been recovered, an unaccented syllable is usually not sung on a note higher than the accented syllable of the same word. We infer that Greek accent was a matter of pitch rather than of stress [103].

10. There are several ways, aside from orthography, in which we may learn that two Greek or Latin words contained similar or identical sounds, although none of them have contributed so much to our knowledge as have the rimes of Chaucer and Shakespeare. In the case of English rime we know just where the corresponding sounds should appear, and we know approximately what degree of similarity is necessary. Ancient alliterations and puns were bound by no such rules; we are in constant danger of finding alliteration where none was intended, and of overlooking the genuine cases on account of our faulty pronunciation, while no man can say just how much similarity of sound is required for a pun. Under these circumstances we should attach little weight to an alliteration unless it occurs several times, or to an isolated pun. For example, *volt* and *voltis* are several times in the early poets joined with words like *vōs*, *voster*, and *voluptās*, which certainly contained initial *vo*; this is evidence that *volt* had not yet become *vult*. On the other hand Plautus' (Rud. 767) pun on *ignem magnum* and *inhūmānum*, since it stands alone, is at best a very weak argument that we should pronounce *g* before *n* as a velar nasal. It sometimes happens that a scrap of evidence of this kind is canceled by similar evidence on the other side of the question. Plautus' pun on *socius* and *Sōsia* (Amph. 383), which has been thought to indicate the pronunciation *sosius*,[2] is neutralized by the pun on *arcem* and *arcam* (Bacch. 943).

A misunderstanding indicates similarity between two words or sentences, as when Marcus Crassus understood a street vendor's cry *Cauneās* "(Figs) from Caunus" as *cavē nē eās*. *Cavē*, then, can scarcely have contained a spirant [151], and the vowel of *nē* must have been elided.

Occasionally we have other indications of identity or likeness of sound. Since the names of other Greek letters contain the sound represented, it is safe to argue that *εἶ* and *οὖ* the ancient names of *ε* and *o*, were monophthongs of the same quality as *ε* and *o* [29, 44].

11. Every language shows a certain amount of harmony in its system of sounds, and if one sound in a language is modified in a given way all similar sounds in that language are likely to be modified in the same way. Thus most French vowels are articulated farther forward in

[2] Possibly Plautus was burlesquing the Umbrian palatalization of *k* before *e* and *i*, which he certainly knew by virtue of his Umbrian birth.

the mouth than are the English vowels which most nearly resemble them. English *t* is formed with the tip of the tongue against the upper gum, and so are *d*, *n*, *l*, *s*, and *z*. In French the corresponding sounds are formed with the tip of the tongue against the teeth. In English both long vowels of medium openness [e·, o·] have become diphthongs [ej, ow], and the close long vowels [i·, u·] have become diphthongs in the south of England [ij, uw] and elsewhere.

Having discovered, therefore, that Latin *ē* was closer than *ĕ*, we expect to find *ō* closer than *ŏ* [123]. Terentianus Maurus describes the position of *d* quite clearly as a dental; we therefore assume that *t* was a dental, although his description of that sound suggests rather an alveolar [195]. The fact that the Romans did not represent Greek φ by *f* shows that the two sounds differed. It is a probable inference that θ was not like English *th* nor χ like German *ch* [90 k]. In Attic and Ionic of the fifth century B.C. the original diphthong ει and the lengthened ε (sometimes called in our grammars the improper diphthong) were identical in sound. Since the general tendency of the Greek language is toward the simplification of diphthongs, it is more likely that the diphthong had become a long close *e* than that the lengthened ε had become a diphthong [21, 23].

12. Of very great importance is the evidence furnished by phonetic change. Since, as far as our knowledge goes, only languages with a strong stress accent are subject to extensive loss of unaccented vowels, the extensive syncope of prehistoric Latin is strong evidence for a stress accent resting upon the only syllable of the word which never shows syncope, namely the first [207 a]. Upon the loss of a short vowel by syncope consonantal *u* became the second member of a diphthong in *fautor* : *faveō*, *lautus* : *lavō*, *naufragus* : *nāvis*, etc. It is therefore probable that consonantal *u* was [w] rather than [β] or [v] [150]. The product of the contraction of two vowels must, if a monophthong, be identical in quality with one of the two, or else intermediate between them. Since, therefore, ε + ε = ει, ει must have the same quality as ε. The contraction of ε + α to η presents a more complicated problem; η cannot be equivalent to *ā*, because these sounds are consistently distinguished in writing; it cannot be equivalent to long ε, because, as we have just shown, long ε is written ει, and ει is not confused with η in early inscriptions. Therefore η must be intermediate between ε and α; it must be a relatively open *e* and ε a relatively close *e*. It follows also that ει is a relatively close long *e* [20–23].

13. In combining and interpreting the several items of evidence as to any sound, two principles must be constantly borne in mind.   In the first place, most of the available evidence falls short of definite proof; it is therefore important to gather every scrap of evidence upon each point.   In other words the force of our evidence is cumulative; while it might be possible to doubt the validity of each item taken separately, the inference from all the items combined is in many cases practically certain.

14. In the second place, we must never neglect chronology.   The prehistoric phonetic change of *favitor* to *fautor* is valid evidence on the nature of consonantal *u* in prehistoric Latin.   Crassus' misunderstanding of *Cauneās* as *cavē nē eās* throws light upon the pronunciation of the Ciceronian period; Priscian's connection of *caelibem* with *vītam* shows that *v* had become a spirant by the sixth century A.D.   Even if we had no conflicting evidence from Plautus himself, it would be impossible to argue from the pun on *socius* and *Sōsia* that *c* before *e* and *i* was already a sibilant; for, aside from possible alliterations in Ps.-Quintilian and Ausonius,[3] and an isolated form in an inscription of 392 A.D., there is no other evidence of a sibilant element in *c* until the sixth century.   Even then we have to assume an affricate [ts] or [tš]; the pure *s*, which some would read in Plautus' *socius*, did not exist in such words even in the earliest French, and it has not yet developed in the Italian of the twentieth century.

15. The available evidence does not permit us to do more than determine the approximate pronunciation of Greek and Latin.   We can show that Latin *ē* was closer than *ĕ*, and that Greek *η* was more open than *ε*; but we cannot tell how great the interval between the two members of each pair was.   We have no means of knowing whether or not Latin *ĕ* and Greek *η* were identical in quality, or whether Latin *ĕ* was equivalent to English *e* in *men* or to French *è* or whether it differed from them both.

When, therefore, it is stated in the following pages that a given ancient sound was "similar to" a given modern sound, that phrase must not be interpreted as meaning "identical with."

[3] See Hey, ALL, 14.112; Becker, ibid., 15.146.

CHAPTER II

THE GREEK VOWELS

A

16. In Modern Greek α has approximately the sound of *a* in English *father*. Such a value is indicated for Ancient Greek also by the correspondence with Latin *a* [111], and similarly by Greek loan-words in other languages (Skt. *āpoklima-* for the astrological term ἀπόκλιμα[1]; Goth. *alabalstraún, apaústaúlus* for ἀλάβαστρον, ἀπόστολος; Arm. *p'aɫarik* for φαλαρίς), and by foreign loan-words in Greek (Ἄριοι, Δαρεῖος for OP *Ariyā, Dārayavahuš*; βραχμανες, Γαγγης, Γανδαραι or Γανδαριοι for Indic *brahmānas, Gaṅgā, Gandhārās*).

In several dialects and at various times Greek α changed, under certain conditions, in the direction of [e]. In prehistoric Ionic-Attic ā became η. A shift of α toward [e] is indicated for Elean by the fact that original η was often written α and by the change of original ε to α before and after ρ and before final ν. Other West Greek dialects also show α for ε before ρ. In Attic-Ionic α + ε contracts into ā while α + ο yields ω (ἐτιμᾶτο : ἐτιμῶντο), and this indicates that at the time of the contraction α inclined toward [e] rather than toward [o]. (Other dialects, however, show η from α + ε.) The Hellenistic and later change of αι to [ε] [49] was never matched by a change of αυ to [ɔ], and this again suggests that α was nearer to [e] than to [o]. Since there is no conflicting evidence, it seems probable that α, at least in Attic-Ionic, West Greek, and Hellenistic, was more like French *a* in *patte* and *part* than in *pas* and *pâte*.

While long and short α sometimes underwent dissimilar changes, there is no clear evidence that they differed in quality.

Ancient Gk. ă was apparently [a] and ā [aˑ].

I

17. While in Modern Greek ι, η, ει, οι, υ, and υι all have the same value (approximately that of *i* in English *machine*), they are, with

[1] Wackernagel, Altindische Grammatik 1.3. The frequent use of Skt. *a*, a considerably closer vowel than *ā*, for Greek short α is natural enough, but it is not significant for our purpose.

certain exceptions to be noted below, kept quite distinct in ancient orthography. Furthermore each of them has different correspondences in the related languages; e.g. ἴδμεν : Lat. *video*; ἔθηκα : Lat. *fēcī*; δείξω : Osc. *deicum*, Lat. *dīcere*; οἰνή : Lat. *ūnus* (earlier *oino*); ὗς : Lat. *sūs*; ἰδυίας : Skt. *vidúṣyās* (-νι- from Pre-Gk. *-usy-*). There can be no doubt, then, that our six letters and digraphs originally denoted as many phonemes.

As to ι alone among these phonemes Modern Greek and etymological considerations are in harmony. Gk. ι, furthermore, usually corresponds to *i* in loan-words (*Ilium, philosophus*, κιρκος, Τιτος; Indic *Diyamedasa*[2] for Διομήδου, Χαβηρις for Indic *Kāverī*; Goth. *Israel, Filippus*).

In Attic and Hellenistic Greek long and short ι did not differ in the same way as Latin long and short *i*. (1) The analogy of the *e*-sounds would make natural either identical quality of the long and short phonemes, as in ε and ει [21, 23, 29, 33]; or a long vowel more open than the short, as η was more open than ε. There would be no analogy in Classical Attic Greek for a short vowel more open than the corresponding long. (2) Latin ĭ is frequently represented by ε in loan-words; e.g. κομετιον, Καικελιος (other examples in [116 e]). This correspondence can be understood only if Lat. ĭ was at least as near to Gk. ε as to Gk. ι in sound.

There is some evidence that ī was an open *i*-sound. (1) In several words it is represented by Lat. ĭ (*crĕpĭda* from κρηπῖδα) or even ē (*Chrestus* is common in inscriptions, *bōlētus* for βωλῑ'της). (2) The Romance languages indicate open *i* in Greek loan-words inherited from Vulgar Latin[3] (It. *cresima*, Fr. *crème* from χρῖσμα; Fr. *chrétien* from Χρῑστιανός; *armoise* from Ἀρτεμῑσία; It. *artetico* from ἀρθρῑτικός).[4]

The above facts are most readily explained by assuming that the several Greek and Latin phonemes stood in some such relation to one another as is indicated in Figure 1.

FIGURE 1

Greek	ĭ	ī	ε	η
Latin	ī	ĭ	ē	

Gk. ι has always been [i]. The long vowel seems to have been somewhat more open than the short vowel in Attic and Hellenistic.

[2] Gardner, Indian Coins 31.
[3] Claussen, Rom. Forsch. 15.855–7.
[4] Of the instances of Lat. *e* for Gk. ī several may be due to popular etymology and the remaining are too few to be significant.

H, E, AND EI

18. In the earliest form of the Greek alphabet and in most dialects at the beginning of our records, E represented an *e*-vowel of either quantity and of any origin, and EI was a true diphthong. H usually has the value [h] in early Attic inscriptions and in many of the other local alphabets.   In eastern Ionic and in the earliest inscriptions of Crete H is a vowel, and in early inscriptions of Thera, Melos, Sparta, Rhodes, etc., it is sometimes a vowel and sometimes a consonant. Finally there are sporadic instances of H as a syllabic sign for *h*ε or *h*η (Naxian ΗΚΗΒΟΛΟΙ = *h*εκηβόλοι, SGDI 5423.1; ΗΡΑ, ΗΡΑΚΛΕΣ on early Attic vases; ΗΡΜΑΙΟΣ = *H*ερμαῖος, Excavations in the Athenian Agora 3.87 No. 105).

19. The history of the letter H must have been substantially as follows.   The Greeks adopted the Hebrew-Phoenician *cheth* [χεθ] for the spirant that yielded the rough breathing of historic times [74]; the consummation of this change gave the Greek letter the name of ῆτα [hε·ta].   From the beginning, probably, the Greeks used this and other consonantal symbols sometimes for the consonant alone, and sometimes for the consonant and a following vowel; this was normal Semitic practice with all consonants no matter what vowel followed, and there are traces of the usage in Etruscan, Lycian, and Lydian.   No doubt, then, the use of H for *h*ε and *h*η is a survival of the old Semitic system limited by the fact that the initial consonant was followed by the *e*-vowel in the name of the letter.   Since several dialects, notably Asiatic Ionic and Cretan, had lost the rough breathing before the time of our records, their speakers pronounced the name of the letter ῆτα [ε·ta], and they had use for it only in the vocalic value, which was the inevitable remainder of the old syllabic value.[5]   In many dialects, including Asiatic Ionic, there were two *e*-vowels, and the new vowel letter thus served a useful purpose.   This innovation and the corresponding use of Ω [39] are the essential features of the Ionic alphabet, and their convenience, added

---

[5] Scholastic theory prefers to say that the Hebrew-Phoenician alphabet does not indicate the vowels at all, but of course both writer and reader of any sentence knew clearly enough in each case which vowel was meant. Bréal, MSL 6.209–11, long ago saw the connection between the Semitic system and the syllabic value of Gk. H. Kretschmer, Vaseninschriften 97 f., pointed out the connection between the syllabic and vocalic values of H. One may note in passing that, since early Greek had no glottal stop and no aspiration (see [79]), a similar explanation is available for the vocalic use of A and E.

to the prestige of Ionic and later of Attic culture and literature, spread that alphabet over the entire Greek world.

20. The vowel sound first denoted by η must have been different in quality from ε; for in the earliest Ionic inscriptions ε denotes not only the short vowel but also the long vowel that had resulted from the lengthening of ε or from the contraction of ε + ε (ὅτι ἂν οἱ μνήμονες εἰδέωσιν, τοῦτο καρτερὸν ἔναι, SGDI 5726.20 f., Halicarnassus, before 454 B.C.). Since η was used not only for inherited ē but also for original ā (μνήμονες corresponds to μνάμονες of other dialects), it is clear that η differed from ε in being nearer to α; that is, it was a more open sound than ε was. The same conclusion follows from the Ionic contraction of ε + α to η (ἦν from ἐάν); for the product of contraction must be identical in quality with one of the original sounds or intermediate between them, and the former alternative is in this case excluded by the orthography. Hence in early East Ionic η = [ε·], ε = [e, e·].

In the Ionic of some of the islands (Naxos, Ceos, Amorgos) original ā had not yet become identical with original ē when the new form of the alphabet was introduced, and so η was used for the sound that had developed out of ā, while ε continued to be used for original ē (Νικάνδρη μ' ἀνέθεκεν, IG 12.5. p. xxiv = SGDI 5423).[6] In these islands, therefore, η must have denoted a very open e-sound; but the vocalic use of the character must have come to them from their eastern neighbors, who had lost the rough breathing, and the islanders undoubtedly applied the character to that one of their phonemes which was most similar to the East Ionic η. Hence we must again infer that η was an open e, i.e. [ε·] in East Ionic.

21. In the meantime ει was used for the inherited diphthong, as in the sentence cited above from SGDI 5726, and for the contraction of ε + ι, as in εἶδον. This orthography must originally have represented the pronunciation (cf. Cyprian pe-i-se-i = πείσει, SGDI 60.12, etc.). In the course of the fifth century, however, ει came to be used also for the result of the contraction of ε + ε (εἶχον, SGDI 5726.30) and for a lengthened ε (εἶναι occurs five times in SGDI 5726 and ἔναι three

---

[6] Schwyzer, Gr. Gramm. 176, 186, following Hatsidakis, argues from the maintenance of distinct accusatives (-εα : -ην) between the s-stems (nom. -ης) and the masculine ā-stems (nom. -ης) until the fifth century in Attic and East Ionic that these dialects also distinguished between original η and η from ā. That the conclusion does not follow from the premises is shown by the retention even later of the distinction between the two declensions in other cases. That East Ionic was unlike Central Ionic in this respect is indicated by the fact that the islanders found it necessary to modify the use of the vowel sign η when they borrowed it.

times).   We must conclude that by this time ει and ε in such words
represented the same sound, and, since the constant tendency of the
Greek language has been to change diphthongs into monophthongs, the
diphthong must have become a close *e*, i.e. [e·].

22. When, in the fifth century, the Athenians borrowed the Ionic
alphabet, they too employed η both for original ā and for inherited ē,
while ε was used for inherited ĕ and ει represented the original diphthong, the result of the contraction of ε + ε, and the lengthened ε.
The inference is that the Attic vowels were virtually identical with the
Ionic in the fifth century; η = [e·], ε = [e], ει = [e·].

23. Further evidence that η was originally an open *e* in Attic is
furnished by the Attic contraction of ε + α to η (γένη from γένεα);
for η must therefore have been intermediate between ε and α.

A particularly cogent proof of the open sound of η in classical times
is furnished by the spelling of a sheep's cry.

> Cratinus 43 Kock:[7] ὁ δ' ἠλίθιος ὥσπερ πρόβατον βῆ βῆ λέγων βαδίζει.
> Aristophanes fr. 642 Kock:[8] θύειν με μέλλει καὶ κελεύει βῆ λέγειν.
> Hesychius: βηβῆν· πρόβατον.

A sheep's cry may be heard as [bɑ], as [ba], or as [bɛ], but not as [be].

In Attic, as in Ionic, the earliest inscriptions distinguish between the
diphthong ει, whether from IE *ei* or from the contraction of ε + ι,
and the lengthened ε (ʰιερεῖον, ἔναι, IG 1².76.39, 23),[9] but during the
fifth century it became more and more usual to write ει for both.   The
considerations that led us to suppose that the Ionic phoneme resulting
alike from ει and from lengthened ε was a monophthong rather than a
diphthong apply equally to Attic.   A monophthong developed from
the diphthong ει must be either an *e*-sound or an *i*-sound, and the constant distinction between ει and ι in the fifth century and the early
fourth century excludes the second alternative, while the constant
distinction between ει and η proves that ει was a relatively close *e*.
Furthermore, Pre-Attic ē̆ tended to become ī if ι stood in a following
syllable (χίλιοι < *χεσλιοι : Ion. χείλιοι; ἱμάτιον < *ἑσματιον : Ion.

---

[7] 'The fool goes about like a sheep saying "ba ba".'

[8] 'He is going to sacrifice me and tells me to say "ba".'

[9] Some of the earliest Attic inscriptions (Shear, Hesperia 5.33—end of the
eighth century; IG 1².460.5—sixth century; etc.) contain the form εἰμί.   Since
there are no other instances of ει for lengthened ε before the fifth century it is
necessary to ascribe this form to the analogy of the second sg. εἶ; see Sturtevant,
JAOS 57.150.

εἱμάτιον; μῑλίχιος beside μειλίχιος).[10] Since Attic η was not subject to any such change (ἡμι-, ἥλιος), it follows that early Attic ε̄ was more similar to ι than η was. Finally the fifth century Attic phoneme ει presently became identical with ῑ [31], while η was still an e-sound. In fifth century Attic, therefore, η was [ε·] and ει (sometimes still written ε) was [e·].

24. When the Ionic alphabet spread over the Greek world its symbols seem everywhere to have been used as nearly as possible in the East Ionic or the Attic values. Thus we assume that those dialects which represent both original ē and lengthened ε by η had only an open ē, while the use of η for original ē and of ει for lengthened ε indicates a distinction similar to that in Ionic and Attic. To the former class belong Arcadian, Cyprian, Elean, Laconian, and Cretan. Most of the others go with Ionic and Attic.

In West Greek and Boeotian contraction of α + ε yielded η (Argive νικῆν = νικᾶν, Boeotian φυσῆτε = φυσᾶτε); in Arcadian we meet κέπι for καὶ ἐπί, and in Thessalian such forms as κέν for καὶ ἐν (both in the native alphabets with ε where η would later have been written).[11] This confirms our conclusion that η denoted an open e wherever it was employed in early times.

In Thessalian and Boeotian even original ē was represented by ει, indicating that the phoneme had become [e·]. The Boeotian vowel system is particularly important, since it furnishes another demonstration of the value of η and ει in Attic. Early in the fourth century the Boeotians borrowed the Ionic alphabet from the Athenians. Since, however, their vowels had developed farther than the contemporary Attic in the direction of Modern Greek, the orthography of particular words differs considerably in the two dialects. The three examples in Figure 2 are typical:

FIGURE 2

	ι	ει	η	αι
Attic		ἔχει	Θηβαῖος	καί
Boeotian	ἔχι	Θειβῆος	κή	

If we assume that the several letters and digraphs have the same value in the two dialects, the Boeotian changes justify us in arranging them in the above order; for in each case Boeotian has shifted the inherited

[10] Wackernagel, IF 25.326–31.
[11] Buck 34, 308.

phoneme one point toward ι. Attic and general Gk. αι was a diphthong [47], and the Boeotian change was a monophthongization. Now the monophthong resulting from [ai] is commonly either [a], as in OE *āgen* (English *own*) : Goth. *aigan*, or open *e*, i.e. [ε], as in Modern Greek and in the Romance languages. The former change cannot be assumed for Boeotian, since the vowel would have been written α. The second phoneme in the series (ει) cannot be a diphthong, since it results in Boeotian from an original monophthong [e·] and develops into a monophthong [i·]; for original *ē*, having passed through the stage represented by ει, came to be written ι in the latest Boeotian inscriptions, as παρῖς for earlier παρεῖς = Attic παρῆν (Buck, 23). Boeotian ει, then, represented a sound between that of η and of ι. We must infer that in the early fourth century, as in the fifth, Attic η was [ε·] and Attic ει was [e·].

25. The evidence is conclusive that the "itacistic" pronunciation of η as [i] was foreign to Attic and to standard Hellenistic Greek until long after the classical period. Says Socrates in Plato's Cratylus 418 C:[12]

νῦν δὲ ἀντὶ μὲν τοῦ ἰῶτα ἢ εἶ ἢ ἦτα μεταστρέφουσιν, ἀντὶ δὲ τοῦ δέλτα ζῆτα, ὡς δὴ μεγαλο-πρεπέστερα ὄντα.

It appears from the context that Plato has in mind an absurd derivation of ἡμέρα (written HEMEPA in the old Attic alphabet) from ἵμερος, but there is no reason to doubt his word when he says that the substitution of η for ι is a change (μεταστρέφουσιν). Even if it be argued that the reference here is to orthography, the adjective μεγαλοπρεπέστερα surely suggests a difference in sound.

26. In the first century B.C. Dionysius of Halicarnassus finds η the most pleasant in sound of all the long vowels except α, and ι the least pleasant.

Comp. Verb. pp. 51.12–52.9:[13] αὐτῶν δὲ τῶν μακρῶν πάλιν εὐφωνότατον μὲν τὸ α ὅταν ἐκτείνηται· λέγεται γὰρ ἀνοιγομένου τε τοῦ στόματος ἐπὶ πλεῖστον καὶ τοῦ πνεύματος ἄνω φερομένου πρὸς τὸν οὐρανόν. δεύτερον δὲ τὸ η, διότι κάτω τε περὶ τὴν βάσιν τῆς γλώττης ἐρείδει τὸν ἦχον ἀλλ' οὐκ ἄνω, καὶ μετρίως ἀνοιγομένου τοῦ στόματος. ... ἔσχατον δὲ πάντων

---

[12] 'But now they change from iota to epsilon or eta, and from delta to zeta, because of course these sounds are more impressive.'

[13] 'Again, of the long vowels themselves the most euphonious is α, when prolonged; for it is pronounced with the mouth open to the fullest extent, and with the breath forced upward to the palate. η holds the second place, inasmuch as it drives the sound down against the base of the tongue and not upwards, and the mouth is fairly open. ... Last of all stands ι; for the impact of the breath is on the teeth as the mouth is slightly open and the lips do not clarify the sound.'

τὸ ι· περὶ τοὺς ὀδόντας τε γὰρ ἡ κροῦσις τοῦ πνεύματος γίνεται μικρὸν ἀνοιγομένου τοῦ στόματος καὶ οὐκ ἐπιλαμπρυνόντων τῶν χειλῶν τὸν ἦχον.

27. Egyptian papyri of the last three centuries before the Christian era show an extensive confusion of η with ε and ει, but the few instances of confusion between η and ι seem not to be phonetically significant.[14] We must conclude that Egyptian Greek did not share the Attic change of ει to [i·] in the middle of the fourth century [31], but rather that this digraph as well as η and ε still denoted an *e*-sound. This evidence indicates that the three sounds tended to approach each other in some way (cf. [30]).

Oriental loan-words indicate that Greek η continued to be an *e*-vowel in the East from Alexander's time until well into the Christian era. Indian coins have *Heliyakreyasa* = Ἡλιοκλέους (ca. 150 B.C.) and *Diyamedasa* = Διομήδου (ca. 120 B.C.), while Μηρός and Χάβηρις represent Indic *Meruş* and *Kāverī*.[15] In Armenian of the fifth century A.D. η is represented by *e* twenty-five times, by *ē* three times, and by *ī* only six times.[16] In the Greek inscriptions of the second and third centuries A.D. found in the Jewish catacombs at Rome departures from traditional orthography generally indicate that η was an *e*-vowel, and Lat. *ē* is regularly represented by η.[17]

The prevailing Gothic representation of η by *ē* and of *ī* and ει by *ei* indicates survival of the old distinction between η and ι in standard Greek of the fourth century A.D.

28. The earliest evidence for the change of η to [i] appears in late Boeotian and Pamphylian.[18] The relatively rare confusion of η with ι in Ptolemaic papyri and Hellenistic inscriptions of the Pre-Christian era perhaps indicate an itacistic pronunciation in some social strata of certain localities; they are not numerous enough to establish a widespread pronunciation of that sort.[19] Similarly the occasional orthographic confusion of η and ι in Greek inscriptions of the Jewish catacombs at Rome indicate that some members of the Jewish community— possibly persons newly arrived from some localities of the Orient—

---

[14] Mayser 62–85.
[15] Kern, Hellas 1.186; Gardner, Indian Coins 23, 31, etc.
[16] Thumb, ByzZ 9.394–6.
[17] Leon, TAPA 58.212–5.
[18] Buck 23; Thumb, Dialekte 302.
[19] Cf. Mayser 82–5; Thumb, Hellenismus 138.

pronounced η as [i] in the second or third century A.D., although the majority still distinguished clearly between η and ι.[20]

In Attic inscriptions the confusion between η and ι begins about 150 A.D.   We cannot assume a very general merging of the two sounds even in the speech of the uneducated before that date.   Indic dīnāra from Lat. dēnārius through Gk. δηνάριον occurred in the original form of the Pañcatantra, which is certainly to be dated earlier than the sixth century A.D.   The word occurs in such a way that it was clearly a very familiar name of a coin, and so we must allow a considerable time for it to spread from some Greek land and to establish itself in common Indian usage.[21]   Perhaps, then, we may set the spread of the itacistic pronunciation of η by the uneducated between 150 and 400 A.D.   It is to be noted, however, that the old distinction of η and ι always survived in a part of Asia Minor; for Pontic Greek still retains it under certain conditions.[22]   The distinction between the two sounds still persisted in the standard pronunciation of Constantinople at the time of the Gothic translation of the Bible in the fourth century, as is shown by Greek loan-words (swnagoge, Iesus, Israel).   By the ninth century, however, Greek H and I were employed as equivalent symbols in the Cyrillic alphabet.

29.   The identical quality of ε and ει in the early fourth century B.C. is shown by the name εῖ for the letter ε in Plato, Cratylus 426 C and 437 A,[23] and in the fifth century by the same name in a fragment of Callias (ap. Athenaeum 453 D).   How old that name of the letter is we do not know, but the spelling of it with the digraph cannot antedate the change of the original diphthong to a close e in the fifth century. Even stronger evidence of the similarity of ει and ε is furnished by their frequent interchange on inscriptions in the position before vowels. The loss of ι from a diphthongal ει might be regarded as analogous to such forms as ἐλάας for ἐλαίας and ποεῖ for ποιεῖ; but that explanation is impossible after the monophthongization of ει in the fifth century; such a form as Δεκελεεύς, IG 2².3056.1 (320 B.C.), must show graphic ε for ει.   Still clearer is the use of ει for ε (εἱαυτο[ν], IG 2².222.14—after 150 B.C.); for no parallels exist in the case of the genuine i-diphthongs.[24]

[20] Leon, TAPA 58.213–6.

[21] Edgerton, The Pañcatantra Reconstructed 2.182.

[22] Thumb, ByzZ 9.395.

[23] If we may trust the manuscripts on such a point; cf. 393 D, where τοῦ ε is written.

[24] Solmsen, KZ 32.513, and Brugmann-Thumb, 77, suggest that ε was closer

Furthermore ε often corresponded to Latin ĭ in loan-words (κομετιον, Καικελιος, *Philumina*—[116 e]); while in the Romance languages Latin ē was confused with ĭ, it is Greek ε that was confused with Latin ĭ. We must arrange the several phonemes of the two languages as in Figure 3 (cf. Figure 1 in [17]).

FIGURE 3

Greek	ī	ĭ	ε	η	α
Latin	ī	ĭ	ē	ĕ	α

30. A confusion between ε and αι begins in carelessly written papyri of the second century B.C. (ὁρᾶτε = ὁρᾶται, P. Eud. 17.11—before 165 B.C.; βαίνεται = βαίνετε, P. Weil 6.2.8—before 161 B.C.). About 100 A.D. ε came to be confused with αι in Attic inscriptions ('Ερικαιεύς, IG 2².2019.12—110 A.D.; Πλατεαῖς, 2².3162.2, 6—between 117 and 134 A.D.), and the confusion became very common about 150 A.D.[25] The two are identical in value in Modern Greek, both representing an open *e* [ε]. As far as quality is concerned the identity dates from about 150 B.C. in Egypt and 150 A.D. in Attica, although the difference in quantity must have persisted longer even in popular speech. The phonemes ε and η thus reversed their original positions as to quality somewhat as indicated in Figure 4.

FIGURE 4

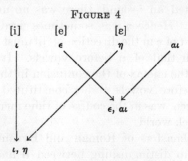

The phonemes ε and η must have had identical quality at some time between the beginning and end of the development, although they must have remained distinct in quantity until a new difference in quality had

---

before a vowel than elsewhere; but if ε was identical in quality with ει in other positions, a closer quality before vowels would not favor confusion with ει, but rather the reverse.

[25] For the similar confusion on Judaean Greek inscriptions at Rome, see Leon, TAPA 58.212 f., 219 f.

developed.   As a matter of fact a confusion between ε and η appears in papyri, beginning with Δεμήτριος, P. Petr.² 56 b 5 (260 B.C.).

31. The further development of ει in Attic from [e·] [23, 24, 29] to [i·] seems to have been rapid.   Even in the fourth century there are a few instances of confusion of ει and ι (συμφέριν, IG 2².558.35).   In the third century it is so common that we must infer identical pronunciation of ει and ι on the part of many persons, and the change must have pene-trated the speech of the whole community by 100 B.C., in view of the great frequency of misspellings.   The Delphian hymns, probably about this date, write the diphthong αι, when sung upon two notes, as α-ει or as αι-ει, where ει must be equivalent to ι.²⁶   The equivalence of ει and ī is presupposed by a remark that Gellius quotes from Nigidius Figulus:

> Gellius 19.14.8:²⁷ Alio deinde in loco scriptum: "Graecos non tantae inscitiae arcesso qui ου ex ο et υ scripserunt, quantae qui ει ex ε et ι;²⁸ illud enim inopia fecerunt, hoc nulla re subacti."

In the position before a vowel, however, ει was after the fourth cen-tury B.C. confused, not with ι, but with η (εὐσεβήας, IG 2².1329.25— before 159 B.C., Γερμανικηοις, 2².1969.25—45 A.D.).   In this position the phoneme ει must still have been a close ē; and since the digraph ει now regularly denoted an *i*-sound, there was no unambiguous way of writing the close ē.   Hence η was sometimes used in this value.   In time the development of η in the direction of [i] must have brought it to a value identical with that of ει before vowels.   It is likely that this stage is marked by the climax of the confusion in the time of Augustus. From then on ει before vowels and η constituted a single phoneme, which, as we have seen, was in the course of time merged with ι through-out most of the Greek world.

The Greek schoolmasters of Roman and Byzantine times devoted as much attention to distinguishing between ει and ι as our teachers devote to the traditional use of *ie* and *ei*.   For example the medieval

---

²⁶ Otto Crusius, Die delphischen Hymnen 94.

²⁷ 'Then in another place he writes: "I do not charge the Greeks with such folly for writing ου with ο and υ as for writing ει with ε and ι; for the former they did of necessity, but the latter under no sort of compulsion." '

²⁸ The text is corrupt, and editors emend variously.   To me it seems that the syntax requires that the antecedent of the second *qui* shall be *Graeci*, and con-sequently that the letters shall be Greek.

dictionary known as Etymologicum Gudianum contains this (289.31 =
Herodian 2.411.27–9 L.):[29]

Κάβιροι· ὁ ᾿Αλεξίων διὰ τοῦ ι, ὡσαύτως ὁ Φιλόξενος· καὶ ῾Ηρωδιανὸς λέγει τὴν παράδοσιν
δίφθογγον ἔχειν καὶ ἴσως συνέδραμε τῷ μάγειρος, πέπειρος, ὄνειρος.

32. The history of ā, η, ει, and ī in Attic and Hellenistic Greek is
roughly diagrammed in Figure 5.

FIGURE 5

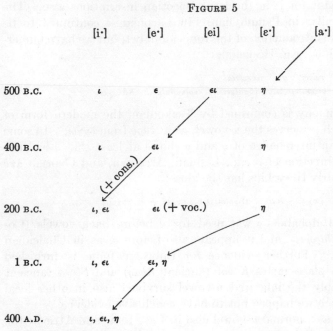

33. In Attic Greek of 400 B.C. η was an open ē, similar to French è
or even to English a in care; ε was a short vowel with about the quality
of French é, and much like the first vowel of Eng. vacation; ει was a
long vowel of the same quality as ε. In brief, η = [ɛ·]; ε = [e]; ει = [e·].

Υ

34. Greek υ corresponds with u of the related languages in inherited
words, as ζυγόν : Skt. yugám, Lat. iugum, Goth. juk; ῦs : Lat. sūs,

[29] ῾Κάβιροι: Alexion writes it with ι, likewise Philoxenus. Herodian says that
tradition gives a diphthong; and (the word) corresponded with μάγειρος, πέπειρος,
ὄνειρος.᾿

OE *sū*. In Modern Greek, however, except for Tsakonian, ancient *υ* has become [i]. While the first stage of the change occurred very early in East Ionic and Attic, possibly before the beginning of our records, several of the ancient dialects retained the inherited [u] or [u·]. In Boeotian inscriptions in the Ionic alphabet from about 350 B.C. on we find *ου* written where earlier inscriptions in the local alphabet had *υ*. Since in Attic of this period *ου* was a normal *u*-vowel [42], we must assume that value for it in the later Boeotian inscriptions also. The situation is similar in Pamphylian. In Laconian *υ* continued to be written after the introduction of the Ionic alphabet, but we have numerous glosses with *ου*; e.g. Hesychius:

> τούνη· σύ. Λάκωνες.
>
> οὐδραίνει (i.e., ὑδραίνει)· περικαθαίρει. Λάκωνες.

This clear testimony is confirmed by Tsakonian, the modern form of Lakonian, which preserves the *u*-vowel, as in *žugo* from *ζυγόν*. In some other dialects an interchange of *υ* and *ο* shows at least that *υ* had not moved in the direction of *ι*, e.g., Lesbian, Arcadian, and Cyprian *ἀπύ* for *ἀπό*. Similarly Hesychius has the gloss:

> μοχοῖ· ἐντός. Πάφιοι (i.e., μοχοῖ = ἐν μυχῷ),

In certain local alphabets *ρ* was used for *κ* before back vowels (Corinthian *καρόν*, *hίρομες*), and it appears also before *υ*, as in Chalcidian *Ϙύρνυς*, *λήρυνθος*).[30] Further evidence for Euboean Ionic is furnished by the modern place-names *Kumi* (ancient *Κύμη*) and *Stura* (ancient *Στύρα*). Probably the inherited *u*-vowel survived also in other local dialects for which we happen not to have conclusive evidence.

35. That *υ* was a normal *u*-vowel also in East Ionic and Attic at the time when those dialects were reduced to writing is indicated by the fact that the character represented [u] as the second member of a diphthong [54, 54 a–d]. The earliest clear evidence for modification of *υ* in East Ionic is furnished by the Persian name *Marduniya*, which Herodotus writes *Μαρδόνιος*, and also by *Μεγαδόστης*, if it contains the root **duš-*,[31] and *Καππαδοκια* if it was taken from the equivalent OP *Katpatuka*. In several other names Herodotus writes *υ* for OP *u* (*Κῦρος* = *Kuruš*, *Καμβυσης* = *Kambujiya*, *Κυαξαρης* = *Huvaxštra*), but the occasional use of *ο* indicates that neither Greek vowel was quite satisfactory for the purpose. Significant also is the use of *υ* for OP *vi-* in

---

[30] Buck, 25 f.

[31] Alvin H. M. Stonecipher, Graeco-Persian Names 46.

Ὑστασπης = *Vištaspa* and Ὑδαρνης = *Vidarna*.[32] Not that υ was an accurate representation of OP *vi-*; but the mere fact that it could be used at all seems to show that υ had some affinity with an *i*-vowel.

35 a. In Indic loan-words from Alexander to the beginning of the Christian era Indic *u* appears sometimes as υ and sometimes as *o*. Greek υ, on the other hand, is regularly represented by *i* on Indic coins; e.g. *Lisikasa* for Λυσίου, *Amitasa* for 'Αμύντου, *Dianisiyasa* for Διονυσίου.[33]

35 b. The use of ου for earlier υ in Boeotian [34] from about 350 B.C. (Πουθίω, IG 7.2418—about 346 B.C.) is proof that Attic υ was no longer normal *u*; for if it had been, the Boeotians would have continued to use the letter in its original value.

35 c. When the Romans came into contact with Attic and Hellenistic Greek there was disagreement about representing υ in Latin. We find such various forms as *Sisipus*, CIL 1².1537; *butirum* (references in the Thesaurus); *Hypolitus*, CIL 1.741; *liquiritia* = γλυκύρριζα; *Quiriace* = Κυριακή, 3.14306, 3; *Moesia* = Μυσία, *lagoena* = λάγυνος, Plautus, Curc. 78. On the other hand Latin *u* is represented by *o* (αἴγορα, IG 2².4115; Σπόριος, 2².1938.40, etc.) or by ου ('Ιούλιος, *passim*), but rarely by υ; while κυ often represents Lat. *qui* ('Ακυλας, IG 2².1806.7; 'Ακυλλιον, 2².4126.8; Τραγκυλλινης, IGRRP 1.672.9, etc.), and there are a few other examples of υ for Lat. *i* ('Αφρυκανην, CIG 1999 b; Βρυτ<αννικου>, IGRRP 1.577.4; μυρμυλλων, 1.773.1, etc.).[34] The difficulty was finally overcome for educated Romans by the adoption of the foreign sound and the Greek letter.

35 d. These facts show that East Ionic, Attic, and Hellenistic υ had shifted from [u] in the direction of [i]. That the change did not go so far in antiquity as it has in Modern Greek is indicated by part of the evidence just cited and also by the following. In Ionic, Attic, and Hellenistic inscriptions and in Ptolemaic papyri υ and ι are rarely confused except in a few words that show assimilation or metathesis (ἥμυσυ, Μιτυληναῖος). Dionysius of Halicarnassus, Comp. Verb. 52.4–9, finds euphonic difference between υ and ι. Demotic papyri of the second century A.D. transcribe υ by *o* rather than by ι.[35] In the fourth century Ulfilas found it necessary to take over the Greek letter υ in writing Greek names; evidently the Gothic *i* was unsatisfactory. Even as late

[32] In these words, as elsewhere in Herodotus, the traditional rough breathing is surely wrong.

[33] Gardner, Indian Coins 29, 51, 61, etc.

[34] Dittenberger, Hermes 6.281–309; Eckinger, Orthographie 40 f., 59 ff., 123 f.

[35] Hess, IF 6.134 fn. 1.

as the tenth century Suidas, in his lexicon, distinguished between υ and ι, although he grouped together all words beginning with η, ι, and ει, since these denoted but a single phoneme, and users of the work would frequently not have known under which letter to search for a particular word.

36. In popular speech, however, the pronunciation [i] had become familiar long before that time, and no doubt in the standard speech of some regions. The occasional confusion of υ and ι in papyri of the second and third centuries A.D. indicates that some speakers pronounced them both alike, although these may have been native Egyptians, who had only normal *u* and *i* in their own language.[36] Greek words in Armenian of the fifth century show sometimes *iu* and sometimes *i* for Gk. υ,[37] and this suggests two approximations to a difficult foreign sound, rather than a variation in Greek itself. A manuscript of the eighth century transcribes υ and οι by Latin *i*,[38] and this apparently represents the pronunciation of standard Greek in the Latin-speaking West.

37. Since Attic υ is sometimes long and sometimes short in verse, it cannot be a diphthong, although Lat. *Moesia*, etc., might suggest that interpretation. Since a preceding syllable ending in a consonant may be either long or short, υ cannot have stood for [wi], as suggested by Ὑστασπης, Κυντος, etc., or [ju], as might be inferred from certain Greek words in Armenian. Probably East Ionic, Attic, and Hellenistic υ was similar to French *u* and German *ü*; such a sound easily develops from *u* and passes into *i*, and it satisfactorily explains most of the evidence given above. Probably the sound denoted by the letter varied in different parts of the Greek world in Hellenistic times as it certainly did in the classical period.[39]

38. In classical times υ was [y] in East Ionic and Attic; in many other parts of the Greek world it was [u].

For υ in diphthongs, see [54–8].

Ω, O, AND ΟΥ

39. The early history of the *o*-vowels was nearly parallel to that of the *e*-vowels. Ω is a modification of the letter O, which was utilized

---

[36] Dieterich, Untersuchungen zur Geschichte der griechischen Sprache 24. Such forms as βιβλίον and ἥμυσυς are earlier and more widespread, but they are due to assimilation.

[37] Thumb, ByzZ 9.397 f.

[38] Staerk, Vizantiĭskiĭ vremennik 15.189–93; cf. Draheim, WKlP 35.406 f.

[39] Thumb, ByzZ 9.398.

to distinguish the open ō, i.e. [ɔ·], from the short close o, i.e. [o]. Probably the distinction between the e-vowels first came to be denoted in writing [19], and then means were found to mark the parallel distinction in the o-vowels. At any rate the Ionic contraction of a + o and of o + a to ω (Παναμύω < -āo, SGDI 5726.12; τὠγῶνος < τὸ ἀγῶνος, 5632 B 32) proves that ω represented a sound between a and o, namely [ɔ·] (cf. the parallel argument concerning η in [20]).

40. In the earliest Ionic inscriptions ου is used exclusively for the original diphthong, while o denotes not only the inherited ŏ but the lengthened o and the product of contraction of o + o and of o + ε; e.g. Προκοννησίō, SGDI 5531 (Proconnesus, sixth century B.C.); τοῦτο τὸ χρόνō τῶν ὀκτωκαίδεκα μηνῶν, 5726.23 f. (Halicarnassus, before 454 B.C.). At first the digraph ου must have denoted a diphthong, namely [ou]; undoubtedly the second member of the diphthong was normal u, as in αυ and ευ [54, 54 a–d]. The same diphthong is clearly indicated for Cyprian by a-ro-u-ra-i = ἀρούραι, SGDI 60.20, o-vo = οὐ 68.3, etc., and for Cretan by σποϝδδάν, 5125.9, <β>οϝσί, 4976, etc.

In the course of the fifth century ου came to be used in Ionic for lengthened o as well as for the original diphthong (βουλεύω and βαρβάρους occur beside κε̄'νō, etc. on SGDI 5632—about 475 B.C.). As in the case of ει and ε̄ [21, 23, 24], this indicates that ου and ō had come to be identical; their value, at least for a time, must have been a close ō, i.e. [o·].

41. Upon the introduction of the Ionic alphabet into Attica ω was used as in Ionic for inherited ō; and in Attica as well as in Ionia the use of ω for the product of contraction of a + o and of o + a (ἐτιμῶντο, ἠδίω) proves that the sound was an open ō, i.e. [ɔ·]. In Attic inscriptions, as in Ionic, ου originally denoted the diphthong [ou] (οὐδὲ, IG 1².39.5—445 or 444 B.C.), while lengthened o and the product of contraction of o + o, o + ε, and also of ε + o were written o (μισθῶντα, IG 1².1.6—sixth century B.C.). We find lengthened o written ου as early as 500 B.C. (Ηερακλέους, IG 1².777), and in the course of the fifth century this became the regular spelling. We must infer that when the confusion began both the original diphthong and lengthened o had the value of close ō, i.e. [o·]. This sound persisted until about 350 B.C.; for until then o was frequently used for lengthened o (Εὐβōλίδō, IG 2².18—394 or 393 B.C.; προέδρōς, 2².109.10—363 or 362 B.C.), and occasionally for the original diphthong (Σπōδίας, IG 1².374.74—408 B.C.; 'ōδένα, 2².111.60 —363 B.C.).

42. At about 350 B.C., when the Boeotians adopted the Ionic alphabet from the Athenians, they took over ου to denote their normal u-vowel

[34], as in ἀργουρίω δραχμὰς μουρίας, IG 7.3172.117. In all probability this reflected the contemporary value of the digraph in Attic, which would seem to date the Attic change from [oʼ] to [uʼ] pretty closely to 350 B.C. At any rate it is certain that in later Attic and Hellenistic Greek, as in the modern language, ου denoted a *u*-vowel. In the Delphic hymns, probably of about 100 B.C., ευ and αυ, if sung upon two notes, have ου for *v*.[40] Conclusive proof comes from the loan-words, e.g. Lat. *būtyrum, Thūcȳdidēs,* Ἰουστος, Ῥουφινος, Goth. *Iudas* for Ἰουδας, Arm. *plakund* for πλακοῦντα. The history of the long *o*-vowels and *ū* in Attic may be pictured as in Figure 6 (cf. Figure 5 in [32]).

FIGURE 6

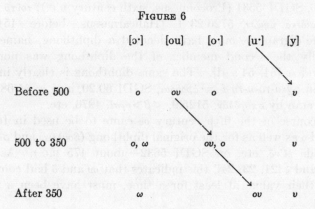

43. After the introduction of the Ionic alphabet into the rest of the Greek world, ω as well as η [24] was everywhere used for the long open vowel. Most dialects distinguished the inherited long vowel from lengthened *o* precisely as Ionic and Attic did, but Laconian, Heraclean, Cretan, and Boeotian employed ω for lengthened *o* and for the product of contraction of *o* + *o* as well as for the original long vowel.

In most dialects the diphthong ου became first a close *ō* [oʼ] and then *ū* [uʼ], as in Ionic and Attic. In Corinthian the original diphthong and lengthened *o* were identical from the time of the earliest inscriptions. In Boeotian ου came to be used not only for the original diphthong (οὖτο, IG 7.3172.150—between 222 and 200 B.C.) but also, from about 350 B.C., for inherited [uʼ] [34].

44. The ancient name of the letter ο was οὖ, and this is shown to have been in use in the fifth century B.C. by a fragment of the Γραμματικὴ Τραγῳδία of Callias (preserved by Athenaeus 453 D), in which the names of the letters are listed as the choreutae. This name, or at

---

[40] Crusius, Die delphischen Hymnen 94.

least its orthography, could have originated only at a time when *o* and *ov* had the same quality. Hence *o* was a close *o* in the dialect (Ionic?) that originated the name of the letter. Attic *o* must have been a close vowel, i.e. [o], at the time of the contraction of *o* + *o* and of the lengthening of *o* under certain circumstances; for otherwise the result would have been *ω*. That *o* was a close *o* in Hellenistic times is indicated by Lat. *amurca, purpura, ampura* [123 e], if these words were borrowed from Greek and not from Etruscan or some other Mediterranean language. Such Greek forms as Μομμιος for *Mummius*, Μαρδονιος for OP *Marduniya*, and Σανδρακοπτος for Indic *Chandraguptas* are at best confirmatory evidence. Greek had no normal *u*, and so an inexact transcription was inevitable; *o* might well have been used even if it had been an open *o*.

45. In Modern Greek *o* and *ω* are identical. Their quantitative identity dates from the loss of the old quantitative distinction after the accent had become a stress accent [109]. The earliest indication of an approach in quality is the occasional confusion of *o* and *ω* in inscriptions and papyri of the third century B.C. (ὀρθῶς, IG 2².1299.48—between 294 and 283 B.C.;[41] οἰκωνόμου, P Rev. L 50.22—258 B.C.). The mistakes in papyri become so common by the second century B.C. that we must infer identical quality for Egyptian Greek. Attic inscriptions do not show any such frequent confusion until the second century A.D. Ulfilas' Gothic of the fourth century A.D. keeps the two sounds distinct in proper names taken from the Greek (*Iairusaulwmeis, Herodes*), and this probably indicates a phonetic distinction in the standard Greek of Constantinople. Greek words in Armenian and in the Hebrew Talmud indicate that *o* and *ω* were identical in the Orient by the fifth century A.D.[42]

46. In Attic of the fifth century B.C. *ω* was an open *o*, similar to Fr. *o* in *tort*, scarcely as open as Eng. *aw* in *law*; in phonetic script it should be written [ɔ·]. Fifth century *o* was similar to *o* in Fr. *pot*, i.e. [o]. Fifth century *ov* was like *o* in Fr. *chose* or Germ. *Sohn*, i.e. [o·]. But about the middle of the fourth century this became [u·].

AI

47. Since the value of the characters A and I in the earliest Greek alphabet is known, the original value of the diphthong is also known,

---

[41] Other examples in Meisterhans-Schwyzer 24. Here and elsewhere Kirchner, IG 2², prints *ω* in the text, but in a footnote records the reading as *o*.

[42] Thumb, ByzZ 9.393; Krauss, Lehnwörter 1.50-2.

and confirmation comes from the Cyprian syllabary (*ta-i ma-ka-i*, etc.). The related languages show *ai*, or a sound developed out of this, in words cognate with Greek words containing αι, as Skt. *edhas*, Lat. *aedēs*, OIr. *aed* : αἴθω; Arm. *aic* : αἴξ; Skt. *sacate* : ἕπεται; Osc. *aeteis* 'partis' : αἶσα. Lat. *laevus* and Gk. λαιός may be loans from some Mediterranean language or languages, but the similarity of vocalism is nevertheless significant. In many other words αι originated in Greek itself in such a way that it must at first have been a diphthong. It resulted from the contraction of α + ι in παῖς (Homeric πάϊς), in κέραι, dat. of κέρας, etc. The αι of the nom. pl. resulted from the analogy of the second declension:

$$\mathring{\alpha}\delta\epsilon\lambda\phi\text{ο}\acute{\upsilon}\text{ς} : \mathring{\alpha}\delta\epsilon\lambda\phi\text{ο}\acute{\iota} = \mathring{\alpha}\delta\epsilon\lambda\phi\acute{\bar{\alpha}}\text{ς} : \mathring{\alpha}\delta\epsilon\lambda\phi\text{αί},$$

and the optative of the first aorist was formed on the analogy of optatives beside indicatives with variable vowel:

$$\mathring{\epsilon}\lambda\text{ί}\pi\text{ο}\mu\epsilon\nu : \lambda\text{ί}\pi\text{ο}\iota\mu\epsilon\nu = \mathring{\epsilon}\lambda\acute{\upsilon}\sigma\alpha\mu\epsilon\nu : \lambda\acute{\upsilon}\sigma\alpha\iota\mu\epsilon\nu.$$

Such processes could occur only in case αι stood in the same relation to ᾰ as οι did to ŏ, and the relationship cannot have been the same unless both αι and οι were diphthongs, since metrical and other evidence proves that they were not dissyllabic.

48. In modern Greek αι has become the same open *e*-sound as ε. It remains to determine when the original diphthong was transformed into the modern monophthong.

The change of αι to ᾱ under certain conditions ('Αθēνάᾳ, IG 1².579— sixth century B.C.) was prehistoric. The crasis of αι with a following ε in κἀκεῖνος, κἄστι, etc., was very early. Both changes would have been impossible after αι became an *e*-vowel.

In Boeotian, before the adoption of the Ionic-Attic alphabet, αι was sometimes written αε, especially at Tanagra ('Ōκίβαε, IG 7.606— sixth century B.C.). This, like Lat. *ae* for earlier *ai* [130], was the first stage of the change to open *e*. The latter stage had been reached in Boeotian by the time the new alphabet was adopted in the fourth century; consequently η was regularly used in place of original αι (κή, Θειβῆος [24]. It is therefore clear that Attic αι had not yet become open *e* in the fourth century.

Numerous Greek words in Latin and Latin words in Greek show that αι continued to be a diphthong in Hellenistic times; e.g. *Achaia*, CIL 1².626, *Menaechmus*, *palaestra*, Καικελιος, Καισαρ. Indian coins of the second and first centuries B.C. have *ay* for αι before a vowel in *Heramayasa* = Ἑρμαίου.[43] Further proof is furnished by Arm. *Kaisr.*

That αι was a diphthong in standard Greek of the Augustan period is implied by a discussion of the euphony of the first paragraph of Thucydides by Dionysius of Halicarnassus.

Comp. Verb. 109.14–20:[44] Ἔτι πρὸς τούτοις ἡ τῶν φωνηέντων παράθεσις ἡ κατὰ τὴν τελευταίαν τοῦ κώλου τοῦδε γενομένη ἐν τῷ ʽκαὶ Ἀθηναίων᾽ διακέκρουκε τὸ συνεχὲς τῆς ἁρμονίας καὶ διέστακεν πάνυ αἰσθητὸν τὸν μεταξὺ λαβοῦσα χρόνον· ἀκέραστοι γὰρ αἱ φωναὶ τοῦ τε ι καὶ τοῦ α καὶ ἀποκόπτουσαι τὸν ἦχον· τὸ δ᾽ εὐεπὲς οἱ συνεχεῖς τε καὶ οἱ συλλεαινόμενοι ποιοῦσιν ἦχοι.

It has to be admitted, however, that Dionysius sometimes discusses euphony on the basis of orthography rather than of the pronunciation of his day. In this same treatise (106.12 f.) he finds ι following itself in ἀγλαΐᾳ ἴδετε, although the diphthong ᾱι had long since lost its final member [62].

49. The confusion between αι and ε begins in carelessly written papyri of the second century B.C. (ὁρᾶτε = ὁρᾶται, P Eud. 17.11—before 165 B.C.; βαίνεται = βαίνετε, P Weil. 6.2.8—before 161 B.C.). In Attic inscriptions αι and ε do not begin to be confused until the second century A.D., and not frequently until about 150 A.D. By the latter date, apparently, the pronunciation as *e* was pretty well established. The Greek inscriptions of the second and third centuries A.D. in the Jewish catacombs at Rome substitute ε for historically correct αι about two thirds of the time.[45]

Sextus Empiricus, who wrote toward the end of the second century A.D., tells us quite explicitly that αι was not a diphthong.

Adv. Gramm. 116–8 (p. 625 f. Bekk., p. 241 Fab.):[46] Τὸ γὰρ στοιχεῖον κριτέον μάλιστα ὅτι στοιχεῖόν ἐστιν ἐκ τοῦ ἀσύνθετον καὶ μονοποιὸν ἔχειν φθόγγον, οἷός ἐστιν ὁ τοῦ α καὶ ε καὶ ο καὶ τῶν λοιπῶν. ἐπεὶ ὁ τοῦ αι καὶ ει φθόγγος ἁπλοῦς ἐστι καὶ μονοειδής, ἔσται καὶ

---

[43] Gardner, Indian Coins 62, etc.

[44] 'Furthermore, the juxtaposition of vowels which is found at the end of this clause in the words καὶ Ἀθηναίων has broken and made a gap in the continuity of the arrangement, by demanding quite an appreciable interval, since the sounds of ι and α are unmingled and there is an interruption of the voice between them; whereas euphony is caused by sounds which are continuous and smoothly blended.'

[45] Leon, TAPA 58.219 f.

The arguments adduced by P. Chantraine, The Link 1.7–10 (1938), for a change of αι to [ε] in Attic prior to 150 A.D. are not convincing. Peculiarly naive is the assumption that monophthongization of αι would yield a short vowel.

[46] 'A primary speech-sound must be judged to be such chiefly from its having an uncompounded sound of a single nature, such as the sound of α, ε, ο, etc. Since

ταῦτα στοιχεῖα. τεκμήριον δὲ τῆς ἁπλότητος καὶ μονοειδείας τὸ λεχθησόμενον· ὁ μὲν γὰρ σύνθετος φθόγγος οὐχ οἷος ἀπ' ἀρχῆς προσπίπτει τῇ αἰσθήσει τοιοῦτος ἄχρι τέλους παραμένειν πέφυκεν, ἀλλὰ κατὰ παράτασιν ἑτεροιοῦται· ὁ δὲ ἁπλοῦς καὶ ὄντως τοῦ στοιχείου λόγον ἔχων τοὐναντίον ἀπ' ἀρχῆς μέχρι τέλους ἀμετάβολός ἐστιν· οἷον τοῦ μὲν ρα φθόγγου ἐν παρατάσει προφερομένου δῆλον ὡς οὐχ ὡσαύτως αὐτοῦ κατὰ τὴν πρώτην πρόσπτωσιν ἀντιλήψεται ἡ αἴσθησις καὶ κατὰ τὴν τελευταίαν, ἀλλὰ καταρχὰς μὲν ὑπὸ τῆς τοῦ ρ ἐκφωνήσεως κινηθήσεται, μεταῦθις δὲ ἐξαφανισθείσης αὐτῆς, εἰλικρινοῦς τῆς τοῦ α δυνάμεως ποιήσεται τὴν ἀντίληψιν. ὅθεν οὐκ ἂν εἴη στοιχεῖον τὸ ρα καὶ πᾶν τὸ ἐοικὸς αὐτῷ. εἰ δὲ τὸν τοῦ αι φθόγγον λέγοιεν, οὐδὲν ἔσται τοιοῦτον, ἀλλ' οἷον ἀπ' ἀρχῆς ἐξακούεται τῆς φωνῆς ἰδίωμα, τοιοῦτον καὶ ἐπὶ τέλει.

Gothic and Armenian show in different ways the equivalence of αι and ε. Gothic orthography, which is largely based upon contemporary (i.e. fourth century) Greek orthography, regularly represents Gk. αι by *ai* in loan-words and frequently employs the same digraph for Gk. ε (*aipiskaupus*) and for native e (*taihun*).[47] Greek loan-words in Armenian have e for αι (*sp'era* = σφαῖρα) as well as for ε and η (*hiuperet* = ὑπηρέτης).

50. In fifth century Attic αι was similar to Eng. *I* and, more precisely, to Ital. *ai* in *mai*; in other words, αι = [ai].

OI

51. The digraph οι must originally have been a true representation of the pronunciation. Furthermore Greek has οι in a number of words whose cognates in the related languages contain vowels or diphthongs normally developed from Primitive IE *oi* (οἶδε : Skt. *veda*, Goth. *wait*; ποινή : Av. *kaēnā*, Lith. *kainé*). In other words οι is the product of contraction within Greek itself of ο + ι. The genitive ending -οιο came from IE -*osyo* (Skt. -*asya*), and the second member of the compound ἑκατόμβοιος from IE -*bowyos*, while classical οἷς was in Homer still

then the sound of αι and of ει is simple and uniform, these also must be elementary speech-sounds. A proof of their simplicity and uniformity is the following: it is characteristic of a composite sound not to continue to its end to be such as when it first strikes the ear, but during its continuance it is altered; while, on the contrary, a simple sound which really has the value of a primary speech-sound is unchanged from beginning to end; for example, if the sound ρα is continuously pronounced, it is clear that the perception of it will not be apprehended in the same way at the end of the pronunciation as at the beginning, but at first perception will be produced by the utterance of the ρ, and afterwards, when this has disappeared, will cause the apprehension of the force of α unmixed with other elements. Wherefore ρα cannot be an elementary speech-sound, nor any sound like it. But if they should speak the sound of αι, there will be no such experience; but the same peculiarity of voice that is heard in the beginning will be heard also at the end.'

[47] For details, see Luft, KZ 35.300, 306 f.

dissyllabic ὄϊς. When the nominative plural ending -οι of the second declension induced -αι in the first, and when -οι- in the thematic optative induced -αι- in the first aorist optative, both must have been diphthongs [47].

51 a. The retention of diphthongal οι in Attic shortly before the beginning of our records is indicated by the contraction of ο + ει and of ο + η to οι (δηλοῖ indicative and subjunctive), the crasis of ο + ι (θοἰμάτιον) and of οι + ε (μοῖστί), and the loss of ι in οι before α, ε, and η (στοάν, Dittenberger, Sylloge² 3—Athenian inscription at Delphi, 460 B.C.).

51 b. When the character ω was introduced, a distinction was made between οι and ωι (i.e. ῳ). Since we have concluded [39] that ω at this time was [ɔ·] and ο was [o], it follows that ωι contained open ο and was approximately like Eng. *oi* in *oil*, while οι contained a close ο.[48]

51 c. That the Modern Greek pronunciation of οι as equivalent to ι was foreign to the Attic of the fifth century appears from Thucydides' account of a certain traditional oracle.

Thuc. 2.54.1–3:[49] Τοιούτῳ μὲν πάθει οἱ Ἀθηναῖοι περιπεσόντες ἐπιέζοντο, ἀνθρώπων τ' ἔνδον θνησκόντων καὶ γῆς ἔξω δῃουμένης. ἐν δὲ τῷ κακῷ οἷα εἰκὸς ἀνεμνήσθησαν καὶ τοῦδε τοῦ ἔπους, φάσκοντες οἱ πρεσβύτεροι πάλαι ᾄδεσθαι 'ἥξει Δωριακὸς πόλεμος καὶ λοιμὸς ἅμ' αὐτῷ.' ἐγένετο μὲν οὖν ἔρις τοῖς ἀνθρώποις μὴ λοιμὸν ὠνομάσθαι ἐν τῷ ἔπει ὑπὸ τῶν παλαιῶν, ἀλλὰ λιμόν, ἐνίκησε δὲ ἐπὶ τοῦ παρόντος εἰκότως λοιμὸν εἰρῆσθαι· οἱ γὰρ ἄνθρωποι πρὸς ἃ ἔπασχον τὴν μνήμην ἐποιοῦντο. ἢν δέ γε οἶμαί ποτε ἄλλος πόλεμος καταλάβῃ Δωρικὸς τοῦδε ὕστερος καὶ ξυμβῇ γενέσθαι λιμόν, κατὰ τὸ εἰκὸς οὕτως ᾄσονται.

If the two words had been alike, there could have been no disagreement about what had been "said" (ὠνομάσθαι, εἰρῆσθαι), and there could

---

[48] In Homer and several of the later dialects ϝ is preserved before οι but not before ο and ω. This has been thought to indicate that ο in οι was a front rounded vowel similar to Fr. *eu* and Germ. *ö*, but if so we should expect confusion between οι and υι. Probably the dissimilative influence of ι served to protect ϝ before οι. At any rate the argument does not apply to Ionic, Attic, or Hellenistic.

[49] 'Through experiencing such a calamity the Athenians were in great distress; people were dying within the city, and the country was being ravaged without. In their misery, as one might expect, they remembered this verse which the old men said had long been recited: "There shall come a Dorian war and a pestilence with it." Now some had contended that not a pestilence (λοιμός) had been named in the verse by their elders, but a famine (λιμός). However, in the actual circumstances the contention that λοιμός was the correct word won the day; for people shaped their memory according to their experience. But, I dare say, if ever there comes another Dorian war hereafter and there happens to be a famine at the same time, probably they will recite the verse in that way.'

have been no variation between the present and the possible future recitation (οὕτως ᾄσονται).

51 d. About 250 B.C. Boeotian inscriptions begin to show υ in place of οι (Βοιωτῦς, IG 7.3083.4—third century). By the end of the century this was the regular orthography except before a vowel. There is no doubt that the sound indicated was a monophthong; the value of Attic υ suggests a front rounded vowel between *u* and *i*, but an easier development from this particular diphthong would be a front rounded vowel between *o* and *e*. In either case Attic οι of the third century B.C. must have differed from υ; otherwise the Boeotians would not have changed from one spelling to the other.

51 e. Greek words in Latin show a diphthong for οι both in early times and in the Ciceronian period (*poena* = ποινή, Plautus; *homoeomeria*, Lucretius 1.830). After Cicero the system of transliteration was so firmly fixed that later loan-words in the standard language throw little light upon current Greek pronunciation.

51 f. Dionysius of Halicarnassus, Comp. Verb. 102.8–12, says that a certain verse ends in ι and the next begins with ε, and that these sounds do not coalesce (συναλείφεται). Since the final word of the former verse is χοροί, this implies that οι was still a diphthong; but Dionysius elsewhere (106.12 f.) speaks similarly of the final ι of ἀγλαίᾳ, although that sound, as we know from other evidence, had already been lost.

52. Confusion between οι and υ begins in the second century B.C. in carelessly written Egyptian papyri (ἀνύγετε, UPZ 1.79.7—160 B.C., λοιμανάμενοι, P Grenf. 1.17.15—after 147 or 135 B.C.). It indicates a monophthongal pronunciation of οι, which was then or ultimately came to be equivalent to that of υ, namely [y]; cf. the similar change in Boeotian [51 d]. The Greek inscriptions of the Jewish catacombs indicate complete identity of οι and υ in the second and third centuries A.D.[50] In Attic inscriptions, however, the two are kept distinct until the third century A.D., when we find Ποιανεψιῶνα, IG 2².2239.82 (between 238 and 244), κυμητήριον and κυμιτίριον on many Christian epitaphs, etc. In the fourth century Ulfilas took over Gk. υ into Gothic to represent both υ and οι in loan-words; he rarely confused either with ι.

For the further change of υ to ι, see [36].

53. In Attic of the fifth century οι represented [oi], a sound somewhat different from that of Eng. *oi* in *oil*.

[50] Leon, TAPA 58.218 f., 224.

AΥ AND EΥ

54. The digraphs aυ and eυ must originally have been used to represent diphthongs, and cognate forms suggest that, at least in certain words, the final member was a normal u (αὔξω : Lat. *augeō*, Goth. *aukan*; αὖ, αὖτε : Lat. *aut, autem*; ζεῦγος : Lat. *iouxmenta* > *iūmenta*; πεύθομαι : Skt. *bódhati*, Goth. *anabiuda*). In those dialects which in historic times had only a normal u in other positions [34], the final member of aυ and eυ must also have been a normal u.

54 a. In East Ionic also there is conclusive evidence that υ as final member of a diphthong was the normal vowel. In that dialect ε + o contracted to a diphthong that is written eυ in our manuscripts (σεῦ : Homeric σέο). In the inscriptions the spelling eυ for originally dissyllabic eo first appears in the fourth century B.C., and from that time on eo and ao were often written for original eυ and aυ (εὀεργέτην, ταὀτα, SGDI 5687—Erythrae, about 357 B.C.). The easiest explanation of these facts is this: ε + o became [eu], but since υ denoted [y], it was clearer to retain the old orthography eo in the new value. Then the spelling eo = [eu] was extended to words with inherited eυ, and analogy gave rise to ao = [au], thus:

$$\epsilon : \epsilon o = a : ao.$$

It is possible that the final member of these diphthongs was actually a close o, as in Germ. *Haus* [haos], but the orthography scarcely provides evidence to that effect. At any rate the second member of our diphthongs in East Ionic was a back vowel, not the [y] denoted by υ in other positions.

54 b. In various dialects the final member of a diphthong is occasionally written with ϝ either alone or combined with υ, as in ἀϝτός, ἀϝτόν, SGDI 4976, 4955, 4962 (Crete); Ναϝπακτίον, IG 9.1.334.40 (Locris, fifth century B.C.); 'Εϝθείας, 4.309 (Corinth); ἀϝυτō, SGDI 5421 (Naxos, seventh or sixth century B.C.); ἀϝυτάρ, IG 1².1012 (Athens, sixth century B.C.); ἀϝυτάν, 9.1.868 (Corcyra); τάϝυρος, ἀμεϝύσασθαι, SGDI 4963, 4964. (Crete). This use of ϝ doubtless stands in some relation to the similar Oscan use of ϝ and of the native character derived from ϝ (usually transcribed v) in writing diphthongs (Aϝδειες, *Avdiis* 'Audius', τωϝτο 'civitas', avt 'at', *lúvkei* 'in luco', etc.). All such spellings must represent a normal u.[51] Even clearer proof of normal u is provided by Λαοδικεούς,

---

[51] I cannot understand Buck's remark (30) that in ἀϝυτάρ, etc., "ϝ indicates the

Inschriften von Olympia 237 (137 A.D.) and γονεοῦσι, Papers of the American School 1.33 (Assos, late Roman times). The occasional use in Cretan of υ for λ preceded by α or ε and followed by a consonant must mean that λ before a consonant was velar *l* and that υ after α or ε was normal *u*. Examples are καυχῷ = χαλκῷ, SGDI 5011, and ἀδευπιαί = ἀδελφαί, 4991.5.18 [87].

54 c. When the Boeotians adopted the Attic alphabet they began to write ου instead of υ for their inherited *u*-vowel [34], but they nevertheless continued to write υ for the final member of the diphthongs αυ and ευ; and they did not depart from this practice even when, a hundred years later, they began to write υ for older οι [51 d]. The reason for this retention of the spellings αυ and ευ is perfectly clear, if we assume that in Attic also υ was a normal *u*-vowel after α and ε.

54 d. While the Romans borrowed Gk. υ (*y*) for use in loan-words, they were nevertheless content to write *au* and *eu* for αυ and ευ. It follows that in these diphthongs υ was more nearly like Lat. *u* than in other positions. Although the Indian coins of the second and first centuries B.C. show *i* for υ in other positions [35 a], they write *E(v)u-krātidasa* for Εὐκρατίδου,[52] and Gk. ταῦρος appears in Sanskrit as *tāvuras* (cf. ἀϝυτάρ, etc. [54 b]).

54 e. That αυ and ευ were still true diphthongs in the Jewish community at Rome in the second and third centuries A.D. is indicated by their constant correspondence with Lat. *au* and *eu* in the catacomb inscriptions, and also by occasional misspellings such as ἀότοῦ, γραματεός, γραμματεούς, γραμματηού(ς).[53]

55. In Gothic of the fourth century A.D. the letter υ is employed (1) as the representative of Gk. υ or οι in loan-words, (2) as the sign for the native bilabial *w*, i.e. [w] (possibly with some tendency toward a spirant pronunciation), and (3) to represent the final element of Gk. αυ and ευ. Since the usual Greek value of υ, namely [y], cannot be the source of the usual Gothic value, namely [w], we must derive the latter from the use of υ in the diphthongs αυ and ευ. But here we are confronted with the apparent difficulty that Greek αυ must have differed from the native Gothic *au*; for while Ulfilas writes *Daweid, Pawlus*, etc. he writes *auso* 'ear', *raus* 'reed', etc. We must conclude that αυ had by

---

natural glide before the *u*-sound"; for such a glide is natural only when the *u*-sound precedes. ἀϝυτάρ is a contamination of the equivalent spellings, ἀϝτάρ and αὐτάρ.

[52] Gardner, Indian Coins 16, 165, etc.
[53] Leon, TAPA 58.224 f.

this time progressed so far from the old value [au] toward the Modern Greek value [av] or [af] that it could not be identified with Goth. *au*. The assumption of a Greek diphthong with final [w] like Eng. *w* and a Gothic diphthong with a more open final member will account for the different treatment of the two and at the same time provide an explanation of the use of Gk. *v* for Goth. *w*. Gk. ευ appears in Gothic as *aiw*, where *ai* stands for [ε] (*aiwlaugia* = εὐλογία, *Aiwneika* = Εὐνίκη); ευ, therefore, was [εw] in the fourth century.[54]

56. There is no convincing evidence of earlier date for a change of αυ and ευ in the direction of the Modern Greek pronunciation [av, εv] or [af, εf]. A certain Egyptian Greek of the second century B.C. has left us the forms ῥάνδους = ῥάβδους, UPZ 1.12.32, 13.25, and ἐμβλένσαντες = ἐμβλέψαντες, P Lond. 1.38.15; but it would be rash indeed to conclude on such evidence that the fully developed Modern Greek pronunciation was current at that early date.[55] Δαβιδ beside Δαυιδ in the Septuagint and epigraphical Φλαβιος beside Φλαουιος merely prove that Greek had no satisfactory way of transcribing Hebrew wau or Latin *v*. An Attic inscription of 120 A.D. (IG 2².2037) reads εὐφήβοισι, but this may stand for εὐεφήβοισι.

57. In classical times αυ was pronounced much as *ow* in English *how*, i.e. [au].[56] The pronunciation of ευ was not like anything in English, French, or German; it was similar to the diphthong of Sp. *ceuta*, i.e. [eu].

ΥΙ

58. The diphthong υι was perhaps inherited in certain cases of υἱός (e.g. gen. υἱός from *suiwós*). Elsewhere υι is due to contraction of υ + ι (ἰδυίας from *idusyās* : Skt. *vidúṣyās*) or to analogy. Its value must originally have been about the same as that of Lat. *ui* [142–4], but *v* in this diphthong seems to have shared the change to [y] [35, 35 a–d]. In Attic the ι was then assimilated to the υ and the two coalesced to form ῡ before the close of the fifth century B.C. Consequently the diphthong does not appear in Attic inscriptions of the fourth century; instead we find ὑύς, Ἰλείθυα, ὀργυᾶς, etc.

In Hellenistic times the diphthong υι was reintroduced into the

---

[54] See especially Jellinek, Zeitschrift für deutsches Altertum 36.266–78.

[55] Cf. Blass 79; G. Meyer, Gr. Gramm.³ 193; Mayser 115. Some other mistakes, no more significant than these, are discussed by Hatzidakis, Ἀναγνώσματα 1.422.

[56] In standard English the diphthong of *how* is [au], but [au] is sometimes heard in standard American English.

κοινή from other dialects, chiefly Ionic.   Consequently the grammarians record the Attic forms as different from their own.

Choeroboscus, 213.8–11 Hilgard:[57] ὅτι ἐν διφθόγγῳ ἐστὶ τὸ ⟨υι ἐν τῷ⟩ τετυφυῖα καὶ γεγραφυῖα δηλοῦσιν οἱ Ἀθηναῖοι τετυφῦα ⟨καὶ γεγραφῦα⟩ λέγοντες· οἱ γὰρ Ἀθηναῖοι τὸ ι τὸ ἐν διφθόγγῳ ἀποβάλλειν πεφύκασιν, οἷον κλαίω κλάω, ποιῶ ποῶ.

The use of yi in Latin to represent υι (e.g. Ilithyia) shows that in Hellenistic as in Ionic and early Attic the prior element of υι was the front rounded vowel [y].

Inscriptions in the Jewish catacombs in Rome show υειός three times, and this must indicate persistence of the diphthongal pronunciation. The single instance of υός is probably an Atticism.[58]

No doubt the Modern Greek pronunciation of υι as [i] resulted from the change of υ to [i], on which see [34, 37].

In Attic of the fifth century υι seems to have been similar to Fr. ui in lui, except that it was probably a falling diphthong [yi] instead of a rising diphthong.   Attic of the fourth century had no diphthong υι, in spite of the occurrence of the digraph in our texts of fourth century authors.

ĀI, ḤI, AND ΩI

59. The Greek diphthongs with long prior member and final ι may, if standing at the end of a word, be inherited (λύκῳ : Av. yasnāi, Skt. devāya, Lat. servō).   In the interior of words always and sometimes in final position they result from contraction or analogy; e.g. κλῇζω from κληίζω.   In ancient times the ι was always written on the line, and it will be convenient to write it so in this section.   The orthography of these diphthongs, as of the others, must originally have represented the pronunciation.   In Homer we actually have variation between diphthongal and dissyllabic pronunciation in some words, as Θρῆικες beside Θρήϊκες, πατρῷον beside πατρώϊον.

60. Attic inscriptions of the early fourth century show ει beside ηι, as in κλείς, IG 2².1414.47 (after 403 B.C.; κλῆις occurs in l. 44), 1425.389 (between 378 and 366 B.C.).   This orthography prevailed in the third and second centuries, and in words which, like κλείς, were not subject to analogical influence from related forms with η, the spelling ει was

---

[57] 'By saying τετυφῦα and γεγραφῦα the Athenians show that υι in τετυφυῖα and γεγραφυῖα is a diphthong; for it is characteristic of the Athenians to drop ι in a diphthong, for example, κλαίω κλάω, ποιῶ ποῶ.'

[58] Leon, TAPA 58.224.

constant in Hellenistic and later times. Since ει in the fourth century denoted a close e [eˑ], that must be what ηι then became. The conclusion is supported by the use of ε in the datives χαλκοθήκε̄ and αὐτε̂, IG 2².120.36 (357 B.C.) and in the nominatives βασιλές and Βρισεές for βασιληίς and Βρισηίς on Attic vases.[59] After ει, i.e. [eˑ], became [iˑ] in the third century B.C. [31], there appeared such spellings as Βρισίς, IG 2.3560, and Ἡρακλίδου, 2011.2.

61. In certain forms, however, analogy restored η. In the dative singular of the first declension the process was this:

χώρᾱ, χώρᾱς, χωρᾶν : χώρᾱι = τιμή, τιμῆς, τιμήν : τιμῆι.

Since -ᾱι was still a diphthong, the analogy demanded a diphthong in τιμῆι, and we find the restored form written consistently with ηι.[60] In the second and third persons singular of the subjunctive the analogical proportion stands:

λύομεν, λύετε : λύεις, λύει = λύωμεν, λύητε : λύῃς, λύῃ.

Since the inducing forms, λύεις and λύει, contained at this time, not diphthongs, but long vowels of the same quality that appeared elsewhere in the paradigm [23, 24], the restored subjunctive forms contained, not ηι, but the η that appeared in the second person plural. Consequently we find very frequently such subjunctives as δοθῇ, P Petr. 2.2.1.10 (260 B.C.). When late inscriptions and papyri spell subjunctive forms with ηι this is due in part to the influence of old documents with ηι in these forms, in part to contracted subjunctives like τιμᾶι and δηλοῖ, and perhaps in part to indicatives of the second and third persons singular with written ει = [eˑ].

62. The diphthongs ᾱι and ωι, and also the restored ηι, lost their second member at various times in different parts of the Greek world. In Attica the loss occurred not far from 200 B.C.[61] The change is reflected in the form of Greek loan-words in Latin; *Thraex, tragoedus,* etc., were borrowed in early times, while *Thrāx, Thrācia, ōdēum* are based upon later Greek forms. We have the testimony of Strabo that ι was silent in the dative singular ⟨of the first and second declensions⟩:

14 p. 648:[62] πολλοὶ γὰρ χωρὶς τοῦ ι γράφουσι τὰς δοτικάς, καὶ ἐκβάλλουσι δὲ τὸ ἔθος φυσικὴν αἰτίαν οὐκ ἔχον.

---

[59] Kretschmer, Vaseninschriften 140.
[60] Meisterhans-Schwyzer 64; Mayser 122.
[61] Meisterhans-Schwyzer 67.
[62] 'For many write the datives without the ι and reject the custom (of writing them) which has no basis in nature.'

When Strabo's contemporary, Dionysius of Halicarnassus, Comp. Verb. 106.12 f., criticised Pindar for following the final ι of ἀγλαΐαι with the initial ι of ἴδετε, either he was unduly influenced by orthography or he recognized that in Pindar's time ᾱι had been a real diphthong although it was such no longer.

63. In Attic of the fifth century ᾱι, ηι, and ωι were all true diphthongs, [a·i], [ɛ·i], and [ɔ·i] respectively, and ᾱι and ωι retained this character in the fourth century. It is noteworthy that ωι rather than οι was similar to Eng. *oi* in *oil*.

ᾹΥ, ΗΥ, AND ΩΥ

64. What we know about the pronunciation of the rare diphthongs with long prior member and final υ is inferred from etymology and orthography. They all result from contractions of simple vowels with diphthongs ending in υ (ἑαυτῷ, Ion. ἑωυτῷ from *ἑοῖ αὐτῷ; ταὐτό, Ion., Dor. τωὐτό from τὸ αὐτό), or from analogy on the basis of short diphthongs in final υ, e.g.:

$$\text{ἐλπίζω} : \text{ἤλπισα} = \text{εὑρίσκω} : \text{ηὑρέθην}.$$

It is a fair inference that υ in these diphthongs as well as in the others was normal *u*; we may assume that ᾱυ was [a·u], ηυ was [ɛ·u], and ωυ was [ɔ·u].

Shortly before the beginning of the Christian Era ᾱυ in Hellenistic Greek lost its final member, as we learn from spellings like ἑατῷ, IG 2 Add. 489 b 15 (between 39 and 32 B.C.).

CHAPTER III

THE GREEK CONSONANTS

Voiced and Voiceless Consonants

65. The Greeks, like the Romans, are silent about the distinction between voiced and voiceless consonants, but there is no doubt that the difference was present in Ancient, as it is in Modern Greek.

The phonetic processes of the language mark off two groups of consonants. Thus, among the mutes, κ, π, τ, χ, φ, and θ frequently stand next one another, as in κόπτω, ζευκτός, ἐκπέμπω, φθάνω, χθών, Ἀτθίς, ἀπφύς, βάκχη, and γ, β, and δ may be combined, as in σμάραγδος and ῥάβδος, but members of one group are never combined with members of the other in the interior of a word, except for etymological reasons, as in compound verbs, such as ἐκδίδωμι. In Attic inscriptions even the preposition ἐκ is sometimes written ἐγ before β or γ, as in ἐγ βουλῆς, IG 2².1672.68, etc., ἐγ Γαργητίων, 3.1636. The similarity of κ, π, and τ with χ, φ, and θ is indicated further by the fact that the latter sounds change to the former upon the loss of their aspiration (τίθημι, πέφευγα, κέχευμαι). The liquids, λ, μ, ν, ρ, are combined with mutes, sometimes of one group and sometimes of the other; but whenever they influence the character of a mute they produce β, δ, or γ; as in δέδειγμαι, ἄμβροτος, μέμβλωκα, ἄνδρα. The grammarians (cited in [98]) tell us that ξ and ψ contain κ and π respectively, while ζ contains δ; and accordingly we find δέδειξαι beside δέδεικται and λέλειψαι beside λέλειπται, but ἐλπίζω beside ἐλπίδα. When ζ became a simple consonant it retained its affinity with β, δ, and γ, as we see from such spellings as πελαζγικόν and Gothic *praizbwtairei*. We thus have two groups of consonants which are rarely combined with each other, namely, β, γ, δ, ζ, and π, κ, τ, φ, χ, θ, ξ, ψ. Furthermore λ, μ, ν, and ρ show affinity with the first group rather than with the second, while σ goes with the second except in words in which ζ is ultimately substituted for it. This state of affairs can scarcely be accounted for except on the hypothesis that the sounds of the first group were voiced and those of the second voiceless. The others, as we shall see, were sometimes voiced and sometimes voiceless.

59

Modern Greek classifies the consonants in the same way, except that π, τ, and κ have come to be voiced after nasals, an exception which indicates that these nasals have all along been voiced.

66. Words borrowed by and from various other languages make available for the argument the independent evidence upon the distribution of voicing in those languages. The connection with Latin is established by numerous words, such as Καπετωλιον, Βασσος, Δομετιος, Γαϊος, *catapulta, basis, Daedalus, Agamemnon, Philippus, Thēsaurus, charta,* and also by some variants from the standard orthography, such as *calx* from χάλιξ, *tūs* beside θύος, *Pilipus* (CIL 1².552, 2400), *Filippus* (3.124), Ἀφφιος, Ἀπφαιος (passim), Σολφικιος (IG 2².4237), Δομεστιχος (3.1133.76, 1230, 1257). The exchanges between India and Greece in the last three centuries B.C. may be illustrated by Γαγγης = *Gaṅgā*, Ταξιλα = *Takṣaśilā*, Γανδαριοι = *Gandhārās*, βραχμανες = *brahmānas*, and the coin legends *Evukrātidasa* = Εὐκρατίδου, *Arkhebiyasa* = Ἀρχεβίου, *Apaladatasa* = Ἀπολλοδότου, *Theuphilasa* = Θεοφίλου. Gothic has *Bēþlaíhaím, Filippus, Gaddarēnus, paíntēkustē, paska.* The confusion between the Greek voiced and voiceless mutes in Coptic and, to a lesser extent, in Armenian and the Rabbinical texts is due to peculiarities of the borrowing languages.

Further details in the matter of voicing or its lack will be brought out in the discussion of the several letters.

P

67. Ancient descriptions of ρ leave no room for doubt that it was a trilled tongue-tip *r*, similar to Italian *r* or the *r* of rural French and German.

Plato, Cratylus 426 D, E:[1] τὸ δὲ οὖν ῥῶ τὸ στοιχεῖον, ὥσπερ λέγω, καλὸν ἔδοξεν ὄργανον εἶναι τῆς κινήσεως τῷ τὰ ὀνόματα τιθεμένῳ πρὸς τὸ ἀφομοιοῦν τῇ φορᾷ· πολλαχοῦ γοῦν χρῆται αὐτῷ εἰς αὐτήν. . . . ἑώρα γαρ, οἶμαι, τὴν γλῶτταν ἐν τούτῳ ἥκιστα μένουσαν, μάλιστα δὲ σειομένην.

Dion. Hal. 54.1–3:[2] τὸ δὲ ρ φωνεῖται τῆς γλώττης ἄκρας ἀπορριπιζούσης τὸ πνεῦμα καὶ πρὸς τὸν οὐρανὸν ἐγγὺς τῶν ὀδόντων ἀνισταμένης.

---

[1] 'The letter *rho*, as I say, appeared to the name-giver to be a fine instrument expressive of motion when he wanted to imitate rapidity; at any rate he often uses it thus. . . . For he saw, I suppose, that the tongue is least quiet and most rapidly shaken in pronouncing this letter.'

[2] 'And ρ is pronounced by the tip of the tongue sending forth the breath in puffs and rising to the palate near the teeth.'

Ibid. 54.10–14:[3] δύναται δ' οὐχ ὁμοίως κινεῖν τὴν ἀκοὴν ἅπαντα· ἡδύνει μὲν γὰρ αὐτὴν τὸ λ καὶ ἔστι τῶν ἡμιφώνων γλυκύτατον, τραχύνει δὲ τὸ ρ καὶ ἔστι τῶν ὁμογενῶν γενναιότατον.

67 a. The grammarians prescribe rough breathing for initial ρ, medial ρρ, and ρ after aspirates.

Herodian 1.546.20 f. Lenz:[4] Τὸ ρ ἀρχόμενον λέξεως δασύνεσθαι θέλει, ῥά, ῥανίς, ῥάξ, χωρὶς τοῦ 'Ρᾶρος (ἔστι δὲ ὄνομα κύριον).

Ibid., 547.5 f.:[5] τὸ ρ, ἐὰν δισσὸν γένηται ἐν μέσῃ λέξει, τὸ μὲν πρῶτον ψιλοῦται, τὸ δὲ δεύτερον δασύνεται, οἷον συρράπτω.

Schol. Dion. Thr. 143.17–22:[6] τοῦτο δὲ ρ οὐ μόνον κατ' ἀρχὰς καὶ ψιλοῦται καὶ δασύνεται, ἀλλὰ καὶ κατὰ τὸ μέσον, οἷον τὸ ἔρραπτον· τὸ μὲν πρῶτον ψιλοῦται, τὸ δὲ δεύτερον δασύνεται· ὡσαύτως καὶ τὰ ὅμοια. οἱ δὲ ἀρχαῖοι γραμματικοὶ τὸ μὲν μετὰ ψιλοῦ εὑρισκόμενον ρ ἐψίλουν, τὸ δὲ μετὰ δασέος ἐδάσυνον· οἷον τὸ 'Ατρεὺς καὶ κάπρος ἐψίλουν, τὸ δὲ χρόνος ἀφρὸς θρόνος ἐδάσυνον.

67 b. Greek inscriptions written in the earlier alphabets show a few traces of this pronunciation, namely Corcyrean ρhοϝαῖσι, IG 9.1.868; Boeotian hραφσα⟨ϝοιδῷ⟩, Eph. Arch. 1896.244;[7] Naxian φhράhσο, SGDI 5423. The spelling τέθριππον from τετρ-ίππο- is merely the converse of the prescription of the "ancient grammarians"; for here as elsewhere τ + h = θ [90]. Probably φροῦδος from προ-ὁδο-, φρούρα from προ-ὁρα-, and φροίμιον beside προοίμιον also get their initial aspirates from a following ῥ. On account of the variant προοίμιον I am inclined to think that the ῥ resulted from ρ + ' upon contraction, but possibly Sommer, Griechische Lautstudien 45–53, is right in thinking rather of an anticipated ' in the uncontracted form. In either case τέθριππον makes it likely that the rough breathing properly belonged to the ρ. Standard Latin orthography inserts *h* after initial *r* and medial *rr* in Greek words, as in *rhētor, Tyrrhēnī,* and Latin inscriptions have many such forms as

[3] 'They cannot all affect the sense of hearing in the same way. λ falls pleasurably on it, and is the sweetest of the semi-vowels; while ρ has a rough quality, and is the noblest of its class.'

[4] 'At the beginning of a word ρ is usually rough (ῥά, ῥανίς, ῥάξ), except 'Ρᾶρος, which is a proper name.'

[5] 'If ρ is doubled in the interior of a word, the first ρ is smooth and the second is rough, as συρράπτω.'

[6] 'And this ρ not only when initial but also when medial is both smooth and rough, ἔρραπτον (the first ρ is smooth and the second rough), and like words in the same way. The ancient grammarians used smooth breathing with ρ occurring after a smooth (mute), and rough breathing after a rough (mute); for example they used smooth breathing in 'Ατρεύς and κάπρος, and rough breathing in χρόνος, ἀφρός, and θρόνος.'

[7] Thumb, IF 8.228.

Crhestos, CIL 3.1656; *Prhygia,* 9.4600; and *Trhacem,* 1424.[8] In Armenian we find *hretor* = ῥήτωρ, *hrog* = ῥόγα, *Hrom* = ῾Ρώμη, but in view of *retin* = ῥητίνη it is likely that the aspiration was only a learned tradition at the time of the borrowing [78].[9]

The variation in the orthographies just cited may be interpreted to mean that the aspiration did not either precede or follow the ρ, but accompanied it throughout. In other words, one may conclude that ῥ was a voiceless trilled *r*. If this was the nature of ῥ, one understands at once how ρ + ʻ could yield ῥ and how this ῥ could then convert a preceding τ into θ in τέθριππον. Further confirmation will come from a study of the other continuants [69, 70, 77, 85]. It is interesting to note that ῥ has yielded a voiceless sound in Tsakonian *šinda* 'root' from Laconian ῥίδδα = Att. ῥίζα as against *adže* 'big' from ἀδρός.[10]

67 c. In many words ῥ- and -ρρ- come from original *sr* (ῥέω, ἔρρει, ἔρρευσα : Skt. *sravati* 'flows'). In other words, as we shall see [85], the unvoicing of ρ appears to be a trace of a lost laryngeal. Furthermore, initial ῥ appears in a limited number of cases to be due to a secondary spread of this articulation, as in the name of the letter, ῥῶ, and in loan words.

68. Without the rough breathing ρ has always been a trilled tongue-tip *r* [r]; ῥ was in ancient times the corresponding voiceless sound [r̥].

Λ

69. The description of λ by Dionysius of Halicarnassus does not tell what part of the tongue and palate were concerned in its production.

Comp. Verb. 53.11–13:[11] φωνεῖται δ' αὐτῶν ἕκαστον τοιόνδε τινα τρόπον· τὸ μὲν λ τῆς γλώττης πρὸς τὸν οὐρανὸν ἱσταμένης καὶ τῆς ἀρτηρίας συνηχούσης.

Probably the articulation in Attic and Hellenistic corresponded with that of τ, δ, and θ.

In Cretan λ before a consonant was occasionally written υ (ἀδευπιαί, SGDI 4991.5.18, αὐκάν· ἀλκήν, Κρῆτες, Hesych.). This must mean that before a consonant Cretan λ approached [u], that is, it was a velarized *l*. Several modern Greek dialects have velarized *l* or contain evidence for such a sound at some time in the past. Greek loan-words in Ar-

---

[8] Other examples are cited by Kretschmer, Vaseninschriften 160 f., and Leumann, Stolz-Schmalz lateinische Grammatik 132.

[9] Thumb, ByzZ 9.415.

[10] See Vasmer, KZ 51.158.

[11] 'They are severally pronounced somewhat as follows: λ by the tongue rising to the palate, and by the windpipe helping the sound.'

menian show sometimes l and sometimes l.[12] Outside of Crete, however, the limits of the velar pronunciation of λ in ancient times cannot be determined.

The development of an ε between λ and a following vowel (ξύλεων) in Cos has been thought to indicate a palatalized l.[13]

There are indications that sl yielded Gk. 'λ, just as sr yielded $ρ$ [67 b, c, 85]; λhαβō'ν, IG 4.177 (Aegina); Λhάβετος, Kretschmer, Vaseninschriften 158 (Attica); *Clhoe*, CIL 5.4721. A similar pronunciation is indicated for λ in a loan word by λhέōν on an Attic vase, Kretschmer, Vaseninschriften 159. Since the grammarians do not prescribe this pronunciation, and since it is rarely reflected in loan words, it cannot have had any such currency as $ρ$. Very likely standard Attic of classical times had no voiceless l.

Attic and Hellenistic λ was probably similar to French l rather than to the English alveolar l; it seems to have been [l].

M AND N

70. Dion. Hal. 53.13–54.1:[14] τὸ δὲ μ (φωνεῖται) τοῦ μὲν στόματος τοῖς χείλεσι πιεσθέντος, τοῦ δὲ πνεύματος διὰ τῶν ῥωθώνων μεριζομένου· τὸ δὲ ν τῆς γλώττης τὴν φορὰν τοῦ πνεύματος ἀποκλειούσης καὶ μεταφερούσης ἐπὶ τοὺς ῥώθωνας τὸν ἦχον.

μ was clearly a labial nasal, while ν involved closure of the oral passage by the tongue, no doubt in the same position in which the dental mutes were formed [96, 97].

The partial or complete assimilation of a nasal to certain following consonants, which is regularly denoted in our printed texts in the interior of a word, occurred also at the end of a word except at the end of a phrase (e.g. τὴμ πόλιν, τὸγ κήρυκα, τὸλ λόγον like σύμμαχος, ἐγγράφω, συλλαμβάνω). The inscriptions frequently indicate assimilation both in the interior and at the end of a word, but etymological spelling is also common in both positions.

It is safe to assume that IE sm and sn became Primitive Gk. 'μ and 'ν just as sr became $ρ$ and sl became 'λ.[15] The existence of voiceless μ

[12] Thumb, ByzZ 9.404–6.

[13] Schwyzer, Griech. Gramm. 212 f., and references.

[14] 'μ is pronounced by the mouth being closed tight by means of the lips, while part of the breath passes through the nostrils, ν by the tongue intercepting the current of the breath, and diverting the sound toward the nostrils.'

[15] See especially Sommer, Griechische Lautstudien 26–44. I differ from him chiefly in positing Primitive Gk. voiceless m and n rather than hm and hn. This is a very slight difference, and it would be foolish to maintain very confidently the actual existence of either nuance rather than the other in a prehistoric period.

(i.e. 'μ-) in some of the historic dialects is evidenced by the following forms: Attic μhεγάλō, IG 1².623 (sixth century B.C.); Megarian Mhεγα[ρεî], SGDI 3045.12; μhειλο[?], IG 7.3493; Pamphylian μhε(ιάλē), SGDI 1266.22. There is no evidence that a voiceless nasal persisted in Attic or Hellenistic Greek after the sixth century B.C.

Throughout the history of the language the usual pronunciation of μ has been similar to that of Eng. *m*, i.e. [m]; ν has probably always been similar to French *n* rather than to the English alveolar *n*; it has always been [n].

AGMA

71. We quote in [178 a] Varro's notice (ap. Priscian 2.30.15–21 K = 201.6–8 GS) of the velar nasal [ŋ], which was written *n* in Latin but γ in Greek.

71 a. Early Greek inscriptions use ν instead of γ (ἐνγύς, IG 1².974.2— ca. 600 B.C.; 9.1.521—Acarnania, fifth century B.C.). The Latin orthography with *n* and the similar spelling of Etruscan, Umbrian, and Oscan words reflect the early usage of Italian Greeks. Originally γγ stood for [g·], and it continued to be used in this value long after γ began to be used for a nasal, as in ἔγγονος = ἔκγονος (frequent in Attic and other inscriptions later than the fifth century B.C.) and in such phrases as ἐγ Γαργητίων, IG 3.1636.

71 b. The use of γ for the velar nasal appears in Attic in the fifth century (Εὐαγγέλō, Στρογγυλίων, IG 1².535—second quarter of the fifth century B.C.). Such a change in orthography is scarcely understandable unless there was an actual change of γ = [g] to a nasal in some position. The only position in which such a change seems at all possible is the position before a nasal; γν and γμ might easily change from [gn, gm] to [ŋn, ŋm], just as βν and βμ became μν and μμ (σεμνός : σέβομαι, τέτριμμαι : τρίβω). The name *agma* for the palatal nasal, which Varro cites from Ion of Chios, implies the pronunciation of γμ as [ŋm]; for most other Greek letter names contain the sound denoted by the letter.

Several epigraphical spellings and the later development of the groups γν and γμ are most easily understood on the basis of the palatal nasal. The clearest cases are Ἀγγνούσιος,[16] IG 2.1698.3, and φθέγγματα,

[16] I cannot extract any meaning from Schwyzer's (Griech. Gramm. 1.214) remark on this form. Does he assume that φθέγμα contained [ŋgm] while our word contained [gn]? But in the preceding sentence he has correctly set up the groups [ŋm] and [ŋn].

CIG 4740.7, 4741.9. The regular development of γν and γμ seems to have been first to [ŋn] and [ŋm] and then to νν and μμ (Attic Ἀριάννη, Kretschmer, Vaseninschriften 171 f., for Ἀριάγνη; Locrian ἐγ Ναυπάκτω, IG 9.1.334; Cretan γιννόμενον, SGDI 5010.2, ψάφιμμα for ψάφιγμα, 5087 b 7; Laconian πούμμα· πυγμή, Hesych.; *σιμμα for σίγμα implied by Lat. *simma* 'semicircular table' and Coptic *sima* = σίγμα).[17] The further development, seen at an early date in γίνομαι and γινώσκω, appears in Ptolemaic and later papyri (πραματείαις corrected to πραγματείαις, UPZ 1.1.25—165 B.C.; τεταμένους, P. Tebt. 1.5.144—118 B.C.)[18] and is regular in colloquial Modern Greek (πρᾶμα from πράγμα). The standard orthography, however, has always been γν and γμ, and no doubt spelling pronunciation has been common among the educated classes from ancient times, as it is today ([gn, gm] in antiquity, [gn, gm] at present).[19]

71 c. The articulation of a nasal before a palatal consonant seems always to have been in the position required for that consonant; nasal γ was in Attic and Hellenistic Greek similar to Eng. *n* in *ink*, i.e. [ŋ].

F

72. Most of the ancient Greek dialects preserve clear traces of the Indo-European phoneme *w*. Frequently the sound is written as ϝ,[20] as in ϝέργον = ἔργον : Eng. *work*. In the traditional text of Homer the phoneme is never written, but its presence or former presence frequently has to be assumed to account for prosodic irregularities.

That the sound was very close to that of *υ* as final member of a diphthong has already been inferred [40, 54b] from the use of ϝ in writing diphthongs (σποϝδδάν, ⟨β⟩οϝσί, ἀϝτός, Ναϝπακτίōν, Ἐϝθείας, ἀϝυτō̄, ἀϝυτάρ, ἀμεϝύσασθαι, etc.). Of similar import is the use of ϝ for the

[17] Schwyzer, KZ 58.189-93.

[18] Other instances in Schwyzer, KZ 58.189 f.

[19] There is no need for or plausibility in Schwyzer's (KZ 61.222–52) theory that νν and μμ have been changed to [gn] and [gm] by a queer kind of dissimilation. Some of the arguments for the change of [gn, gm] to [ŋn, ŋm] by Ebel (KZ 13.264), Brugmann (Curt. St. 4.103 f.), and L. Havet (MSL 4.276) are no longer tenable, but enough remain to make the change practically certain.

Sapir's suggestion (Lang. 14.273 f.) that Greek once had a prevocalic phoneme [ŋ] which was denoted by the letter γ (e.g. in γυμνός and γάλα) has little plausibility and is supported by no evidence whatever. Against it is the fact noted above that the conditioned velar nasal was originally written ν.

[20] We are not here interested in the paleographic varieties of the character, or their origin, or even in the question whether or not they are all to be traced to one original type.

glide after v, i.e. [u], in Cretan τίτυϝος, SGDI 4976, and τιτουϝέσθω, 5128.

73. The Oscans and Umbrians took over, through Etruscan mediation, the Greek ϝ in the form ⊐, and used it for the consonant that they represented by V when they employed the Latin alphabet. Modern scholars transcribe Oscan ⊐ by v and Latin V by u, and so we have the nom. sg. of the Oscan word for 'via' cited as *víú*, whereas the Oscan cognate of Lat. *vincō* is written in Latin letters as *uincter*. The Oscan character ⊐ is also used to represent the glide between u and a following dissimilar vowel (*eítiuvam* in the native alphabet is equivalent to *eituam* in the Latin alphabet). When Oscan is written in Greek letters ϝ is used in the same way (Διουϝει ϝερσορει 'Iovi versori'). In view of the known value of Latin v [148–52], all this clearly indicates that ϝ was similar to Eng. *w*.

74. The tradition of the end of the last century B.C. also identified ϝ with Lat. v, as appears from the following:

Dion. Hal., Ant. Rom. 1.20:[21] καὶ διδόασιν αὐτοῖς χωρία τῆς ἑαυτῶν ἀποδασάμενοι τὰ περὶ τὴν ἱερὰν λίμνην, ἐν οἷς ἦν τὰ πολλὰ ἑλώδη, ἃ νῦν κατὰ τὸν ἀρχαῖον τῆς διαλέκτου τρόπον Οὐέλια ὀνομάζεται. σύνηθες γὰρ ἦν τοῖς ἀρχαίοις Ἕλλησιν ὡς τὰ πολλὰ προτιθέναι τῶν ὀνομάτων, ὁπόσων αἱ ἀρχαὶ ἀπὸ φωνηέντων ἐγίνοντο, τὴν ου συλλαβὴν ἑνὶ στοιχείῳ γραφομένην. τοῦτο δ' ἦν ὥσπερ γάμμα διτταῖς ἐπὶ μίαν ὀρθὴν ἐπιζευγνύμενον ταῖς πλαγίαις, ὡς ϝελένη, καὶ ϝάναξ, καὶ ϝοῖκος, καὶ ϝανήρ, καὶ πολλὰ τοιαῦτα.

Cassiodorus 7.148.5–10 K = Varro 208.19–209.3 GS:[22] Est quaedam littera in F litterae speciem figurata, quae digamma nominatur quia duos apices ex gamma littera habere videatur. Ad huius similitudinem soni nostri coniunctas vocales digammon appellare voluerunt, ut est *votum, virgo*. Itaque in prima syllaba digamma et vocalem oportuit poni, ϝotum, ϝirgo; quod et Aeolii fecerunt et antiqui nostri; sicut scriptura in quibusdam libellis declarat. Hanc litteram Terentius Varro dum vult demonstrare, ita perscribit, *vau*.

---

[21] 'And apportioning them a part of their own domain, they assigned them the district about the sacred pond, where most of the land was marshy (ἑλώδης), which now is named according to the ancient fashion of the language *Velia* (Οὐέλια). For it was the common practice of the ancient Hellenes to prefix to words beginning with a vowel the syllable ου written with one letter. This was like gamma with two cross strokes joined to one upright stroke, as ϝελένη, ϝάναξ, ϝοῖκος, ϝανήρ, and many similar words.'

[22] 'There is a letter shaped like F, which is named digamma because it seems to have two outlines of gamma. According to the likeness of this sound our ancestors wanted to call digamma such groups of vowels as appear in *votum* and *virgo*. Therefore in the initial syllable digamma and a vowel should have been written; this the Aeolians and our ancestors did, as the spelling in certain books shows. In the attempt to indicate this letter Terentius Varro spells ⟨the name⟩ *vau*.'

The same tradition persisted in the first century A.D.; for Quintilian 1.4.8 (quoted in [152]) identifies consonantal *u* with digamma.

75. East Ionic was one of the first dialects to lose the phoneme ϝ, and consequently words from other dialects which contained this sound appear in Ionic, from Homer down, either with loss of ϝ or with the substitution of some other sound.[23] The vowel *v* represents ϝ in ὑάκινθος (ὑάκινθον, Il. 14.348; ὑακινθίνῳ, Od. 6.231 = 23.158). When the substitution was first made no doubt *v* was [u] without aspiration; but this *v* was later modified as were all others in the dialect, and when the word was transferred to Attic it was inevitably subjected to the universal Attic aspiration of initial *v*. In Homeric Ὀιλεύς, Ὀιλιάδης beside Hesiod's Ἰλεύς, Pindar's Ἰλιάδης, etc., and in Οἴτυλον, Il. 2.585, beside Βίτυλα, Ptolemy 3.14.43, *o* has been substituted for digamma (probably after the change of *v* to [y]). From later Ionic may be cited the name of the Ionic colony in Italy, which varies between Ἐλέα, Ἐλῆ and Ὑελῆ (on coins also Ϝελ⟨ητέων⟩).[24]

76. When the Ionic alphabet was adopted by the speakers of dialects that retained ϝ, they were confronted with a similar, but purely orthographic, difficulty. In some cases they wisely retained their own ϝ alongside of the Ionic letters, but frequently they left the phoneme unwritten or substituted *v* or *o*, as in Cretan ὑέργων, SGDI 5072 b 5, 8, for ϝέργων, beside ἕκαστος and ἴκατι, on the same inscription; Ὀράτριον = Ϝράτριον, 5041.13, 19; Ἄξος or Ὀάξος for Ϝάξος; Arcadian ὀλοαῖς = ὀλϝαῖς, IG 5.2.514.15; Cyprian ὕεσις· στολή, Πάφιοι, Hesych.

Another device, which became a favorite in Laconia and with the later lexicographers, was to substitute for ϝ an Ionic letter of more or less similar shape, much as early English printers substituted *y* for *þ* in such words as *ye* = *þe* = *the*, just because it resembled the required character more nearly than any other in fonts of type imported from the continent. No one can doubt that this is the explanation of the use of Γ and P for ϝ; but many scholars have assumed that whenever B is similarly used we must assume that both ϝ and β have been changed to [v]. It is entirely possible that in one place or another these two changes actually occurred in ancient times; the Modern Gk. change of β to [v] is familiar [95], and ϝ has yielded the same sound in Tsakonian *vànne* 'lamb' < Laconian *ϝαρνίον = βαρνίον· ἀρνίον, Hesych.[25] We

[23] Kretschmer, Wiener Eranos 118–21; cf. Glotta 3.321. See also Eva Fiesel, Namen des griechischen Mythos im Etruskischen 14 f.

[24] W. Schulze, KZ 33.395–7 = Kleine Schriften 395 f.

[25] Thumb, IF 9.296; Meillet, MSL 13.35 f.

shall see that β became the regular representative of Lat. v at about the time when we may suppose on other grounds also that both phonemes had become [v]. In general, however, the substitution of β for ϝ upon the introduction of the Ionic alphabet is not cogent evidence for a spirant pronunciation of either.[26]

77. While initial w of Primitive Indo-European regularly yields Attic smooth breathing (ἰδεῖν : Lat. *videō*; ἔπος : Lat. *vōx*, Skt. *vacas*), initial *sw* appears in Attic as rough breathing (ἔκυρος : Lat. *socer*, Skt. *śvaśuras*, OE *sweger*; ἑ : Skt. *svas*). In Homer we can trace the digamma in words of the first type by apparent hiatus like that before ἴσασι in Od. 2.211:

ἤδη γὰρ τὰ ἴσασι θεοὶ καὶ πάντες Ἀχαιοί.

But words of the second type show not only retention of a preceding short vowel, but also its apparent lengthening, as in Il. 3.172:

αἰδοῖός τέ μοί ἐσσι, φίλε ἑκυρέ, δεινός τε.

Here we need an initial consonant group in ἑκυρέ and in δεινός. A further trace of the variant form of digamma, which comes from *sw-*, has been detected in Boeotian Ϝϝεκαδάμοε, IG 7.593,: Thessalian Ϝεκέδαμος, and in Pamphylian ϝηϝ, SGDI 1266.23. This evidence indicates that IE *sw-* yielded Primitive Gk. voiceless w, i.e. 'ϝ-, just as *sr* > ῥ- [67 b], *sl-* > 'λ- [69], *sm-* > 'μ-, and *sn-* > 'ν- [70]. Further evidence for two w sounds is found by Meillet[27] in the Pamphylian use of two digamma signs; he interprets ϝ as representing the voiceless sound and Ⱳ as representing the voiced sound. The theory necessitates the assumption that initial ϝ before other vowels than οι was always voiceless in Pamphylian.

For Primitive Gk. 'ϝ- and Attic rough breathing due to an original voiceless laryngeal plus w, see [85].

78. For the most part ϝ was a voiced w, namely [w]; but ϝ in the group *hw*, which existed in certain historic dialects and which must have been the immediate source of Attic rough breathing in digamma words, was doubtless voiceless [w̥].

---

[26] An instance of variation between β and various vocalic substitutes for [w] in the Ionic-Attic-Hellenistic tradition is furnished by the Phrygian Σαβαζιος, Aristophanes +, beside Σαναζιος, Σαουαζιος, Σαοαζ(ι)ος, and Σααζιος (see Kretschmer, Einl. 195 f.). Here it is impossible to interpret β as [v]; but it must be admitted that the Phrygian phoneme may, for all we know, have been [v].

[27] Glotta, 2.26–8.

The Breathings[28]

79. In many words the rough breathing comes from IE *s* (ἑπτά : Skt. *saptá*; ὁ : Skt. *sá*, Goth. *sa*) or from anticipation of medial aspiration from medial *s* (εὕω : Lat. *ūrō* < IE *eusō*). Such an origin might yield at first a sound like the German *ach*-sound, i.e. [x]; cf. Slavic [x] from *s*.[29]

In other words rough breathing has been thought to come from IE *y* (ὅς : Skt. *yás*), but Sapir[30] has shown that we should expect IE *y* to yield a voiced sound in Greek, just as did all the other IE voiced continuants (*r* > ρ, *l* > λ, *m* > μ, *n* > ν, *w* > ϝ). He concludes that ζ- is the normal reflex of IE *y*- (ζυγόν : Skt. *yugám*, Lat. *iugum*). No doubt IE initial *sy*- yielded Gk. rough breathing just as IE *sw*- appears in Attic as rough breathing [77]. Examples are few, to be sure; one is apparently ὑμήν 'membrane' : Skt. *syūma* 'thong'. Medial *sy* after a vowel appears in Homeric Greek as -ι- (τοῖο : Skt. *tasya*, τελείω : τέλος). Probably the first result of the simplification was voiceless *y*, i.e. [ç]. This sound, if medial, may have become voiced; at any rate it is not distinguished from ι as final member of a diphthong in our texts (τοῖο : Skt. *tasya*, μοι: Skt. *me*). In initial position [ç] and [x] had apparently become identical by the time when the alphabet was introduced. At least they were not distinguished by different symbols.

For Primitive Gk. [ç] due to an original voiceless laryngeal plus *y*, see [85 fn. 43].

That Greek actually possessed a spirant, [x] or [ç], instead of mere aspiration at the time when the alphabet was introduced is virtually certain. The Hebrew-Phoenician alphabet had a letter, *hē*, whose value was similar to the later Greek rough breathing. Since this is the source of the Greek E, we must suppose that the Greeks had no such consonant when the alphabet was borrowed; probably they did not hear the Phoenician consonant at all, and supposed that their name of the letter, later written as εἶ [29], was identical with the Phoenician name. The letter H, earlier ⊟, is the Hebrew-Phoenician *chēth*, whose value was either a front-velar or a pharyngeal voiceless spirant. The fact that the Greeks preferred this to the available *hē* shows that the Greek consonant was a relatively strong spirant.

A trace of this value is probably to be recognized in the early Naxian (SGDI 5419, 5423) use of □Σ for ξ, if □ is a differentiation of ⊟, the

[28] Thumb, Untersuchungen über den Spiritus Asper im Griechischen, Strassburg, 1888.
[29] Meillet, Le slave commun 97 f.
[30] Lang. 14.271 f.

Naxian form of H. For the phonetics, compare German *Ochs* = [ɔks], etc.

80. In certain dialects, notably Asiatic Ionic, the rough breathing was lost before our earliest records,[31] and so the Ionic alphabet that was ultimately adopted by all Greek communities [19, 74] had no sign for such a phoneme. Consequently it was usually left undenoted in most of the dialects that still retained it; but occasionally, regularly in Heraclea and Tarentum, it was represented by the first half of the letter H, namely ⊢.

81. Aristophanes of Byzantium adopted this sign (writing it above the vowel letter) as a diacritic mark to distinguish words that were homonyms except for the breathing.[32] For example he wrote ὈΡΟΣ when he wanted to warn against reading ὄρος. Since he used the diacritic only when he wanted to make clear some such distinction, he obviously needed a device to enforce the alternative reading; accordingly, in order to caution his readers against saying ὄρος, he wrote ὈΡΟΣ with the second half of the letter H written above the line. The origin and value of the breathing marks are described by the later grammarians; e.g.:

Schol. Dion. Thr. 142.30–143.2:[33] τοῦτο δέ φησι μόνον, ὅτι τὸ σημεῖον τῆς δασείας, ἤτοι τὸ διχοτόμημα τοῦ Η τὸ ἐπὶ τὰ ἔξω ἀπεστραμμένον, τίθεται ἐπάνω φωνήεντος δασυνομένου, ἤγουν ἐκ τοῦ θώρακος μετὰ πολλῆς τῆς ὁρμῆς ἐκφερομένου· τὸ δὲ ἕτερον τοῦ αὐτοῦ στοιχείου διχοτόμημα, τὸ ἐπὶ τὰ ἔσω ἐστραμμένον, ἐπάνω φωνήεντος ψιλουμένου, ἤτοι ἐξ ἄκρων τῶν χειλέων προφερομένου.

82. The rough breathing is called by the grammarians πνεῦμα δασύ or more briefly δασεῖα (sc. προσῳδία) and the smooth breathing is named πνεῦμα ψιλόν; the same words and their derivatives are applied to initial vowels, e.g. φωνήεντος δασυνομένου in the passage just cited. This pair of adjectives and their derivatives must, when contrasted, denote respectively the abundance or absence of some feature: hair upon

[31] Otherwise K. Meister, Homerische Kunstsprache 209–26; but see E. Hermann, GGL 1922.139–41; Eva Fiesel, Namen des griechischen Mythos im Etruskischen 29.

[32] See Laum, Al. Akzent. 99–118, 128–34. In the first edition of this book I followed Blass, 90, in thinking that Aristotle, El. Soph. 177 b 3 ff., referred to the mark of the rough breathing when he said that a παράσημα was placed beside the word ὄρος or ὅρος; but Laum, 105 f., shows that παράσημα means a mark in the margin to indicate that the passage involves a grammatical problem.

[33] 'This means merely that the mark of the rough breathing, that is the half of H that is turned outwards, is placed above a vowel pronounced with aspiration, that is, expelled from the breast with much force; and that the other half of the same letter, the one that is turned inwards, is placed above a vowel pronounced without aspiration, that is, expelled from the tips of the lips.'

animals, feathers upon birds, trees upon a hill or a plain. By the grammarians they are used not only of initial vowels but also, from about 200 B.C., of the rough and smooth mutes [90 b] and, beginning apparently with Aristarchus, of the two kinds of ρ [67 a]. The only way to harmonize these three bits of phonetic description is to make δασύς refer to an audible puff of breath preceding or following another sound while ψιλός must indicate the absence of such a puff of breath.[34]

82 a. Greek loan-words in various foreign languages confirm our conclusion that the rough breathing was aspiration. Of the very abundant material we need cite only a few typical examples: Latin *Hinnad*, CIL 1².608 (212 B.C.), *hieroceryx*, 6.500 (377 A.D.), *Herculēs*, *historia*, *hymen* (Plautus +); Etruscan-Latin *Hercle*; Osc. *Herekleis*; Indic[35] *Heliyakreyasa* = 'Ηλιοκλέους, *Hipastratasa* = 'Ιπποστράτου, *Hermayasa* = 'Ερμαίου; Hebrew[36] *hegmon* = ἡγεμών, *hili* = ὕλη; Syriac[36] *hereticos*, *Hellas*, *Hermes*; Palmyrene[36] *hippica*, *hipatīcā* = ὑπατικός; Coptic[37] *hina* = ἵνα, *hoplon* = ὅπλον, *hoste* = ὥστε; Goth. *Haíbraius*, *Herodes*; Armenian *hymenaios*.

82 b. While the Ionic-Attic-Hellenistic graphic tradition provides information about aspiration of the initial vowel of final members of compounds only in cases where κ, τ, or π at the end of the prior member is aspirated (ἀνθίστημι, ἔφιππος) the early non-Ionic alphabets provide a number of forms such as εὐhορκô(ν), IG 1².34.6; πάρhεδροι, 127.19; ἐνhēβō'hαις, 5.1.213.33; πενταhετηρίδα, 14.645.105. Similar spellings with the sign ⊢ occur on the Heraclean tables and in literary papyri. From the similar forms on Latin inscriptions we may cite *Euhemerus*, *Polyhymnia*, *Synhistor*, CIL 9.4644 (5 B.C.); *pentaheterici*, 2.4136; *Euhodus* 5.6711. Wackernagel, Glotta 14.66 f., cites similar forms of Greek loanwords from Oriental languages. The Homeric scholia contain many notices on this topic;[38] their statements are of course based in part upon oral tradition and in part upon the pronunciation of Hellenistic and later times. There is no doubt that Attic and Hellenistic Greek often preserved the aspiration of the second member of a compound.

83. The lack of a letter for the rough breathing, combined with many

[34] It has been held by a number of scholars that the smooth breathing was a glottal stop, similar to that of German and to Hebrew *aleph*; but there is no evidence whatever in favor of the theory, and the phenomena of elision and crasis definitely disprove it. See Sturtevant, TAPA 68.112-9.

[35] Gardner, Indian Coins 23, 59, 62, etc.

[36] Thumb, Untersuchungen über den Spiritus Asper 85 f.

[37] Thumb, loc. cit.; Blok, Zeitschrift für ägyptische Sprache und Altertumskunde 62.57 f.

[38] Laum, Al. Akzent. 358-60.

local differences in the treatment of the phoneme, early gave rise to a grammatical literature on the subject, and the ultimate loss of the sound led the schoolmasters to redouble their efforts. The character of this literature is sketched in Schol. Dion. Thr. 154.3–9:[39]

τινὲς τῶν γραμματικῶν ἐξ ἐμπειρίας κανόνας ἐποιήσαντο κατὰ τὰς εὑρημένας παραδόσεις λέξιν ἑκάστην μεταχειρισάμενοι καὶ τὰ ἐν ταῖς λέξεσιν φωνήεντα ἀκριβωσάμενοι, πότε καὶ ὁπόσα δασύνονται καὶ ὁπόσα ψιλοῦνται. καὶ ἔστι τεχνολόγημα περὶ τούτων, πότε τὸ α πρὸ τοῦ β καὶ πρὸ τοῦ γ καὶ τῶν λοιπῶν στοιχείων δασύνεται ἢ ψιλοῦται. ὁμοίως καὶ τὸ ε καὶ τὰ λοιπὰ φωνήεντα πρὸ τῶν αὐτῶν στοιχείων πότε δασύνονται καὶ πότε ψιλοῦνται.

Our best criterion for determining the geographical and chronological limits of aspiration and loss of aspiration (psilosis) after the introduction of the Ionic alphabet is the epigraphical treatment of κ, π, and τ before closely connected words with rough breathing. Such forms as οὐχ οὗτος, ἐφ’ ᾧ, and ἀνθ’ οὗ indicate retention of the rough breathing, while οὐκ οὗτος, ἐπ’ ᾧ, and ἀντ’ οὗ (even if, as in the case of medieval manuscripts, the breathing is written) indicate its loss. This criterion shows[40] that the sound was generally preserved in Hellenistic Greek until the second century A.D., after which time it gradually dropped out of use.

Confirmation of this conclusion comes from the use of the signs for the breathings in the literary papyri. While they were originally used chiefly to distinguish between words that were written with the same letters but differed in aspiration (e.g. ὅρος : ὄρος), the second and especially the third century A.D. saw a gradual increase in their use.[41] Undoubtedly one reason for this was the increasing loss of aspiration before a vowel in ordinary speech while scholastic tradition still retained it, so that it became more and more important to inform the reader where to use the rough breathing and where not. As is usual in such cases the grammarians who supplied the diacritic marks had their own difficulties; they occasionally wrote ὀκτώ, ἔτυμον, ὀδόντων, etc.

Errors in recording the rough breathing in Gothic, Hebrew, and Armenian indicate that by the fourth or fifth century it was preserved

[39] 'Some of the grammarians have established standards of correctness based upon knowledge, having treated each word according to the traditions which they have found, and having accurately determined which vowels in the various words have rough breathing and when, and which have smooth breathing and when. There is also a system of rules about these matters; when α before β and before γ and so forth is rough or smooth, and when ε and the other vowels before the same letters are rough and when smooth.'

[40] Thumb, Untersuchungen über den Spiritus Asper 73–8.

[41] Laum, Al. Akzent. 454–6.

only as a scholastic tradition. This tradition, however, has persisted in writing throughout the Byzantine period and down to the present.

84. In classical Attic the rough breathing was an important phoneme similar to Eng. *h*, i.e. [h]. The smooth breathing was a grammarian's device to indicate absence of aspiration.

VOICELESS SEMIVOWELS

85. We have seen that IE *sr*- yielded Gk. ῥ and -*sr*- Gk. -ρῥ- [67 c], that IE *sl*- apparently yielded Gk. 'λ- [69], and also that IE *sm*- and *sn*- probably yielded Gk. 'μ- and 'ν- [70]. Similarly IE *sw*- yielded Attic rough breathing and 'ϝ in some at least of the digamma dialects [77], and IE *sy* became Greek rough breathing in the initial position [79]. In all these cases Greek possessed a voiced sound (ρ, λ, μ, ν, ϝ, ζ) coming from an IE semivowel unaccompanied by *s* (ἄροτρον : Lat. *arātrum*, λευκός : *lūceo*, μήτηρ : *māter*, νῦν : *nunc*, αἰϝεί : *aevum*, ζυγόν : *iugum*).

It has long been known that the voiceless members of the pairs ϝ- : 'ϝ- (Attic ' : ') and ζ- : '- frequently appear even in words which in Primitive Indo-European had no *s* before the *w* or *y* (ἔννυμι : *vestis*, ὅς : Skt. *yas* 'who, which').[42] There is reason to believe that ῥ, 'λ, 'μ, and 'ν also once existed in Greek words which had not lost an *s* before the semivowel. In many such words there is independent evidence that a laryngeal consonant has been lost before the semivowel, and since three of the four laryngeals of Pre-Indo-European were voiceless, we have here an explanation of the alternation between voiced and voiceless continuant in Greek.[43]

Σ

86. Gk. σ represents IE *s* in many words (ἐστί : Lat. *est*, Skt. *ásti*; γένος : Lat. *genus*, Skt. *jánas*), and there is no indication that σ of

[42] The material on the rough breathing from IE *w*- is collected in Sommer, Griechische Lautstudien 83–136; his conclusions must certainly be rejected in favor of the laryngeal theory. For the latter see especially Kuryłowicz, Études indoeuropéennes 1.30–76, 253 f. (with references), Prace Filologiczny 17.79–96; Sapir, Lang. 14.269–74. Of particular significance for the Greek voiceless continuants is a Princeton dissertation (not yet published) by W. M. Austin.

[43] In my opinion the laryngeals, ', ', *x*, and γ, should be ascribed to Indo-Hittite. They were lost in Pre-Indo-European; but any one of the first three unvoiced an immediately following semivowel. I should therefore assume for Primitive Indo-European as well as for Primitive Greek the following voiceless continuants: 'r, 'l, 'm, 'n, 'w, 'y (= [ç], cf. [79]).

other origin had a different value. In Modern Gk. σ initial, intervocalic, and before or after voiceless consonants is a voiceless dental sibilant.

We have a description of the sound by Dionysius of Halicarnassus.

Comp. Verb. 54.3-6:[44] τὸ δὲ σ (φωνεῖται) τῆς μὲν γλώττης προσαγομένης ἄνω πρὸς τὸν οὐρανὸν ὅλης, τοῦ δὲ πνεύματος διὰ μέσων αὐτῶν φερομένου καὶ περὶ τοὺς ὀδόντας λεπτὸν καὶ στενὸν ἐξωθοῦντος τὸ σύριγμα.

This might serve as a description of English or French s or sh (ch), i.e. [s] or [š].

That σ was an s-sound rather than an sh-sound, [s] rather than [š], is shown by the treatment of Greek words in languages that have sounds of both types. In Indic we have the coin legends Lisikasa for Λυσίου, Dianisiyasa for Διονυσίου, Hipastratasa = Ἱπποστράτου;[45] Coptic presents numerous forms like Diomētos = Διομήδης, systadikē = συστατική, apoklēsis = ἀπόκρισις.[46]

Additional evidence that σ in most positions was a voiceless sound is furnished by Greek words in languages that distinguish between a voiced and a voiceless sibilant, e.g. Goth. Aíleisabaíþ = Ἐλισαβετ, aípiskaúpus = ἐπίσκοπος; Armenian skiptōs = σκηπτός; Rabbinical Hebrew 'isqerīṭī = ἐσχαρίτης.[47]

87. Nevertheless there is evidence that several ancient Greek dialects possessed a voiced s, i.e. [z]. In Elean and later Laconian final s appears as ρ; and it is safe to say that an intermediate stage in the change was [z]. In Elean this stage may have passed before our earliest records; but it is likely that final s in most Laconian inscriptions should be read as [z]. Eretrian medial ρ for σ similarly implies an earlier (i.e. prehistoric) [z]. It should be noted, however, that intervocalic σ in Laconian must always have been voiceless; for here the later change is to h. There is also some evidence for a change of σ to ρ before voiced consonants, namely Eretrian Μίργος = Μίσγος, Cretan κόρμοι = κόσμοι, Thessalian Θεόρδοτος, Laconian Θιοκορμίδας,[48] and we may assume earlier

[44] 'And σ is pronounced by the entire tongue being carried up to the palate and by the breath passing between tongue and palate, and emitting, round about the teeth, a thin, hissing sound.'

[45] Gardner, Indian Coins 29, 51, 59. (These coin legends employ all three Sanskrit sibilants.)

[46] Other examples can be found in any list of Greek loans in Coptic; these are taken from Blok, Zeitschrift für ägyptische Sprache und Altertumskunde 62.55, 57.

[47] Krauss, Lehnwörter 1.100, 106.

[48] Buck 53.

forms with [z]. In this position later Attic and Hellenistic Greek had [z]; for from about 330 B.C. we find ζ intruding more and more upon the earlier σ in such words (Πελαζγικόν, IG 4.583—between 331 and 307 B.C.; Ζμυρναῖος, 2².2314.19—after 191 B.C.).[49] Lucian, Iudicium Vocalium 9, makes Sigma refer to this as one of his grievances:[50]

ὅτι δὲ ἀνεξίκακόν εἰμι γράμμα, μαρτυρεῖτέ μοι καὶ αὐτοὶ μηδέποτε ἐγκαλέσαντι τῷ ζῆτα σμάραγδον ἀποσπάσαντι καὶ πᾶσαν ἀφελομένῳ Σμύρναν.

Languages that distinguish between a voiced and voiceless sibilant transcribe Greek σ or ζ before a voiced consonant with their symbol for the voiced sibilant; e.g. Goth. *praizbwtaírei* = πρεσβυτέριον, Armenian *zmelin* = σμιλίον, Rabbinical Hebrew *qōzmīn* = κόσμιον. It remains entirely possible, however, that before the middle of the third century B.C. Attic σ before a voiced consonant was a voiceless sound.

88. Before voiceless consonants σ is often written double in inscriptions of various dialects: Αἰσσχύλō, IG 1².571; Ἀσσκληπ⟨ίῳ⟩, 2².4377; αἰσσχρός, 12.5.40; Ἀρίσστα, SGDI 1920.9; ἐπίσστευε, 2188.12; Δίσσκος, 2190.5; ἀσσφάλειαν, 2736.10; Νέσστωρ, Kretschmer, Vaseninschriften 174; Αἰσσχίνου, Inschr. von Magnesien 111.[51] This orthography has often been thought to indicate syllable division within the sibilant; but it is unlikely that so obscure and difficult a matter as syllable division attracted the attention of the scribes. In the first edition of this book it was suggested that σ was a stronger sound in this position than in others. Another possibility is that σσ is intended to distinguish [s] from the [z] of consonant groups such as σβ, σγ, and σμ. If so, the few similar doublings before a voiced consonant (Λέσσβον, IG 2².107.32) must also indicate a voiceless sibilant; they may have been a sort of protest against the new pronunciation [zb], etc. If this suggestion is adopted, Attic [z] before a voiced consonant must be dated somewhat earlier than would otherwise be necessary.

89. The normal value of σ was always about that of English, French, or German *s*, i.e. [s]. In various dialects at different times σ in certain positions had also the value of French *z*, i.e. [z]; in particular this was

[49] See other examples in Meisterhans-Schwyzer 88 f.; Lademann, De Titulis Atticis 56 f.; Mayser 204.

[50] 'That I am a long-suffering letter, you yourselves are my witnesses, since I have never brought suit against Zeta for taking an emerald from me and robbing me of all Smyrna.'

[51] Others in G. Meyer, Griech. Gramm.³ 304 f. A few similar forms are cited from Ptolemaic papyri by Mayser 216 f.

the sound of σ before a voiced consonant in later Attic and in Hellenistic Greek.

THE ASPIRATES[52]

90. Most scholars are convinced that Ancient Gk. φ, θ, and χ were aspirates somewhat similar to Eng. *p*, *t*, and *k*, i.e. [ph, th, kh], but Collitz[53] has advocated a return to the older opinion that they were spirants as in Modern Greek, like Eng. *f*, *th* (in *thin*), and German *ch* (in *ach*). He gave no reason beyond the fact that "Grimm's law" runs more smoothly if the Indo-European, Greek, and Sanskrit sounds corresponding to the initials of Eng. *bear*, *do* and *yesterday* were spirants comparable with the English and German spirants just mentioned; only by this device could Grimm arrange his successions of consonants in the form of a circle.[54] The argument is not cogent even for Indo-European, and the Greek sounds need not be identical with their Indo-European sources. Nevertheless Collitz's revival of an old opinion makes it advisable to state the arguments for the aspirate pronunciation quite fully.

90 a. The earliest known classification of the Greek consonants is the one by Dionysius Thrax 11.5–12.4:[55]

τούτων ⟨συμφώνων⟩ ἡμίφωνα μέν ἐστιν ὀκτώ, ζ ξ ψ λ μ ν ρ σ, ... ἄφωνα δὲ ἐστιν ἐννέα; β γ δ κ π τ θ φ χ.

The only way to make this classification understandable is to assume that the mutes are all momentaneous sounds while the semivowels are either continuants or, in the case of the first three, contain continuants. If so, the last three mutes cannot be spirants.

This argument, however, is considerably weakened by the existence of another classification, which is most clearly stated by Sextus Empiricus (second century A.D.), Adv. Gramm. 102 (p. 621.28 ff. Bekk., p. 238.21 ff. Fab.):[56]

[52] Compare the paragraphs on the classes of mutes [96, 97].

[53] Lang. 2.179 f. Cf. Prokosch, Comparative Germanic Grammar 39 f.

[54] This is not the place to discuss Collitz's suggestion about the value of Skt. *gh*, *dh*, and *bh*; but we may properly point out that *bh* cannot have been very close to Gk. φ, or we should not find βαρυγαζα, Ptolemy +, for *Bharukaccha*, or Ἀβισαρης, Arrian +, for *Abhiṣara*. At any rate *bh* was a voiced consonant and φ was not.

[55] 'Of these ⟨consonants⟩ eight are semivowels, ζ, ξ, ψ, λ, μ, ν, ρ, and σ. ... Nine are mutes, β, γ, δ, κ, π, τ, θ, φ, and χ.'

[56] 'Of the consonants some are in themselves semivocalic and others mute;

τῶν δὲ συμφώνων τὰ μὲν ἡμίφωνά ἐστι κατ' αὐτοὺς τὰ δὲ ἄφωνα, καὶ ἡμίφωνα μὲν ὅσα δι'
αὐτῶν ῥοῖζον ἢ σιγμὸν ἤ τινα παραπλήσιον ἦχον κατὰ τὴν ἐκφώνησιν ἀποτελεῖν πεφυκότα,
καθάπερ τὸ ζ, θ, λ, μ, ν, ξ, ρ, σ, φ, χ, ψ, ἤ, ὥς τινες, χωρὶς τοῦ θ καὶ φ καὶ χ τὰ λειπόμενα
ὀκτώ. ἄφωνα δέ ἐστι τὰ μήτε συλλαβὰς καθ' ἑαυτὰ ποιεῖν δυνάμενα μήτε ἤχων ἰδιότητας,
αὐτὸ δὲ μόνον μετὰ τῶν ἄλλων συνεκφωνούμενα, καθάπερ, β, γ, δ, κ, π, τ, ἤ, ὡς ἔνιοι, καὶ τὸ θ,
φ, χ.

We may probably ascribe the classification of φ, θ, and χ with the continuants to a spirant pronunciation that had developed out of the earlier
aspirate pronunciation by the second century A.D. The fact remains,
however, that Diogenes Laertius, 7.57, ascribes the system of six mutes
to "the Stoics"; we do not really know how ancient it is. May the
puff of breath after these consonants have made them comparable to
the double consonants even in Hellenistic times?

90 b. The earliest description of all the mutes is by Dionysius Thrax,
12.5–13.2:[57]

τούτων (i.e. ἀφώνων) ψιλὰ μέν ἐστι τρία, κ π τ, δασέα τρία, θ φ χ, μέσα δὲ τούτων τρία,
β δ γ. μέσα δὲ εἴρηται ὅτι τῶν μὲν ψιλῶν ἐστι δασύτερα, τῶν δὲ δασέων ψιλότερα.

The description by Dionysius of Halicarnassus, cited in [96], is in full
agreement with this, but it adds certain details about the position of
articulation in which we are not interested at the moment.

Even earlier than Dionysius Thrax is a passage in Ps.-Aristotle,
De Audibilibus (plausibly ascribed to Straton, head of the Peripatetic
school about 200 B.C.) 804 b 8–11:[58]

δασεῖαι δ' εἰσὶ τῶν φωνῶν ὅσαις ἔσωθεν τὸ πνεῦμα εὐθέως συνεκβάλλομεν μετὰ τῶν φθόγγων,
ψιλαὶ δ' εἰσὶ τοὐναντίον ὅσαι γίγνονται χωρὶς τῆς τοῦ πνεύματος ἐκβολῆς.

The word φωνή in itself applies equally to vowels and to consonants, but
the expulsion of breath after the sounds cannot be ascribed to vowels

---

the semivowels are those which in their pronunciation are by themselves able
to produce a whizzing or hissing or some similar sound, as ζ, θ, λ, μ, ν, ξ, ρ, σ,
φ, χ, ψ, or, as some writers say, the other eight without θ, φ, and χ. Mutes are
those which cannot by themselves produce syllables or their peculiar sounds,
but which are merely pronounced with the others, as β, γ, δ, κ, π, τ, or, as some
writers say, also θ, φ, and χ.'

[57] 'Of these ⟨mutes⟩ three are smooth, κ, π, and τ, three rough, θ, φ, and χ,
and three intermediate between these, β, δ, and γ. They are called intermediate
because they are rougher than the smooth ⟨mutes⟩, but smoother than the
rough ⟨mutes⟩.'

[58] 'Those sounds are rough in connection with which we expel the breath
immediately after their sound; those are smooth on the contrary which are produced without the expulsion of breath.'

with the rough breathing. Hence we have here a treatment of consonants, and all will agree that the rough mutes are more likely to be meant than liquids with rough breathing. We have found [77] that the only possible meaning of the adjective δασύs in its grammatical use, is 'accompanied by breath, aspirated'. It would be possible, then, to depart from the traditional rendering of δασύs and ψιλόs and to substitute 'aspirate' for 'rough' and 'non-aspirate' for 'smooth' in our translations of the two Greek passages just cited.

90 c. The early alphabets of Crete, Thera, and Melos lack symbols for φ and χ. In Crete π and κ are used instead (πυλά = φυλή, κρόνος = χρόνος); in Thera and Melos we meet the more accurate spellings πh, κh, and ϙh, and also in Thera the quite unnecessary θh (Theran Πhειδιπίδας, IG 12.3.536; 'Αρκhαγέτας, 762; Θhαρύμαϙhος, 763). These spellings suggest the aspirate pronunciation; but if we suppose, for the sake of the argument, that the speakers of these dialects had the phonemes *f* and *ch* while their alphabet had no corresponding signs, we must admit that they might have written as they actually did.[59]

90 d. The prehistoric dissimilation of aspirates (τρίχες : θρίξ, ἀρκεθέωρος : ἄρχω, πέφευγα from *φεφευγα) implies the possession of some common element by the three phonemes, which element is lost if two of them stand near together. It is difficult to see what this element can be except aspiration. Furthermore the process extends to words in which rough breathing is followed by an aspirate (ἔχω : ἕξω, ἄ-λοχος : ἀ-πλός). Here the aspiration in the mute caused dissimilative loss of the aspiration before the vowel. Unquestionably our three phonemes were aspirates when these changes occurred.

90 e. In Attic Greek of the early historic period there was a tendency in the reverse direction, yielding assimilated forms such as hέχει, IG 1².678 (early sixth century B.C.); hέχον, 1².180.75 (422 B.C.); Ηισθμοῖ, 1².77.12 (after 450 B.C.); ἰχθύs, Aulus Gellius 2.3 (quoted [183]); 'Ανθίλοχος, φαρθένος, Διοφείθης, Kretschmer, Vaseninschriften 149 f.[60] Similar forms occur occasionally in other parts of the Greek world, as φαρθένō, IG 5.2.262.28, 31 (Arcadia, fifth century B.C.); θυφλός, 14.865 (Cumae, sixth century B.C.); θύχαι, SGDI 5015.2, 5018 a 1 (Gortyn). It is obvious that a spirant could not induce the initial aspiration of the

---

[59] Such forms as αἰτρίαν, πωνή, οὐκί, ascribed to Scythians by Aristophanes, and Στένελος, Πίλων, etc., on Attic vases are no more significant for Attic pronunciation than the various foreign mispronunciations of *th* are for English pronunciation.

[60] Further examples in Kretschmer, Ath. Mitth. 21.413 ff.

first four examples. The proof is scarcely less cogent in the remaining words, since it is unlikely that a spirant could induce a spirant of different articulation; [θ] could scarcely change a neighboring [p] to [f].

90 f. The metathesis of aspiration offers equally good evidence for those dialects for which it is citable; namely Ionic (κιθών, κίθρα, ἄχαντος), Cretan (καυχός for χαλκός), Thessalian (Πετθαλός = Φετταλός).[61]

90 g. Perhaps even more cogent is the dissimilated Θαλήύβιος from Θαλθύβιος from Ταλθύβιος of Attic vases;[62] for the loss of τ from θ here leaves aspiration.

90 h. The spelling στ for σθ is common in the North-West Greek dialects and in Hellenistic documents, and there are occasional early instances in Doric dialects (Locrian χρῖσται, IG 9.1.334.19; Phocian πρόστα, SGDI 2561 C 39; Elean λυσάστω, πεπάστω, SGDI 1168.7, 8; Cretan μιστῶ, SGDI 5125 A 11). Similarly we find Delphian Σπαῖρος for Σφαῖρος and Elean πάσκω for πάσχω. Almost certainly these forms indicate loss of aspiration after σ (cf. Eng. [sp, st, sk] beside [ph, th, kh] in most other positions). At any rate such spellings preclude the possibility that the concurrent (traditional) writings σθ, σφ, σχ contained spirants.[63]

90 i. Particularly clear proof that φ, θ, and χ are aspirates is furnished by the fact that in all dialects that retain rough breathing final π, τ, κ become φ, θ, χ before aspirated vowels (ἐφ' ἡμῖν, ἀνθ' οὗ, οὐχ οὗτος). Particularly cogent are epigraphic instances in alphabets that have a sign for h, which is nevertheless omitted; thus the Heraclean tables present such phrases as ἐφ' ἑκατέρω, 1.91; ἐφ' ἑκάστας, 2.28; ἀφ' ἇς, 2.30; καθ' ἀ 1.153; καθ' ὡς, 1.169. It appears that ΚΑΘΑ was completely equivalent to ΚΑΤΗΑ. Similar phrases occur frequently on early Attic inscriptions that employ Η = h elsewhere (ἐφ' ἱερᾶι, IG 1².313.163; καθ' ἑμέραν, 1².84.40).[64]

90 j. Greek, like the related languages, sometimes lengthened consonants, particularly in nursery words, nicknames, and onomatopoetic formations (ἄττα, πιππίζω, φίλλιος, Σθέννις). In the case of χ, θ, and φ

[61] Hellenistic forms of this kind may be Ionisms; see Mayser 184.

[62] Kretschmer, Vaseninschriften 150, Ath. Mitth. 21.414.

[63] Thumb's explanation (IF 31.222–9) of the στ forms by analogy has been refuted by Kretschmer, Glotta 6.295. Buck's suggestion (55) that θ had in West Greek become a spirant except after σ is precluded by the fact (pointed out by Kretschmer) that the forms with στ got into the κοινή from West Greek. For the κοινή surely had an aspirate θ in other positions.

[64] The tautological spelling of our printed texts originated in the Byzantine extension of the breathing signs to all initial vowels.

such lengthening yielded forms like ἰακχή beside ἰαχή; τιτθή 'nurse' beside τιθηνός, τιθηνέω, ἐτιθήνατο; Ψαπφώ beside ψᾶφος, ψῆφος.[65] Evidently the closure of the oral passage was held for a time, but the puff of breath was unaltered. That the lengthening of spirants would yield affricates is most improbable.

90 k. The Latin transcription of χ by c or ch and of θ by t or th is scarcely valid evidence for the character of the Greek sounds; since Latin had neither aspirates nor spirants of the palatal and dental series, only a rough approximation to the Greek sounds was possible.

On the contrary the representation of φ by p (*Pilipus, Pilonīcos*) and later by ph (*Philippus, philosophia*) is made significant by the fact that Latin had an f. Even if one supposes that Greek φ was a bilabial spirant and Latin f a labio-dental (but see [188 b]), we should still expect to find φ represented by f rather than by p, if not regularly at least in some of the pre-Christian instances.[66]

90 l. We have, in fact, Quintilian's explicit statement that Latin f, in contradistinction to the Greek aspirates, is merely similar to (not equal to) aspiration.

1.4.14:[67] . . . quin fordeum faedosque pro aspiratione velut simili littera utentes; nam contra Graeci aspirare solent, ut pro Fundanio Cicero testem qui primam eius litteram dicere non possit irridet.

Quintilian, 12.10.28 f., says that f has a sound that is not Greek; similarly Terentianus Maurus, 6.332.227–9 K (quoted in [188 a]).

90 m. While the standard method of transcribing Latin with Greek letters uses π, τ, and κ respectively for Latin p, t, and c, the Greek aspirates are occasionally used (Σολφικιος, Ὀφφιανος, Ἀφφιος, Ἀπφαιος, Ἀφφιανος, Ἀπφιανος, Ἀντισθεια, Δομεστιχος). What led to these transcriptions is not altogether clear; but it is at least certain that spirants could not have been used in this way. In one word Latin itself provides a reason for the Greek aspirate; *cohors, chors, cors* is written χωρς, χορς, χωρτη as well as κωρτη and κοορτη.

---

[65] The occasional spelling of such words with φφ, θθ, or χχ is not surprising; λ : λλ = π : ππ = φ : φφ.

[66] This argument cannot be answered by citing the Greek representation of Lat. f by φ (Φλαμινιος, Φαβιος); since Greek had no spirant, it was necessary to make an inexact substitution, and of course the aspirate was preferable to the non-aspirate.

[67] '. . . (the early Romans) even ⟨said⟩ *fordeum* and *faedi* ⟨for *hordeum* and *haedi*⟩, using in place of aspiration what is in a way a similar letter; for, on the contrary, the Greeks have many aspirates, as ⟨for example⟩ Cicero in defending Fundanius makes fun of a witness who cannot pronounce his initial.'

90 n. The Iranian spirants, *f*, *θ*, and *x*, were usually represented by Gk. *φ*, *θ*, and *χ*; but this fact is not any more significant than the use of *φ* for Lat. *f* [90 k fn. 66]. Sometimes, however, *σ* or *τ* was used for Iranian *θ* (Σατασπης, Hdt., : θατα 'hundred'; 'Αρτασουρας, 'Αρτασυρας, Plut. +, : θura- 'strong'; Μιτρογαθης, Aesch., Pers. 43 +, beside Μιθρα-[68]). These spellings are enough to show that the usual orthography was somehow unsatisfactory, and thus they support the theory that Gk. *θ* was an aspirate.

90 o. Indic coins of the second and first centuries B.C. regularly show *kh*, *th*, and *ph* for *χ*, *θ*, and *φ* (*Arkhebiyasa* = 'Αρχεβιου, *Agathukreyasa* = 'Αγαθοκλεους, *Apulaphanasa* = 'Απολλοφανου).[69] The sign of the zodiac, παρθενος, appears in Sanskrit as *pāthenas*. It is true that the Indic languages have no spirants like [x, *θ*, f], and therefore they might naturally represent Greek spirants in this way; but it is significant that Gk. *θ* is never represented by a sibilant.[70]

90 p. Gk. σακχαρ, σακχαρις 'sugar' from Prakrit *sakkhara*[71] is evidence for the aspirate pronunciation of *χ*; it is closely parallel to ουχ ουτος [90 i]. Παλιβοθρα for *Pātaliputram*, the name of the chief city of Magadha, reminds one of 'Αντισθεια for Lat. *Antistia*, but very likely the word was connected with βοθρος 'trench' by popular etymology. As far as it goes the spelling favors aspirate pronunciation of *θ*.

90 q. A Gnostic text of the second century A.D., written in Demotic Egyptian,[72] contains a large number of interlinear Greek transliterations of Demotic words. In these the digraphs *ph* and *kh* (also *gh*, since *g* and *k* are interchangeable) are represented by *φ* and *χ* respec-

---

[68] In Old Persian general Iranian *θr* is written by a special sign of doubtful phonetic value, but the Greeks probably learned their Iranian from nearer neighbors than the Persians.

[69] Gardner, Indian Coins 11, 32, 54, etc.

[70] No evidence can be got from Δαχιναβαδης, Periplus Maris Rubri 50, 51, for Prakrit *Dakhinābadha* from Skt. *Dakṣiṇāpathas*. If Greek had no voiceless aspirate a spirant *χ* might well have rivaled *κ* as the substitute for Indic *kh*.

βραχμανες for Skt. *brahmānas* does not counterbalance the above evidence; Hellenistic Greek no longer had the consonant group *hμ* [88], and so there was no satisfactory equivalent for the Indic *hm*. It is, to be sure, surprising that the Indic voiced *h* did not lead to the use of a Greek voiced sound; perhaps we should assume some intermediary language with voiceless *h*.

[71] Wackernagel, Altindische Grammatik 1.115.

[72] Hess, IF 6.123–32.

Undoubtedly there is evidence upon the pronunciation of the Greek aspirates in earlier Egyptian transcriptions of Greek words and in the numerous Egyptian personal names in Ptolemaic Greek papyri, but this material the Egyptologists have not yet made available for use by other scholars.

tively, while the Demotic characters for the spirants *f* and *ḥ* are kept even in the Greek transliterations. Gk. *θ* represents the Demotic digraph *th* except before *ι* and *ει*, where it usually stands for *ts*. The inference is clear that *φ* and *χ*, and *θ* also except before front vowels, were aspirates.

90 r. These conclusions are confirmed by the use of the Greek letters *φ*, *θ*, and *χ* in Coptic writing. In Bohairic Coptic they represent the inherited voiceless mutes *p*, *t*, and *k* in accented syllables; these seem, therefore, to have been aspirated. In Sahidic Coptic they stand respectively for *p*, *t*, and *k* plus the separate phoneme *h*. For instance, if a Greek loan-word with initial *h* representing the rough breathing is preceded by the feminine article *t*, the result is *θ* (transliterated *th*), as *thorasis* = ἡ ὅρασις.[73] Some have hesitated to accept this really inescapable conclusion because they have supposed that Gk. *φ*, *θ*, and *χ* must, on other evidence, have become spirants by the third century, when the earliest Coptic documents were composed. There are two possible ways of disposing of this objection. (1) Gk. *φ*, *θ*, and *χ* were certainly aspirates when the language was introduced into Egypt, and they might easily persist there longer than in some other parts of the Greek world. (2) If the Coptic alphabet was invented by churchmen they may well have employed the standard pronunciation of the schools, which prescribed aspirate pronunciation of *φ*, *θ*, and *χ* for some six centuries longer [92 b].

90 s. The Armenian alphabet was formed, largely on the basis of the Greek, about 400 A.D., and the letters *φ*, *θ*, and *χ* were employed to denote the aspirates *p'*, *t'*, and *k'*, while *π*, *τ*, and *κ* were used for the corresponding non-aspirates *p*, *t*, and *k*. Accordingly Greek loan-words in Armenian show such forms as *k'art* = χάρτης, *at'letaik* = ἀθληταί, *p'alang* = φάλαγξ. Since Armenian had a velar spirant [x] but no [f] or [θ], it is the identification of Gk. *χ* with Armenian *k'* that is really significant for us. Greek was never established in popular use in eastern Asia Minor, and so it is safe to say that the ecclesiastics who originated the Armenian alphabet based it upon the standard usage of the schools. The Greek loan-words in Armenian are also learned words. We therefore have here evidence for standard Greek

[73] Blass 104; Hopfner, Ueber Form und Gebrauch der griechischen Lehnwörter in der koptisch-sa'idischen Apophthegmenversion (Denkschriften der Wiener Akad. 62.2) 6 f.; Worrell, Coptic Sounds 83–7. The fact that Sahidic *p*, *t*, and *k* were voiceless or half-voiced lenes does not affect our argument, since the dialect had only one order of mutes.

pronunciation, and in view of the circumstances of the time, the standard pronunciation of Constantinople.[74]

90 t. The Georgian ecclesiastic alphabet was introduced at about the same time as the Armenian, and there is internal evidence that it was formed under the same influences. Here again Greek χ was employed for an aspirate, although the language had a velar spirant [x].[75]

ΦΘ AND ΧΘ

91. The available evidence indicates that the aspirates had their usual values in the groups φθ (φθάνω) and χθ (χθών).[76] The orthography itself forbids us to suppose that the pronunciation was πθ and κθ; for such groups would certainly have been written phonetically as were the groups πφ, τθ, and κχ. Besides, a conventional use of φθ and χθ for πθ and κθ would have been betrayed by frequent misspellings; whereas the substitution of π and κ for φ and χ is scarcely more common before θ than in other positions. The spelling ἠνείχθεισαν on an Ephesian inscription of the sixth century B.C. rules out the (otherwise most improbable) theory of graphic assimilation.[77]

The Hellenistic Greek of Egypt seems to have changed these groups to πθ and κθ respectively (ἔκθρας, P. Tebt. 1.5.259—118 B.C.; δαινεκθέντες, 1.25.17—117 B.C.; ὀπθαλμῷ, P. Grenf. 1.45.5—19 B.C.).[78] A similar tendency in Italian Greek is indicated by ἐκθρῶν in the papyrus manuscript of Philodemus, De Ira 16.24, 19.11, 23.30, 32.25; *Apthonetus*, CIL 5.735 Add., 12.408; *Apthoni*, 9.6078.36; and by the orthography of Latin manuscripts.[78]

THE ASPIRATES BECOME SPIRANTS[79]

92. In Laconian σ begins to be written for earlier θ in inscriptions of the fourth century B.C., and this is anticipated by Alcman's σιῶν = θεῶν,

---

[74] Thumb, ByzZ 9.411 f.; Trubetzkoy, Glotta 25.252-6.

[75] Trubetzkoy, Glotta 25.253.

[76] Some have mistakenly supposed that an aspirate could not be pronounced before a mute. Kretschmer, Glotta 4.316, 6.295 f., has effectively answered them.

[77] Kretschmer, Glotta 4.316.

[78] See Rahlfs, SBPA 1912.1040.

[79] It has been suggested (G. Meyer, Griechische Grammatik³ 287 f.) that the first stage of the change of φ, θ, and χ from the old aspirate pronunciation was the development into affricates [pf, tθ, kx]. The forms cited as evidence (ὄκχος, ὀκχέω in Pindar; ἰακχή, ἰακχέω in the tragedians; φιλόσοφον with long penult in Aristophanes; *bracchium* in Plautus, etc.) are probably instances of the colloquial doubling mentioned above [90 j], in spite of the occurrence of some of them in serious poetry.

1.36 Diehl, and quotations of Laconian speech in Aristophanes (σιός = θεός, Lys. 81) and Thucydides (σύματος, 5.77). While σ in literature may be due to a grammarian's recension, the epigraphical σ must stand for a contemporary spirant. Whether this was [s], as in Tsakonian, or [θ], as elsewhere in Modern Greek, is uncertain.

The use of θθ in Gortynian in words and formative elements that earlier had σθ or ζ has often been cited as evidence that θ was a spirant.[80] It is, however, equally possible to suppose that earlier σθ and ζ = [ts] became [t·h]. The occasional writing τθ instead of θθ in the later period rather points in this direction (cf. τίτθη, etc. [90 j]).

Other alleged evidence for spirants in Greek before the Christian era seems to me even less persuasive.[81]

92 a. The earliest indication of the spirant pronunciation in Hellenistic Greek is the use of f for φ in a few carelessly written Latin inscriptions of the first century A.D. at Pompeii (*Dafne*, CIL 4.680; *Fileto*, 2402, *fisica*, 1520, 6865—cf. *Ruphus*, 4615).

In the second century A.D. we find Demotic Egyptian *ts* before *i* transcribed by Gk. θ [90 q].

The inscriptions of the second and third centuries A.D. in the Jewish catacombs at Rome show thorough equivalence of φ and Latin f (*Afrodisia*, Φαυστινος); but θ and χ, for which, however, Latin could not supply an equivalent if they were spirants, correspond with Latin *th* and with *ch* or *c* respectively. That θ and χ were still heard as aspirates is shown by such forms as χῖτε and χεῖθε for κεῖται.[82] Possibly we should infer that the spirant pronunciation was common, while some speakers affected the traditional sounds, but without being able to distinguish aspirate from non-aspirate. In the fourth century A.D. Lat. f was the regular transcription of φ; and in the same century Ulfilas represented φ and θ by Gothic f and þ (*Filippus* = Φίλιππος, þomas = Θωμᾶς).

92 b. Nevertheless the schools of Constantinople inculcated the aspirate pronunciation for several centuries longer. We have already seen [90 s] that this pronunciation is evidenced by Greek words in the Armenian of the fifth century. The Glagolitic alphabet, invented in the ninth century to write Church Slavic, retained Greek χ in its proper alphabetic position and introduced a new sign to write the Slavic velar spirant. Although the few extant documents preserved in the original

---

[80] See especially Krause, KZ 49.121–6; Kretschmer, Glotta 23.1–17.

[81] But see Schwyzer, Gr. Gramm. 205–7 and references. Birt's suggestion (Glotta 14.113 f.) cannot be taken seriously.

[82] Leon, TAPA 58.228 f.

form of the Glagolitic alphabet do not directly prove that the original χ-sign had the aspirate value, that hypothesis alone can account for its preservation alongside of the new sign for the spirant.[83]

92 c. The spirant pronunciation is clearly described by a Byzantine grammarian.

Schol. Dion. Thr. 43.14–21:[84] τοῖς μὲν ἄκροις χείλεσι πιλουμένοις ἐκφωνεῖται τὸ π, ὥστε σχεδὸν μηδ' ὅλως πνεῦμά τι παρεκβαίνειν· ἀνοιγομένων δὲ τῶν χειλέων πάνυ καὶ πνεύματος πολλοῦ ἐξιόντος ἐκφωνεῖται τὸ φ· τὸ δὲ β ἐκφωνούμενον ὁμοίως τοῖς ἄκροις τῶν χειλέων, τουτέστι περὶ τὸν αὐτὸν τόπον τοῖς προλεχθεῖσι τῶν φωνητικῶν ὀργάνων, οὔτε πάνυ ἀνοίγει τὰ χείλη, ὡς τὸ φ, οὔτε πάνυ πιλοῖ, ὡς τὸ π, ἀλλὰ μέσην τινὰ διέξοδον τῷ πνεύματι πεφεισμένως δίδωσιν.

92 d. Standard pronunciation treated φ, θ, and χ as aspirates in Hellenistic and Byzantine Greek until the ninth century A.D. The spirant pronunciation began in popular speech as early as the first century, at least in Italy, and gradually spread.

THE VOICELESS MUTES

93. The passage quoted in [90 b] from Dionysius Thrax, 12.5–13.2, shows that κ, π, and τ were non-aspirates. We have already presented evidence to show that they were voiceless [65, 66]. Comparison of Greek words with their cognates in the related languages indicates that both characteristics were inherited from Primitive Indo-European (ἑκατόν : centum; πατήρ : pater, Skt. pitā; τίς : quis; τρεῖς : trēs, Skt. trayas). Both are retained, also, in Modern Greek.

In Hellenistic and Roman times κ and τ regularly transcribe the Semitic emphatic consonants q and ṭ, while χ, θ, and φ are as regularly used for Semitic k, t, and p.[85] In all probability the sounds of the latter series were aspirates,[86] but, at any rate, the emphatics were neither

[83] Trubetzkoy, Glotta 25.248–56.

[84] 'π is pronounced with the edges of the lips tightly compressed so that scarcely any breath escapes. φ is pronounced with the lips fully open and much breath escaping. β, which is likewise pronounced with the edges of the lips, that is, with the same part of the vocal organs as the sounds just mentioned, does not either open the lips fully, as does φ, or close them tight, as does π, but sparingly provides a moderate passage for the breath.'

[85] For late Akkadian, see Ungnad, Meissner Festschrift, 220. For Aramaic, see Rosenthal, Die Sprache der Palmyrenischen Inschriften = MVAG 41.1.36 f. For the Septuagent and Hexapla, see Sperber, Hebrew Union College Annual 12–13.128–32. The use of Phoenician ṭ for Lat. t (Harris, A Grammar of the Phoenician Language 22) strengthens the argument.

[86] The West Semitic spirant pronunciation of k, p, and t after vowels would scarcely hold for Akkadian even of the latest period, and besides we definitely know that Gk. χ, θ, and φ were not normally spirants before the Christian era.

aspirated nor voiced; these transcriptions therefore confirm our conclusion.[87]   Greek κ, π, and τ seem to have been similar to the corresponding sounds of Modern French.[88]

THE VOICED MUTES[89]

94. The statement in Dionysius Thrax, 12.5–13.2 [90 b], that β, δ,
and γ are intermediate between κ, π, and τ and θ, ϕ, and χ in respect
to aspiration,[90] when combined with the inference that we have already
drawn in [65, 66], seems to define their character rather closely.   These
sounds must have been voiced aspirates more or less like those still to
be heard in India.[91]

I cannot find any important evidence in support of this definite
declaration of Dionysius.   The fact that $\delta + h = \delta$ in οὐδείς and μηδείς
is perhaps a trifle clearer if δ was an aspirate; but the writing is not
hard to understand anyway.   The fact that β, γ, and δ, like ϕ, χ, and θ,
have now become spirants gives us a harmonious development of voiced
and voiceless aspirates; but it is not necessary to assume parallel development.   The use of Greek β, γ, and δ to represent Thracian-Phrygian,
Macedonian, and Illyrian sounds developed out of IE bh, gh, and dh
is well known.   It has always been assumed that these languages had
lost the aspiration of the primitive Indo-European voiced aspirates as

[87] On the other hand τ, at least, evidently did not closely resemble Phoenician
ṭ at the time when the alphabet was borrowed.

[88] Cf. Meillet, MSL 19.164, whose phonetics, however, need revision.   My
former attempt (TAPA 48.49–62) to show that κ, τ, and π were lenes was not
successful; cf. [94 fn. 89].

[89] The theory proposed by me in TAPA 48.49–62 and followed in the first edition of this book that Gk. β, δ, and γ were fortes, has to be abandoned.   The
evidence upon which it was chiefly based is fallacious; the Latin words which
show p, t, and c corresponding to Gk. β, δ, and γ are loans from Etruscan or
another Mediterranean language rather than from Greek.   In any case the
theory itself is incredible.   See Fohalle, Mélanges linguistiques offerts à M. J.
Vendryes 157–78.

[90] Ammann's suggestion (Glotta 24.158–61) that the more explicit second
sentence quoted above from Dionysius is not original, and that the adjective
μέσα was intended to describe β, δ, and γ as intermediate between the semivowels
and the mutes, is not convincing.   Ammann does not explain how these three
sounds came to be grouped with the mutes, and actually to be put last among
them, even in Dionysius' text as emended.   Furthermore, Plato, Theaet. 203 B,
who, according to Ammann, followed the same classification as Dionysius, pretty
clearly includes β among the mutes.

[91] So Kretschmer ap. Gercke-Norden, Einleitung in die Altertumswissen-
schaft[3] 1.6.15.   Otherwise Ammann, Glotta 24.158–61.

Slavic and Iranian did; it is equally possible, but by no means necessary, to assume that the Greek letters here, as well as in Greek itself, stood for voiced aspirates.

The regular equivalence of β, γ, and δ to voiced non-aspirates in loan-words causes no difficulty in case the other language concerned has no voiced aspirates. It is a bit disturbing to find on Indic coins *Arkhebiyasa* instead of **Arkhebhiyasa* for Ἀρχεβίου, *Diyamedasa* instead of **Dhiyamedhasa* for Διομήδου, etc.[92] This evidence, however, does not necessarily count against Dionysius; the breath in the Indic voiced aspirates is known to have been voiced, while that which followed β, γ, and δ may have been voiceless. At any rate we must assume some difference between Gk. β and Indic *bh*, Gk. δ and Indic *dh*, which prevented them from being perfect equivalents.

95. The earliest indication of spirant pronunciation of any voiced stop is the occasional omission of γ or the substitution of ι for it after front vowels in various ancient dialects; e.g. Boeotian ἰώ = ἐγώ, Aristophanes, Ach. 898, etc.; Arcadian Φιαλείας = Φιγαλείας, IG 5.2.419, 420; Pamphylian μhειάλε, SGDI 1267.9, 10, 23; Tarentine ὄλιος, Herodian 1.141.19 L. Similar forms appear in Attic in the latter part of the fourth century B.C. (ὀλιαρχίαι, IG 2².448.61—318 B.C.; ὀλίον, 1325.22—Macedonian period.)[93] It is quite clear, however, that this pronunciation of γ did not become the standard in Attic or Hellenistic Greek for some centuries. Latin had [j] initial and [j·] medial (*iugum, eius*), but Greek γ is regularly represented by *g* (*Sigēum, Aegīna*) and when Latin is written in Greek characters *g* is represented by γ (Γαιος, Ἀγριππας) while consonantal *i* appears often as ι (Ἰουλιος, Ἰανουαριος), rarely as ζ (Ζουλια, κοζους = *coiux*), but scarcely ever as γ. Even in the inscriptions of the second and third centuries A.D. in the Jewish catacombs, γ is represented by Lat. *g* and it is retained in Greek orthography except in three occurrences of γερουσιάρχης which show initial γιε-, ιε-, and ειε-.[94]

The use of β to transliterate Lat. *v* does not necessarily prove that

[92] Gardner, Indian Coins 31, 32, 167; cf. Wackernagel, Altindische Grammatik 1.115.

[93] Other evidence that has been alleged for an early spirant pronunciation of the voiced mutes (e.g. Meillet, MSL 19.165 f.) seems inconclusive. In particular the use of ζ for δ in early Elean inscriptions indicates that ζ had become [d] and had thus become equivalent to δ; the later use of δ in the same words does not then indicate either a phonetic change or a falsification of the record (Lagercrantz, Zur griechischen Lautgeschichte 109).

[94] Leon, TAPA 58.226 f.

either had become a bilabial spirant [β] or a labio-dental spirant [v]. Since Attic and Hellenistic Greek had no such sound as Classical Lat. *v*, namely [w], a substitution was necessary and the choice lay between *ου* and *β*. For a long time the former was preferred; but as [β] became a more and more frequent pronunciation of *v*, the digraph *ου* became less and less appropriate to represent it. This may be the whole explanation of the increasing preference for *β* which, by the second or third century A.D., led to its regular use as the substitute for Lat. *v*. Nevertheless we know that *β* did ultimately become [β], and there is no reason against assuming that the process was already complete in the second century A.D.[95]

In the fourth century A.D. Gothic orthography employed *b*, *d*, and *g* to denote spirants, at least in the interior of the word. It is probable that this reflects the standard Greek usage of the time, although no other course would have been open to Ulfilas even if *β*, *δ*, and *γ* had still been mutes.

The use of *β* for Slavic [v] in the Cyrillic alphabet, while a modified *β* was used for [b], proves that *β*, at least, was a spirant in the ninth century.

THE CLASSES OF MUTES

96. As to the position in which the several classes of mutes were articulated, our most important evidence comes from Dionysius of Halicarnassus.

Comp. Verb. 55.11–57.8:[96] τῶν δὲ καλουμένων ἀφώνων ἐννέα ὄντων τρία μέν ἐστι ψιλά, τρία δὲ δασέα, τρία δὲ μεταξὺ τούτων· ψιλὰ μὲν τὸ κ καὶ τὸ π καὶ τὸ τ, δασέα δὲ τὸ θ

---

[95] Leon, TAPA 58.227 f., argues that *β* had not yet become a spirant at the date of the inscriptions in the Jewish catacombs, because "in Latin transcriptions of Greek words it is invariably represented by *b*." He cites, however, only one example (*theosebes*), which has besides a medial *b*, and Lat. medial *b* was by this time [β]. Even including a few Hebrew words in which Gk. *β* (no doubt substituted for Hebrew [b] or [β]) appears as Latin *b*, this evidence is scarcely sufficient to establish the thesis.

[96] 'Of the so-called "mutes," which are nine in number, three are smooth, three rough, and three between these. The smooth are κ, π, τ; the rough θ, φ, χ; the intermediate β, γ, δ. They are severally pronounced as follows: three of them from the edge of the lips, when the mouth is compressed and the breath, being driven forward from the windpipe, breaks through the obstruction. Among these π is smooth, φ rough, and β comes between the two, being smoother than the latter and rougher than the former. This is one set of three mutes, all three spoken with a like configuration of the organs, but differing in smoothness and

καὶ τὸ φ καὶ τὸ χ, κοινὰ δὲ ἀμφοῖν τὸ β καὶ τὸ γ καὶ τὸ δ. φωνεῖται δὲ αὐτῶν ἕκαστον τρόπον τόνδε· τρία μὲν ἀπὸ τῶν χειλῶν ἄκρων, ὅταν τοῦ στόματος πιεσθέντος τότε προβαλλόμενον ἐκ τῆς ἀρτηρίας τὸ πνεῦμα λύσῃ τὸν δεσμὸν αὐτοῦ. καὶ ψιλὸν μέν ἐστιν αὐτῶν τὸ π, δασὺ δὲ τὸ φ, μέσον δὲ ἀμφοῖν τὸ β· τοῦ μὲν γὰρ ψιλότερόν ἐστι, τοῦ δὲ δασύτερον. μία μὲν αὕτη συζυγία τριῶν γραμμάτων ἀφώνων ὁμοίῳ σχήματι λεγομένων, ψιλότητι δὲ καὶ δασύτητι διαφερόντων. τρία δὲ ἄλλα λέγεται τῆς γλώττης ἄκρῳ τῷ στόματι προσερειδομένης κατὰ τοὺς μετεώρους ὀδόντας, ἔπειθ᾽ ὑπὸ τοῦ πνεύματος ἀπορριπιζομένης καὶ τὴν διέξοδον αὐτῷ κάτω περὶ τοὺς ὀδόντας ἀποδιδούσης· διαλλάττει δὲ ταῦτα δασύτητι καὶ ψιλότητι· ψιλὸν μὲν γὰρ αὐτῶν ἐστι τὸ τ, δασὺ δὲ τὸ θ, μέσον δὲ καὶ ἐπίκοινον τὸ δ. αὕτη δευτέρα συζυγία τριῶν γραμμάτων ἀφώνων. τρία δὲ τὰ λοιπὰ τῶν ἀφώνων λέγεται μὲν τῆς γλώττης ἀνισταμένης πρὸς τὸν οὐρανὸν ἐγγὺς τοῦ φάρυγγος καὶ τῆς ἀρτηρίας ὑπηχούσης τῷ πνεύματι, οὐδὲν οὐδὲ ταῦτα διαφέροντα τῷ σχήματι ἀλλήλων, πλὴν ὅτι τὸ μὲν κ ψιλῶς λέγεται, τὸ δὲ χ δασέως, τὸ δὲ γ μετρίως καὶ μεταξὺ ἀμφοῖν. τούτων κράτιστα μέν ἐστιν ὅσα τῷ πνεύματι πολλῷ λέγεται, δεύτερα δ᾽ ὅσα μέσως, κάκιστα δὲ ὅσα ψιλῶς· ταῦτα μὲν γὰρ τὴν αὐτῶν δύναμιν ἔχει μόνην, τὰ δὲ δασέα καὶ τὴν τοῦ πνεύματος προσθήκην, ὥστ᾽ ἐγγύς που τελειότερα εἶναι ἐκείνων.

While this passage does not help us to decide whether δ, θ, and τ were alveolars or dentals, or whether γ, κ, and χ were palatals or velars, it does determine the relative position of the three classes of mutes. The last sentence of the passage cited [98] from Archinus ap. Syrianum indicates that κ was formed far back in the mouth. That δ, θ, and τ were dentals rather than alveolars is made probable by their articulation in Modern Greek. The same inference may be drawn from their correspondence with the Indic dentals (examples in [90 o, 94]) rather than with the cerebrals,[97] as is the case with the alveolars of Modern English (Laṇḍaṇa = London). In other respects the loan-words (examples above) tend to confirm the statements of Dionysius but add nothing to them.

97. From the discussions in [90–6] we may infer the following statements as to the several mutes of Attic and standard Hellenistic Greek.

---

roughness. The next three are pronounced by the tongue being pressed hard against the extremity of the mouth near the upper teeth, then being blown back by the breath, and affording it an outlet downwards round the teeth. These differ in roughness and smoothness, τ being the smoothest of them, θ the roughest, and δ medial or common. This is the second set of three mutes. The three remaining mutes are spoken with the tongue rising to the palate near the throat, and the windpipe echoing to the breath. These, again, differ in no way from one another as regards formation; but κ is pronounced smoothly, χ roughly, γ moderately and between the two. Of these the best are those which are uttered with a full breath; next those with moderate breath; worst those with smooth breath, since they have their own force alone, while the rough letters have the breath also added, so that they are somewhere nearer perfection than the others.'

[97] Bendall, JPh. 29.201.

κ was a voiceless velar non-aspirate similar to French *c* before a back vowel, i.e. [k].

γ was a voiced velar, probably followed by a weak puff of breath, i.e. [g‘], for which [g] may ordinarily be written.

χ was a voiceless velar aspirate, similar to English *k* initial, i.e. [kh].

τ was a voiceless dental non-aspirate, similar to French *t*, i.e. [t].

δ was a voiced dental, probably followed by a weak puff of breath, i.e. [d‘], for which [d] may ordinarily be written.

θ was a voiceless dental aspirate, similar to English *t* initial, i.e. [th], except that it was dental, like Fr. *t*, and not alveolar.

π was a voiceless labial non-aspirate, similar to French *p*, i.e. [p].

β was a voiced labial, probably followed by a weak puff of breath, i.e. [b‘], for which [b] may ordinarily be written.

φ was a voiceless labial aspirate, similar to Eng. *p* initial, i.e. [ph].

Ξ AND Ψ

98. The ancients tell us that ξ, ψ, and ς represent combinations of mutes with σ. Syrianus cites such descriptions from Archinus, the man who, in the archonship of Euclides, proposed the decree that the Ionic alphabet should be employed in state inscriptions. The later grammarians are more explicit.

Syrianus, in Metaph. 191.29–35 Kroll:[98] ταύτῃ δὲ τῇ ἀποδόσει καὶ ᾿Αρχῖνος ἐχρῆτο, ὡς ἱστορεῖ Θεόφραστος· ἔλεγε δὲ ὁ ᾿Αρχῖνος ἢ ἔξω τι παρὰ τὴν μύσιν τῶν χειλῶν ἐκφωνεῖσθαι, ὥσπερ τὸ π, καὶ διὰ τοῦτο τὸ ψ πρὸς τῷ ἄκρῳ γεννᾶσθαι τῆς γλώττης ὡς ἐκ τοῦ π σ συγκείμενον· ἢ τῷ πλάτει τῆς γλώττης παρὰ τοὺς ὀδόντας, ὥσπερ τὸ δ, καὶ διὰ τοῦτο τὸ ς κατὰ ταύτην γεννᾶσθαι τὴν χώραν· ἢ τῷ κυρτῷ πιεζομένῳ ἐκ τοῦ ἐσχάτου, ὥσπερ τὸ κ, ὅθεν τὸ ξ προϊέναι.

Dion. Thr. 14.4–6:[99] ἔτι δὲ τῶν συμφώνων διπλᾶ μέν ἐστι τρία, ς ξ ψ. διπλᾶ δὲ εἴρηται ὅτι ἓν ἕκαστον αὐτῶν ἐκ δύο συμφώνων σύγκειται, τὸ μὲν ς ἐκ τοῦ σ καὶ δ, τὸ δὲ ξ ἐκ τοῦ κ καὶ σ, τὸ δὲ ψ ἐκ τοῦ π καὶ σ.

---

[98] 'Archinus also used this explanation, as Theophrastus says. Archinus said that either a sound is pronounced outside near the point where the lips touch, as π, and for this reason ψ is produced near the tip of the tongue as being composed of π and σ; or with the blade of the tongue near the teeth, as δ, and for this reason ς is produced in this place; or with the arched tongue pressed upon from the back of the mouth, as κ, whence comes ξ.'

[99] 'Furthermore three of the consonants are double, ς, ξ, and ψ. They are called double because each one of them is composed of two consonants, ς of σ and δ, ξ of κ and σ, ψ of π and σ.'

Dion. Hal., Comp. Verb. 53.1–7:[100] διπλᾶ δὲ τρία, τό τε ζ καὶ τὸ ξ καὶ τὸ ψ. διπλᾶ δὲ λέγουσιν αὐτὰ ἤτοι διὰ τὸ σύνθετα εἶναι, τὸ μὲν ζ διὰ τοῦ σ καὶ δ, τὸ δὲ ξ διὰ τοῦ κ καὶ σ, τὸ δὲ ψ διὰ τοῦ π καὶ σ συνεφθαρμένων ἀλλήλοις ἰδίαν φωνὴν λαμβάνοντα, ἢ διὰ τὸ χώραν ἐπέχειν δυεῖν γραμμάτων ἐν ταῖς συλλαβαῖς παραλαμβανόμενον ἕκαστον.

Etymologically ξ results from the junction of any velar mute with σ (φύλαξ, φάλαγξ, θρίξ), and ψ from the junction of any labial mute with σ (λείψω, νίψω, γράψω), but, if we are to believe the grammarians, β and γ were unvoiced and φ and χ lost their aspiration. On the latter point the statement of the grammarians is confirmed by the phenomena of dissimilation; while *θριχός and *ἔχω were dissimilated into τριχός and ἔχω, the corresponding forms with ξ retained the aspirate or the aspiration (θρίξ, ἔξω). Similarly we have τρέφω but θρέψω. The unvoicing of β and γ is evidenced also by early inscriptions in alphabets that lacked signs for ξ and ψ, as in Cretan δικακσάτō beside δικάδδω, SGDI 4991 passim; Ϝέρκσιεν, 4982; Theran Ῥεκσάνōρ, IG 12.3.762; Attic ἄχσει, IG 1².56.28; βλάφσōσι, 184.5. On the other hand early inscriptions in Attic, Boeotian, and some other dialects regularly employ the aspirates φ and χ before σ, and thus seem to conflict with our conclusion that aspiration was lost before σ. In addition to the two words last cited we may illustrate with Attic ἔδοχσεν, passim; χσυγγράφσει, IG 1².24.14; Boeotian Ϝάναχς, φεφύλαχσο, Buck 197; Locrian Ἐχσαίνετος, IG 9.1.293. The same pronunciation is reflected in Armenian transcriptions such as kʻset = ξέστης, kʻsipʻiē = ξιφίας, pʻsenas = ψῆνας, pʻsiatʻ = ψίαθος.[101] We cannot escape the conclusion that while the relatively strong aspiration of χ, θ, and φ was reduced before σ, all mutes were in this position pronounced with a weak aspiration; ψ was [pʻs] and χ was [kʻs], but ordinarily one may be content with writing [ps] and [ks].

Z

99 a. The passages cited above [98] from Attic and Hellenistic grammarians group ζ with ξ and ψ as a double consonant. It is noteworthy, however, that while ξ and ψ are said to consist of κ and σ and of π and σ respectively, the σ in ζ is put first in the group and it is followed by the

[100] 'Three are double, ζ, ξ, and ψ. They are called double either because they are composite, receiving a distinctive sound through the coalescence respectively of σ and δ into ζ, of κ and σ into ξ, and of π and σ into ψ; or because they occupy the room of two letters in the syllables where they are found.'

[101] Thumb, ByzZ 9.414.

voiced instead of the voiceless dental mute. We have found reason to
believe that σ sometimes stood for a voiced s, and, in view of the tendency of the language to extend voice or voicelessness through an entire
consonant cluster, it is safe to interpret σ and δ as [zd]. This value of
ζ is indicated also by several other considerations. (2) In a number of
words ζ resulted from the combination of σ and δ. 'Αθήναζε and
θύραζε come from *'Αθηνανσ-δε and *θυρανσ-δε (cf. οἰκόν-δε). Διόζοτος is a
graphic variant of Διόσδοτος. Attic ὄζος, Lesbian ὕσδος 'bough' is cognate
with Gothic asts, German Ast, while ὄζος 'comrade' is probably for
*ὄ-σδος with zero-grade of ὁδός.[102] (3) The regular loss of nasals before σ
appears also before ζ ('Αθήναζε, θύραζε, συζεύγνυμι, σύζυξ, πλάζω from
*πλαγγψω, Delphian ἀζετωθέωντι from *αν-ζετω-).[103] (4) By the loss of
σ, i.e. [z], between consonants (cf. δέκτο from *δέξτο, βδέω from *βσδέω)
*ϝέρζω became Aeolic and Ionic ἔρδω and *ἀμέρζω became Aeolic ἀμέρδω.
(5) Gk. ζ sometimes represents sibilant plus d in loan-words ('Ωρομαζης =
OP Auramazda; 'Αρταβαζος, Herodotus, 'Αρταοζος, Xenophon, = OP
*Artavazda; 'Αζωτος, Herodotus, = Hebrew 'Ašdōd). These arguments
establish the pronunciation [zd] for primitive Greek and for several
of the later dialects, including Attic and Ionic.

99 b. On the other hand, etymology more often indicates that the
sibilant must have developed in the first place after the δ; δy (ἐλπίζω,
πεζός, Ζεύς : Skt. Dyauṣ) and γy (πλάζω : πλάγξαι; ἁρπάζω : ἅρπαξ;
μέζων : μέγας) must have yielded [dz] rather than [zd] in Primitive
Greek. Since [zd] in ὄζος is inherited from Primitive Indo-European,
it seems necessary to assume that Primitive Greek had both [dz] and
[zd]. Furthermore the dialects that later changed δι into a sound or
sound-group written ζ must at first have pronounced [dz] rather than
[zd] (Aeolic ζα- = δια-, Lesbian Ζόννυσος, κάρζα, Cyprian κορζία). Lesbian
pretty clearly had both sounds (ὕσδος : κάρζα), and some dialect or dialects probably transported the sound [dz] to Italy; for Lat. z is used in
that value in inscriptions, as it still is in It. orzo = [ordzo], etc.; see [203].

99 c. In some early Cretan inscriptions ζ is written for the consonant
group resulting from τy and θy (ὄζος from *ὄτyος, μέζατος from *μέθyατος).
We cannot suppose that voiced y here made the whole group voiced,
so that we might interpret ζ as standing for [dz]; for in later inscriptions
of the same dialect we have such forms as ὄττοι 'ὄσοι' and μέττον 'μέσον'.
Here at least ζ must have been written for [ts] as well as for [dz]. It is
possible, then, that the use of ζ = [ts][104] in Oscan and Umbrian may

---

[102] Brugmann-Thumb 149.
[103] Ibid. 87.
[104] Kretschmer, Glotta 23.1 f.

rest upon a closely similar Greek usage, rather than upon the better known value [dz].

99 d. Beginning about the middle of the fourth century B.C. Attic inscriptions show confusion between σ and ζ (imperfect ἐπεψήφισεν, IG 2².233 a 3—340 B.C.; συναγωνισζόμενος, 743.8—before 260 B.C.; Ζμυρναῖος, 2314, 1.19—ca. 191 B.C.[105]). The change of ζ to a voiced sibilant, i.e. [z], which such confusion indicates, is reflected in Aristotle's hesitant description of it.

Aristotle, Metaph. 993 a 4–7:[106] ἀμφισβητήσειε γὰρ ἄν τις, ὥσπερ καὶ περὶ ἐνίας συλλαβάς· οἱ μὲν γὰρ τὸ ζα ἐκ τοῦ σ καὶ δ καὶ α φασὶν εἶναι, οἱ δέ τινες ἕτερον φθόγγον φασὶν εἶναι καὶ οὐθένα τῶν γνωρίμων.

Hellenistic ζ appears in Latin as *s* or *ss* (*massa, Setus*) and Lat. consonantal *i* is sometimes represented by ζ (κοζους = *coiux*, IG 14.968, 1516, 1910 a, 2192; Ζουλιαι, 1349; Ζουλιανη, 1910 a). Both transcriptions would be strange if ζ stood for [zd] or [dz], but they are natural enough if ζ was [z]. Languages that distinguish between [s] and [z] apply the distinction more or less neatly to Hellenistic loan-words (Coptic *esthesis* 'feeling', *agōnize* 'to fight for'; Gothic *Xristus, praizbwterei*; Armenian *skiptos* = σκηπτός, *zmelin* = σμίλιον but also *prot'esmiōs* = προθέσμιος). We may conclude, then, that in Attic and Hellenistic Greek from the middle of the fourth century B.C. ζ was commonly pronounced as a voiced sibilant, as it is in Modern Greek, although the pronunciation as a double consonant [zd] was for a long time prescribed by the grammarians (see the passage quoted from Dionysius of Halicarnassus in [98]).

100. In Attic of the fifth and early fourth century ζ was a double consonant; it stood for σδ, that is [zd]. From about the middle of the fourth century Attic ζ was similar to French *z*, that is [z].

[105] Other examples in Meisterhans-Schwyzer 88, 92. On σζ, see Schwyzer, Gr. Gramm. 217 f. On ζ before voiced consonants, see [81].

[106] 'For one might be in doubt, just as about certain syllables; for some say that ζα consists of σ, δ, and α, while others say that it is a different sound and not one of the well known sounds.' It must be noted, however, that ζα is here an emendation for σμα, and δ in the next line for μ.

CHAPTER IV

THE GREEK ACCENT

101. The earliest extant reference to Greek accent is in Plato.

Cratylus 399 A:[1] πρῶτον μὲν γὰρ τὸ τοιόνδε δεῖ ἐννοῆσαι περὶ ὀνομάτων, ὅτι πολλάκις ἐπεμβάλλομεν γράμματα, τὰ δ᾽ ἐξαιροῦμεν, παρ᾽ ὃ βουλόμεθα ὀνομάζοντες, καὶ τὰς ὀξύτητας μεταβάλλομεν. οἷον Διὶ φίλος· τοῦτο ἵνα ἀντὶ ῥήματος ὄνομα ἡμῖν γένηται, τό τε ἕτερον αὐτόθεν ἰῶτα ἐξείλομεν καὶ ἀντὶ ὀξείας τῆς μέσης συλλαβῆς βαρεῖαν ἐφθεγξάμεθα.

The change of accent here mentioned is the loss of the accent of φίλος in the compound Δίφιλος, and it is described as pronouncing a grave (βαρύς) syllable instead of an acute (ὀξύς) syllable. If we should interpret ὀξύς as 'loud', then βαρύς would have to mean 'faint, weak', and βαρύς has no such meaning. In fact, it is sometimes applied to unusually loud sounds, provided they are of low pitch; in Od. 9, 257 the voice of the Cyclops is called φθόγγος βαρύς, and Zeus is βαρυβρεμέτης, βαρύγδουπος, βαρύκτυπος, βαρύοπα, etc. We must understand ὀξύς and βαρύς in the Cratylus passage as we do when Plato speaks of music.

Phaedrus 268 D:[2] ἀλλ᾽ ὥσπερ ἂν μουσικὸς ἐντυχὼν ἀνδρὶ οἰομένῳ ἁρμονικῷ εἶναι, ὅτι δὴ τυγχάνει ἐπιστάμενος ὡς οἷόν τε ὀξυτάτην καὶ βαρυτάτην χορδὴν ποιεῖν, οὐκ ἀγρίως εἴποι ἄν. . . .

The Greek acute accent was therefore high pitch and the grave accent was low pitch.[3] And if the second ι of Δίφιλος has grave accent, then grave accent is simply lack of accent [106 c].

The grammarians consistently use the words ὀξύς and βαρύς in this way, and they agree in prescribing a third kind of accent.

[1] 'For in the first place we must make some such observation as this about words, that when we derive a word from whatever we please, we often put in additional letters, and take others out, and alter the accents. For example, in order that Διὶ φίλος may be a word instead of a phrase, we have taken out one of the two iotas, and in place of the acute middle syllable we have come to pronounce a grave syllable.'

[2] 'But as a musician, if he should meet a man who thought he was skilled in music just because he understood how it is possible to give a chord the highest pitch and the lowest, would not furiously say. ... '

[3] For the history of the words ὀξύς and βαρύς in earlier Greek, see P. Hanschcke, De Accentuum Graecorum Nominibus 10–31 (Bonn, 1914).

102. Dion. Thr. 6.15–7.2:[4] τόνος ἐστὶ φωνῆς ἀπήχησις ἐναρμονίου, ἡ κατὰ ἀνάτασιν ἐν τῇ ὀξείᾳ, ἡ κατὰ ὁμαλισμὸν ἐν τῇ βαρείᾳ, ἡ κατὰ περίκλασιν ἐν τῇ περισπωμένῃ.

What the nature of the circumflex was appears very clearly from other passages.

Dion. Hal., Comp. Verb. 41.5–7:[5] τῶν δὲ ἀμφοτέρας τὰς τάσεις ἐχουσῶν αἱ μὲν κατὰ μίαν συλλαβὴν συνεφθαρμένον ἔχουσι τῷ ὀξεῖ τὸ βαρύ, ἃς δὴ περισπωμένας καλοῦμεν.

Ps.-Sergius 4.529.4–7 K.:[6] Athenodorus duas esse prosodias putavit, unam inferiorem, alteram superiorem; flexam autem—nam ita nostra lingua περισπω-μένην vocavimus—nihil aliud esse quam has duas in una syllaba.

The passage quoted below [107] from Theodosius of Alexandria is even more explicit, and, although it was written after the character of the accent had been essentially changed, it certainly preserves a sound tradition from Alexandrian times.

That the high pitch of a circumflex syllable differed from that of a long acute syllable in that it came near its beginning is shown also by its behavior in the language itself. (a) If an acute syllable contracts with a following syllable, the result is a circumflex (ἡδέες > ἡδεῖς); but if an acute syllable contracts with a preceding syllable, the result is an acute (ἑσταώς > ἑστώς). (b) The recessive accent of the vocative produces Ζεῦ beside nom. Ζεύς like πάτερ beside πατήρ. (c) Similarly the recessive accent of Lesbian yields nom. Ζεῦς.

According to the Alexandrian grammarians, then, the acute (ὀξύς) accent was characterized by a rise in pitch and the circumflex (περισπώμενος) accent by a rise plus a fall in pitch. The grave (βαρύς) "accent" was low pitch, i.e. lack of accent.

103. The correctness of this doctrine is strikingly confirmed by the few extant remains of ancient musical scores, notably the fragments of hymns preserved on stone at Delphi; for, according to these documents, an accented syllable is usually sung on a higher note than any unaccented syllable in the same word, and scarcely ever does an unaccented syllable have higher pitch than the accented syllable of its word. Furthermore a circumflexed syllable is usually sung on two notes, of

---

[4] 'Accent is a modification of the musical voice, by elevation in the acute, by leveling in the grave, by bending (or deflection) in the circumflex.'

[5] 'Of the ⟨words⟩ that have both pitches, some have the grave fused with the acute on one and the same syllable—those which we call circumflex.'

[6] 'Athenodorus thought there were two accents, one lower and one higher; and that the circumflex—for thus we translate περισπωμένη—was nothing but these two in one syllable.'

which the first is most frequently the higher.[7] Dionysius of Halicarnassus, to be sure, tells us (Comp. Verb. 41.18–42.14) that music
subordinates the words to the tune and in support of the statement he
analyzes the melody of a song in Euripides where, he says, three suc-
cessive words are sung to one note and several words have unaccented
syllables sung on higher notes than the accented syllable gets. This
passage merely proves that the careful retention of speech accent in
song was not universal. The argument that has been drawn from the
practice of the Delphian hymns is not thereby weakened.

104. That the Greek accent had had this character from the
earliest times is indicated by the fact that it generally corresponds
with the Sanskrit accent, which was similarly described in terms of
pitch by the Hindu grammarians. The following pairs of words are
typical: *pitā́* : πατήρ; *pitáras* : πατέρες; *bhrā́tā* : φρᾱ́τωρ; *úttaras* : ὕστερος;
jánas : γένος; *jánasas* : γένεος; *bháranti* : φέροντα; *gurúṣ* : βαρύς; *janitā́* :
γενετήρ; *hitás* : θετός; *ákṣitas* : ἄφθιτος; *pā́das* : πόδες; *padás* : ποδός.
Where Sanskrit and Greek accent diverge the reason is sometimes the
specifically Greek limitation of the accent to the last three syllables of
the word, and sometimes that an original variation within a paradigm
has been leveled in one way in Sanskrit and in another way in Greek.
While many differences remain unexplained, there is no doubt that the
two systems are fundamentally the same.

Since, therefore, the Greek accent system and the Sanskrit system
are clearly somewhat divergent developments of the same original
system, and since both the Greek accent and the Sanskrit accent are
described as variations in pitch, it is fair to conclude that Greek inherited
a musical accent. Furthermore some of the related languages preserve
traces of the same system.

105. But to say that the Greek accent was musical does not mean
that Greek was habitually sung. We might be sure without any specific
evidence that the melody of speech was more flexible—less precisely
regulated—than that of music. We have besides the testimony of
Aristoxenus, the best of the Greek writers on music, that during speech
pitch constantly changed, whereas in music each note was held for a
time and then the voice leaped at once to another note.

Harmonica Stoicheia 1.9 = 101.19–102.7, 102.20–25 Macran:[8] πάσης δὲ φωνῆς
δυναμένης κινεῖσθαι τὸν εἰρημένον αὐτὸν τρόπον δύο τινές εἰσιν ἰδέαι κινήσεως, ἥ τε συνεχὴς

---

[7] Crusius, Die delphischen Hymnen 113 f.

[8] 'While every voice is capable of change of position, as we have said, there
are two kinds of change, continuous change and change by intervals. In con-

καὶ ἡ διαστηματική. κατὰ μὲν οὖν τὴν συνεχῆ τόπον τινὰ διεξιέναι φαίνεται ἡ φωνὴ τῇ αἰσθήσει
οὕτως ὡς ἂν μηδαμοῦ ἱσταμένη μηδ' ἐπ' αὐτῶν τῶν περάτων κατά γε τὴν τῆς αἰσθήσεως φαντασίαν,
ἀλλὰ φερομένη συνεχῶς μέχρι σιωπῆς. κατὰ δὲ τὴν ἑτέραν ἣν ὀνομάζομεν διαστηματικὴν
ἐναντίως φαίνεται κινεῖσθαι· διαβαίνουσα γὰρ ἵστησιν αὐτὴν ἐπὶ μιᾶς τάσεως εἶτα πάλιν
ἐφ' ἑτέρας καὶ τοῦτο ποιοῦσα συνεχῶς—λέγω δὲ συνεχῶς κατὰ τὸν χρόνον—ὑπερβαίνουσα
μὲν τοὺς περιεχομένους ὑπὸ τῶν τάσεων τόπους, ἱσταμένη δ' ἐπ' αὐτῶν τῶν τάσεων καὶ φθεγγο-
μένη ταύτας μόνον αὐτὰς μελῳδεῖν λέγεται καὶ κινεῖσθαι διαστηματικὴν κίνησιν. . . . τὴν μὲν
οὖν συνεχῆ λογικὴν εἶναί φαμεν, διαλεγομένων γὰρ ἡμῶν οὕτως ἡ φωνὴ κινεῖται κατὰ τόπον
ὥστε μηδαμοῦ δοκεῖν ἵστασθαι. κατὰ δὲ τὴν ἑτέραν ἣν ὀνομάζομεν διαστηματικὴν ἐναντίως
πέφυκε γίγνεσθαι· ἀλλὰ γὰρ ἵστασθαί τε δοκεῖ καὶ πάντες τὸν τοῦτο φαινόμενον ποιεῖν οὐκέτι
λέγειν φασὶν ἀλλ' ᾄδειν.

Aristoxenus' statement carries complete conviction since the same
difference between the melody of speech and that of song is to be observed in the languages of the present day. It is, in fact, probable
that spoken Greek did not sound very unlike a modern European
language in point of melody; the chief difference may have been that
the rise and fall in pitch was a function of the word rather than, as in
English, of the sentence.

106 a. Dionysius of Halicarnassus, in an often quoted passage, seems
flatly to contradict Aristoxenus on this point. A real difference of
opinion about so important a feature of their native language can
scarcely be ascribed to two such excellent observers; we must find some
interpretation of Dionysius' words that will harmonize with Aristoxenus.

Comp. Verb. 40.17–41.12:[9] διαλέκτου μὲν οὖν μέλος ἑνὶ μετρεῖται διαστήματι τῷ λεγομένῳ
διὰ πέντε ὡς ἔγγιστα, καὶ οὔτε ἐπιτείνεται πέρα τῶν τριῶν τόνων καὶ ἡμιτονίου ἐπὶ τὸ ὀξὺ οὔτ'

---

tinuous change of position the voice seems to the senses to traverse a certain
space in such a manner that it does not become stationary at any point, not
even at the extremes—according to our sense-perception, at least—but moves
continuously until silence intervenes. In the other species, which we call change
by intervals, the voice seems to move in the opposite manner; for step by step
the voice halts upon one pitch and again upon a second, doing this continuously
—continuously in time, I mean. Stepping over the spaces bounded by the
pitches while stopping upon the pitches themselves and sounding only these, the
voice is said to sing and to change by intervals. ... Continuous change we call
the change of speech, as in speaking the voice changes its position in such a way
that it does not seem to remain stationary at any point. The reverse is the
case with the other change, which we designate change by intervals; for, on the
contrary, the voice seems to remain stationary, and all men say that a person
who is evidently doing this is singing rather than speaking.'

[9] 'Now, the melody of spoken language is measured by a single interval, which
is approximately that termed a fifth. When the voice rises toward the acute,
it does not rise more than three tones and a semitone; and when it falls toward
the grave, it does not fall more than this interval. Further, the entire utterance

ἀνίεται τοῦ χωρίου τούτου πλέον ἐπὶ τὸ βαρύ. οὐ μὴν ἄπασα λέξις ἡ καθ' ἓν μόριον λόγου
ταττομένη ἐπὶ τῆς αὐτῆς λέγεται τάσεως, ἀλλ' ἡ μὲν ἐπὶ τῆς ὀξείας, ἡ δ' ἐπὶ τῆς βαρείας, ἡ δ'
ἐπὶ ἀμφοῖν. τῶν δὲ ἀμφοτέρας τὰς τάσεις ἐχουσῶν αἱ μὲν κατὰ μίαν συλλαβὴν συνεφθαρμένον
ἔχουσι τῷ ὀξεῖ τὸ βαρύ, ἃς δὴ περισπωμένας καλοῦμεν· αἱ δὲ ἐν ἑτέρᾳ τε καὶ ἑτέρᾳ χωρὶς
ἑκάτερον ἐφ' ἑαυτοῦ τὴν οἰκείαν φυλάττον φύσιν. καὶ ταῖς μὲν δισυλλάβοις οὐδὲν τὸ διὰ μέσου
χωρίον βαρύτητός τε καὶ ὀξύτητος· ταῖς δὲ πολυσυλλάβοις, ἡλίκαι ποτ' ἂν ὦσιν, ἡ τὸν ὀξὺν
τόνον ἔχουσα μία ἐν πολλαῖς ταῖς ἄλλαις βαρείαις ἔνεστιν.

Dionysius must mean that the high point of an accented syllable was
higher than the low point in the same word by approximately one fifth,
not that the voice leaps over this interval at any point in the word.
When he says that in dissyllables there is no space intermediate between low pitch and high pitch, he must mean merely that there is only
one unaccented (low-pitched) syllable and only one accented (high-
pitched) syllable.[10] This amounts to saying that in such a word only
two pitches were of linguistic importance; as modern scholars would
put it, only these two varieties of pitch were phonemic in dissyllables.
He therefore says nothing at all about the pitch of those parts of the
word which must, according to Aristoxenus, have been spoken with
pitch gradually rising from grave to acute or falling from acute to
grave.

106 b. It is significant, however, that Dionysius limits this statement to dissyllables. He implies that in polysyllables there is τὸ διὰ
μέσου χωρίον βαρύτητός τε καὶ ὀξύτητος. Since this cannot mean merely
Aristoxenus' pitch-glide between grave and acute (for if it did, it would
apply equally to dissyllables), it would seem to be a sort of lower acute
or higher grave; Dionysius apparently knew that some of the grave
syllables of a polysyllable might have higher pitch than others. He
implies something analogous to the secondary accent that is familiar
in languages, like English, with a stress accent.

106 c. This is probably the middle accent which is mentioned a few
times in our ancient sources.

---

during one word is not delivered at the same pitch of the voice throughout, but
one part of it at the acute pitch, another at the grave, another at both. Of the
words that have both pitches, some have the grave fused with the acute on one
and the same syllable—those which we call circumflexed; others have both pitches
falling on separate syllables, each retaining its own quality. Now in dissyllables
there is no space intermediate between low pitch and high pitch; while in poly-
syllabic words, whatever their number of syllables, there is but one syllable
that has the acute accent (high pitch) among the many remaining grave ones.'

[10] It must be admitted that this meaning is not clearly discernible in Dionysius'
words; but any other interpretation would be mere nonsense, as well as flat con-
tradiction of Aristoxenus.

Aristotle, Rhet. 1403 b 24–9:[11] δῆλον οὖν ὅτι καὶ περὶ τὴν ῥητορικὴν ἔστι τὸ τοιοῦτον ὥσπερ καὶ περὶ τὴν ποιητικήν, ὅ περ ἕτεροί τινες ἐπραγματεύθησαν καὶ Γλαύκων ὁ Τήιος. ἔστι δὲ αὐτὴ μὲν ἐν τῇ φωνῇ, πῶς αὐτῇ δεῖ χρῆσθαι πρὸς ἕκαστον πάθος, οἷον πότε μεγάλῃ καὶ πότε μικρᾷ καὶ πότε μέσῃ, καὶ πῶς τοῖς τόνοις, οἷον ὀξείᾳ καὶ βαρείᾳ καὶ μέσῃ.

Poet. 1456 b 30–4:[12] ταῦτα δὲ ⟨τὰ στοιχεῖα⟩ διαφέρει σχήμασίν τε τοῦ στόματος καὶ τόποις καὶ δασύτητι καὶ ψιλότητι καὶ μήκει καὶ βραχύτητι, ἔτι δὲ ὀξύτητι καὶ βαρύτητι καὶ τῷ μέσῳ· περὶ ὧν καθ' ἕκαστον ἐν τοῖς μετρικοῖς προσήκει θεωρεῖν.

Many scholars have assumed that the middle accent was the circumflex, since in Aristotle and elsewhere it is named along with grave and acute as the third kind of accent. But "intermediate" would be a peculiarly inept name for an accent which contained within itself both the extremes. Furthermore, Wackernagel[13] has shown that in Soph. El. 179 a 14 Aristotle referred to οὗ as ὀξύτερον as against οὐ, which was βαρύτερον; for him both acute and circumflex syllables were ὀξύς.

The fullest account of the middle accent is rather confused, since it is combined with a statement about certain varieties of the circumflex and a reference to a wholly mysterious μονότονον.

Ps.-Sergius 529.10–12, 530.9–23 K. = Varro 214.5–9, 215.5–22 GS:[14] Tyrannio vero Amisenus, quem Lucullus Mithridatico bello captum Lucio Murenae con-

---

[11] 'It is clear, then, that there is a kind of skill similar to that in regard to poetry, and this has been treated by Glaucon of Teos and others. It has to do with the voice; how one should use it for each emotion, as, for example, when one should make it loud and when soft and when intermediate, and how one should use the accents, namely the acute, the grave, and the middle accent.'

[12] 'And these speech sounds differ in the configuration of the mouth, in the place of articulation, in roughness and smoothness (i.e. aspiration or the lack of it), in length and shortness, and also in the acute, grave, and middle accent; each of which topics should be discussed in connection with metrics.'

[13] Beiträge zur Lehre vom griechischen Akzent 8–12.

[14] 'But Tyrannio Amisenus, whom Lucullus captured in the Mithridatic war and gave to Lucius Murena, and who was presented by the latter at the same time with his liberty and the citizenship, writes that there are four accents, grave, middle, acute, and circumflex. ...

'It is necessary to understand that this theory is no recent invention, but of all who before Varro and Tyrannio have left any notice of accent, the majority and all the distinguished writers have mentioned this middle accent, all of whom Varro says were his authorities; of the grammarians, Glaucus of Samos and Hermocrates of Iasus, and likewise the Peripatetic philosopher Theophrastus, which name he got from his divine eloquence, and also Athenodorus of the same sect, a man of the keenest insight, who calls a certain accent the monotone (it seems to be none other than the middle accent, although under a different name). Some have thought that there are more than four accents, as Glaucus of Samos, by whom six accents were proposed under these names, low, middle, high, broken,

cessit, a quo ille libertate simul et civitate donatus est, quattuor scribit esse prosodias, βαρεῖαν, μέσην, ὀξεῖαν, περισπωμένην. . . . Scire enim oportet rationis huius recens non esse commentum, sed omnium qui ante Varronem et Tyrannionem de prosodia aliquid reliquerunt plurimos et clarissimos quosque mediae huius fecisse mentionem, quos omnes sibi fuisse auctores Varro commemorat; grammaticos Glaucum Samium et Hermocratem Iasium, item philosophum Theophrastum peripateticum, cui divina facundia nomen adscivit, nec non eiusdem sectae Athenodorum, summi acuminis virum, qui quandam prosodiam μονότονον appellat quae videtur non alia esse quam media licet diverso vocabulo. Nec desunt qui prosodias plures esse quam quattuor putaverint, ut Glaucus Samius, a quo sex prosodiae propositae sub hisce nominibus, ἀνειμένη, μέση, ἐπιτεταμένη, κεκλασμένη, ⟨ἀνακλωμένη,⟩ ἀντανακλωμένη. Sed hic quoque non dissentit a nobis; nam cuivis ex ipsis nominibus intellectu proclive est tres primas esse simplices et non alias quam βαρεῖαν, μέσην, ὀξεῖαν, postremas autem tres duplices et quasi species unius flexae, quae est genere una.

Unfortunately we know nothing further about this middle or secondary accent beyond the mere fact of its existence. No illustrations are given by any of our authorities, and we cannot be certain that this accent rested upon any particular syllable of any Greek word.

106 d. In the first edition of this book it was suggested, after Ehrlich and others, that the middle accent of the grammarians should be ascribed to the syllables marked grave in our texts, namely the final syllables of oxytones within a phrase. These cannot have been the syllables referred to by Dionysius of Halicarnassus [106 a], since he definitely prescribes acute accent for the polysyllables which, by implication, contain the intermediate accent. Furthermore, Dionysius elsewhere (Comp. Verb. 42.4–6) says that λευκὸν within a certain phrase has an acute syllable, and there are many similar remarks in the grammatical literature.[15]

It may be suggested, however, that the finals of oxytones within the

---

bent, reflected. But he also agrees with us; for it is easy to understand from the names themselves that the first three are simple and no other than the grave, middle, and acute, while the last three are composite and, so to speak, three species of a single genus, which is the circumflex.'

[15] Laum, Al. Akzent., has held that the finals of oxytones within the phrase were, with certain exceptions, pronounced as other acute syllables, and that the use of the grave sign on such syllables originated about 400 A.D. as a result of a misunderstanding of earlier accented texts. It has since been shown (Joseph Giessler, Prosodische Zeichen in den antiken Handschriften griechischer Lyriker, Giessen dissertation, 1923; Jakob Wackernagel, IF Anz. 43.59; A. Debrunner, ByzZ 29.50–5; Eduard Hermann, Phil. Woch. 50.228–33), however, that earlier papyri regularly leave finals of oxytones within the phrase unmarked or mark them grave.

phrase had a somewhat lower accent than other acute syllables, so that they might be compared to the secondary or middle accents of polysyllables. Such a situation might give rise to the use of the grave sign in the way that is still in use. The grave sign was not restricted to this use before 400 A.D.; but the earlier literary papyri show that it always tended to stand on finals of oxytones within the phrase.

107. A Byzantine fragment, very likely from the pen of Theodosius,[16] makes Aristophanes of Byzantium the inventor of the accent marks and also of the breathings. The most important part of the text follows:[17]

κατὰ τοῦτο καὶ ὁ Ἀριστοφάνης σημεῖα ἔθετο τῷ λόγῳ πρῶτα ταῦτα, ἵν' ἅμα συλλαβῆς καὶ λέξεως γενομένης κανών τις ἔποιτο καὶ σημεῖον ὀρθότητος· ἔπειτα τρίχα τεμὼν τὴν κίνησιν τῆς φωνῆς τὸ μὲν εἰς χρόνους, τὸ δὲ εἰς τόνους, τὸ δὲ εἰς αὐτὸ τὸ πνεῦμα. καὶ τοὺς μὲν χρόνους τοῖς ῥυθμοῖς ἤκασε, τοὺς δὲ τόνους τοῖς τόνοις τῆς μουσικῆς. καὶ σημεῖα ἔθετο ἐφ' ἑκάστῳ καὶ ὀνόματα, τοῖς μὲν χρόνοις τὸ βραχὺ καὶ τὸ μακρὸν ἐπονομάσας καὶ σχήματα οἰκεῖα ποιησάμενος, τῷ μὲν μακρῷ τὴν εὐθεῖαν γραμμὴν καὶ ἀποτεταμένην ⁻, τῷ δὲ βραχεῖ τὴν συνεστραμμένην καὶ συνέχουσαν ὥσπερ ἑκατέρωθεν τὴν φωνὴν ˘· τῶν δὲ τόνων τὴν μὲν ἄνω τείνουσαν καὶ εὐθεῖαν καὶ εἰς ὀξὺ ἀπολήγουσαν ἐοικυῖαν τοῖς βέλεσι τοῖς ἐφιεμένοις ὀξεῖαν ἐπονομάσας ', τὴν δὲ ἐναντίαν ταύτῃ βαρεῖαν ˎ· ἐπεὶ δὲ ἑώρα τὴν ἔξω τοῦ μέλους λέξιν οὐ κατὰ τὸ βαρὺ μόνον οὐδ' ἐν τῷ ὀξεῖ

[16] The entire passage is reprinted from Arcadius 186–91 by Lentz, Herodian XXXVIII–XXXX, and by Laum, Al. Akzent. 99.

[17] 'In this way also Aristophanes applied to speech first these diacritic marks, so that at the same time when syllable and word were written there might accompany them a standard and symbol of their correct pronunciation; then he observed the triple modification of the voice in respect to quantity, accent, and breathing. Quantity he compared with rhythm, and accent with the tones of music. He also assigned marks and names to each, he named the quantities short and long, and invented appropriate marks, for the long quantity the straight, extended line (⁻), for the short the curved line that seems to hold the sound back from both directions (˘). Of the accents, the straight one pointing upwards and ending in a point (?) like an arrow being aimed (') he named acute, and the one pointing in the opposite direction (`) he named grave. Since he saw that speech which is not sung does not confine itself merely to the grave and the acute, but that it needs also a third accent, namely the circumflex, first he observed the character of the voice itself. And since it proved that in circumflexed words the voice at first gives an acute sound and then turns downward approximately to the grave pitch, he thought that the circumflex is nothing but a mixture and mingling of them both, namely the acute and the grave, and in this way he invented a mark for it. For, having joined together the two straight accents, that of the acute and that of the grave (^), he said that this was the circumflex, thus naming it ὀξυβάρεια (acute-grave) from the two accents of which it consisted. But since the mark of the accent was going to resemble one of the letters, namely Λ, fearing that when it was written along with the letters it would confuse the reading, he broke the angle of the straight lines a little and bent them into a semi-circle, and while changing the mark he also changed the name into the more suitable and euphonious name of circumflex.'

καταμένουσαν, ἀλλὰ καὶ τρίτου τινὸς δεομένην τόνου, τούτου δὴ τοῦ περισπωμένου, πρότερον
αὐτῆς τῆς φωνῆς τὴν δύναμιν ἐσκοπεῖτο.   καὶ ἐπεὶ συνέβαινε ταῖς περισπωμέναις λέξεσιν εὐθὺς
ἀρχομένην τὴν φωνὴν ὀξύ τι ὑπηχεῖν, κατατρέπειν δὲ ὡς εἰς τὸ βαρύ, οὐδὲν ἄλλο ἢ μίξιν καὶ
κρᾶσιν ἐξ ἀμφοῖν, τοῦ τε ὀξέος καὶ τοῦ βαρέος, ἡγησάμενος εἶναι τὸ περισπώμενον, οὕτως αὐτῷ
καὶ τὸ σχῆμα ἐποιήσατο.   ἐφαρμοσάμενος γὰρ ἀλλήλαις τὰς εὐθείας ἑκατέρας, τήν τε τοῦ ὀξέος
καὶ τὴν τοῦ βαρέος ταύτην εἶναι τὴν περισπωμένην ἔλεγεν, ὧδέ πως αὐτὴν ἐξ ἀμφοῖν τοῖν τόνοιν
ἐξ ὧν ἐγένετο ⁁ ὀξυβάρειαν ὀνομάζων.   ἐπεὶ δὲ ὁμοιότητα τὸ σχῆμα τοῦ τόνου πρὸς τῶν γραμμάτων ἔμελλεν ἕξειν τὸ Λ, δεδοικὼς μή τι ἄρα ἐν τῇ παραθέσει τῶν γραμμάτων παραμιγνύῃ
τὴν ἀνάγνωσιν, βραχύ τι τῶν εὐθειῶν τὴν γωνίαν κλάσας καὶ περιτείνας αὐτὰς εἰς ἡμικύκλιον,
ἅμα τῷ σχήματι τῆς περισπωμένης καὶ τὸ ὄνομα ἐπὶ τὸ οἰκειότερόν τε καὶ εὐφωνότερον μετέβαλεν.

The last sentence in this passage cannot be based upon a sound tradition, since the early papyri write the circumflex with an angle; the
alteration to a semicircle in early Byzantine times was no doubt a mere
reflex of writing the whole mark with one stroke of the pen.

107 a. The early literary papyri and the Homeric scholia show that
the accent marks were originally used to help inexperienced readers distinguish between words that might otherwise be confused (ἄλλα : ἀλλά,
πόλεις : πολεῖς), and, since there was no effort to mark all accented
syllables, it was more convenient to write ᾹΛΛΑ than ΑΛΛΆ, since the
former gave the reader the needed hint at the earliest possible moment.
This was the reason why the grave mark, which merely indicated lack
of accent, was needed; if all accented syllables had been marked, there
would have been no point in marking any unaccented syllables.

108. There is very little evidence about stress in ancient Greek, and
that little is chiefly negative.

108 a. The Greek vowel system is more conservative than that of
any other Indo-European language of which we have extensive remains.
In particular there is very little loss of vowels and nothing at all resembling the vowel-weakening in Latin.   Since these are the characteristic effects of strong stress falling constantly upon a given syllable,
it seems safe to say that Greek had no strong distinctions of stress or,
if it had any, that the stress must have fallen sometimes on one syllable
and sometimes on another (in other words, it must have been a function
of the phrase).

108 b. A fixed stress accent associates itself with the rhythm of
speech and verse; either it forms the basis of the rhythm, as in the
modern languages of western Europe, or it tends to coincide with the
time beats, as in Latin.   In ancient Greek there is no correspondence
between the written accent and rhythm.   Consequently there can have
been no considerable increase of stress upon the syllables with the

known accents—probably they were quite without a regular increase of stress at the early period when the several types of verse finally developed into the forms we know. There is here no argument against a stress accent independent of the pitch accent and resting upon different syllables of the word according to the structure of the phrase.

108 c. Modern Greek accent is, in large part, a stress accent resting, in general, upon the same syllables that in ancient times carried the pitch accent. This fact proves that at some time the two kinds of accent must have been combined upon the same syllables, and that the element of stress must have become relatively stronger until the modern condition was reached. It does not follow, however, that any increase of stress was combined with the rise of pitch in the fifth century B.C., or at any date before clear evidence for such stress appears.

109 a. Several scraps of evidence for stress in Greek of classical or Hellenistic times have been alleged by various scholars, but the only item that seems worthy of mention applies to the dialect of the Athenian mob of the fourth century B.C. The comic poet Amphis, 30 Kock, ridicules a fish-dealer for saying 'ττάρων 'βολῶν and 'κτὼ 'βολῶν. The verb σκορακίζεσθαι (first in Ps.-Demosthenes 11.11) presupposes an imprecation 's κόρακας. But all of these lost vowels were initials, and so their loss may have had no relation to stress. Possibly we should write 'κτώβολῶν, assuming crasis, whence 'βολῶν was extended to 'ττάρων 'βολῶν, and similar phrases may be responsible for 'κτώ and for 's from ἐς. Again we may have something like Eng. 'fraid not, 'fact is and French 'turellement for naturellement, 'tends tu? for entends tu?, etc.

109 b. Kretschmer's[18] dating of the change from pitch to stress at about 200 B.C. has been widely accepted, but is not tenable. He based his argument upon the tendency to confuse ε with η and ο with ω in Hellenistic papyri, but this confusion is rather due to changes in vowel quality [30, 45]. The fact that η and ω appear for ε and ο in unaccented syllables as well as in accented syllables from the early part of the third century on is fatal to Kretschmer's theory.

Vulgar Latin tended, as early as the third century B.C., to retain the position of the Greek accent in proparoxytone loan-words, even if the penult had to be shortened (áncŏra, póĕsis, Phílĭppus). It was argued in the first edition of this book that the Romans must have heard considerable stress in these words, or they would not have identified the Greek accent with their own. It is more likely, however, that

[18] KZ 30.591–600. Cf. Sturtevant, TAPA 42.45–7.

in these cases as elsewhere the Romans were impressed with the pitch that was common to both the Greek and the Latin accent [213]; there is no evidence here for stress in Greek.[19]

109 c. By the second century A.D. erroneous quantities in verse become so common as to indicate that a stress accent is exerting its characteristic influence. In that century we should probably date Babrius, whose choliambics always have an accented syllable in the next to the last place.

It has been thought[20] that a Coptic translation of part of the Old Testament, dated about 350 A.D., indicates a stress accent by spelling Ἰάκωβος with κκ, as against Ἰακώβ with one κ, and by frequently spelling θάλασσα with λλ. The evidence would be much stronger if other instances of doubled consonants after the accent could be cited, either in native Coptic words or in Greek loan-words.

109 d. Nevertheless we must assume that Greek accent in the fourth century A.D. was largely a matter of stress; for in that century Gregory of Nazianzus composed hymns in accentual rhythm.

109 e. The Byzantine grammarians, in sharp contrast to those of the Hellenistic and Roman periods, often speak of the accent in terms that imply stress, e.g. ῥωννύναι 'strengthen', σφοδρῶς 'vehemently'.[21]

110. It is quite certain, therefore, that Greek accent from the beginning until some time during the Roman period was essentially a matter of pitch, and that there were two kinds of accent, a rising (acute) accent and a rising-falling (circumflex) accent. Although the Greek accent is often called a musical accent, there was in Greek as in other languages a sharp difference between the melody of speech and of song; in speaking, pitch constantly changed.

All syllables except those that were acute or circumflex were usually called grave (i.e. heavy or low); but we are told that some of these were higher than the rest, and were sometimes said to bear the middle accent. We do not know which syllables were treated in this way except that they were confined to polysyllables. Perhaps one may infer that middle accent never rested on a syllable next to an acute or circumflex syllable.

There is some reason to suppose that the final syllable of an oxytone

---

[19] For a discussion of other supposed indications of stress in Greek prior to the Christian era, see Ehrlich, Untersuchungen über die Natur der griechischen Betonung.

[20] Rahlfs, Sitzungsberichte der Berliner Akademie 1912.1040 f.

[21] Misteli, Ueber griechische Betonung 28 f.; Laum, Al. Akzent. 8 and fn. 5.

within a phrase had a lower pitch than other acutes. It may have approximated the middle accent.

At some time in or near the second century A.D. Greek came to have a stress accent resting upon about the same syllables that had previously had higher pitch. It is safe to say that the change was gradual, beginning with simultaneous rise of pitch and increase of stress. There is, however, no clear indication of stress upon the "accented" syllables before the second century A.D., and there is some reason to suppose that in the earliest Greek there was little if any stress associated with the higher pitch. There may have been a variation of stress depending upon the structure of the phrase, but there is no direct evidence of that either.

CHAPTER V
THE LATIN VOWELS
A

111. Scholarly tradition is nearly unanimous in making Lat. *a* a low vowel; and the divergent English pronunciation (*a* in *pater* = *a* in Eng. *pate, a* in *iam* = *a* in Eng. *can*) is known to have resulted from changes in the pronunciation of English [1].

The Romance languages usually present a vowel of extreme openness where Latin had *a*. Lat. *ad* appears everywhere as *a*; Lat. *pater* and *māter* yield *padre* and *madre* in Italian, Spanish, and Portuguese; Lat. *amāre* is It. *amare*, Sp. and Port. *amar*. The different French development (*père, mère, aimer*, etc.) is known to be secondary.

Gk. *a* corresponds with Lat. *a* in loan words (Καισαρ, Μαριος, *Platō*, *cōmarchus*). Equally cogent are early Latin loan-words in the Germanic languages, such as Germ. *Wall* and *Strasse*.

112. The ancient descriptions of *a* show quite clearly that it was a low vowel.

> Terentianus 6.328.111–5 K:[1]
> *A* prima locum littera sic ab ore sumit:
> immunia rictu patulo tenere labra,
> linguamque necesse est ita pendulam reduci,
> ut nisus in illam valeat subire vocis,
> nec partibus ullis aliquos ferire dentes.[2]

> Martianus Capella 3.261:[3]
> Namque *a* sub hiatu oris congruo solo spiritu memoramus.

113. Since Italian, Spanish, Portuguese, and Rumanian agree in showing a low central vowel for Latin accented *a*, while only Rhetic

---

[1] '*A*, the first letter, takes its position in the mouth as follows: one must hold the lips parted but not ⟨otherwise⟩ functioning (i.e. unrounded?), and the tongue must be relaxed and withdrawn in such a way that the impulse of the voice may be able to pass over it, nor may the tongue strike any of the teeth in any place.'

[2] Cf. Terentianus 6.329.118–20 K, quoted below [115].

[3] 'For we pronounce *a* with an opening of the mouth suitable only to ⟨this letter and⟩ *h*.'

and French indicate a front vowel, it is perhaps safer to follow the majority and to assume that Lat. *a* was similar to *a* in Italian or German, i.e. [ɑ], rather than like the [a] of Fr. *patte*.

114. Although most other Latin vowels had differences of quality corresponding to their differences of quantity [116, 123], there is no evidence for any qualitative difference between long *a* and short *a*. In fact, Lucilius (9.352–5 M) tells us that there was no such difference:[4]

> *Aa* primum longa, ⟨*a*⟩ brevis syllaba. Nos tamen unum
> hoc faciemus, et uno eodemque ut dicimus pacto
> scribemus *pacem, placide, Ianum, aridum, acetum,*
> ῏Αϱες, ῏Αϱες Graeci ut faciunt.

In the first line Lucilius distinguishes between long and short *a*; but then he proposes to write them alike, "just as we speak". Lucilius is evidently following Greek practice, and he may have overlooked a non-phonemic qualitative difference; at any rate he says there was no such difference.

E and I

115. Tradition is unanimous in making Lat. *e* and *i* front vowels of which *e* is the more open sound. The descriptions of the Roman grammarians confirm this. The best of these is in Terentianus 6.329.116–20:[5]

> *E* quae sequitur vocula dissona est priori
> quia deprimit altum modice tenore rictum,
> et lingua remotos premit hinc et hinc molares.
> *I* porrigit ictum genuinos prope ad ipsos
> minimumque renidet supero tenus labello.

116 a. The evidence is clear that both *e* and *i* differed in quality according as they had long or short quantity. Accented *e* and *i* develop in the Romance languages as is indicated by the typical words included in Table 1.

---

[4] 'To begin at the beginning, *aa* is a long and *a* a short syllable. Nevertheless we shall make them one; and in one and the same way as we speak, we shall write *pacem, placide, Ianum, aridum, acetum*, just as the Greeks write ῏Αϱες, ῏Αϱες.'

[5] 'The next vowel, *e*, differs from the previous one ⟨i.e. *a*⟩, in that it lessens the opening of the mouth to some extent, and the tongue touches the back molars on both sides. *I* extends the contact almost to the wisdom-teeth themselves and produces a slight smile along the upper lip.'

TABLE 1

	ĕ	ē	ĭ	ī
Latin	mel	vērum	pira	vīvere
Italian	miele	vero	pera	vivere
Sicilian	meli	viru	pira	. . . . .
French	miel	voire (vērē) plein (plēnus)	poire sein (sinus)	vivre
Spanish	miel	vero	pera	vivir
Portuguese	mel	crer (crēdere)	pera	viver
Sardinian	mele	kreere (crēdere)	pira	raigina (rādīcīna)

In every Romance language, except in Sardinian, accented ē and ĭ have merged in a single phoneme, while accented ĕ and ī have everywhere been kept distinct. It follows, at least in accented syllables, that the quality of Vulgar Latin ē was nearer an *i*-sound than was that of ĕ, and that the quality of ĭ was nearer *e* than was that of ī. In other words ē was a closer vowel than ĕ, and ī than ĭ. The conclusion is confirmed by the fact that accented ī is everywhere retained as an *i*-sound; it was so close a vowel as to avoid the tendency to develop into an *e*-sound.[6]

116 b. If this inference is correct we may expect to find in Latin inscriptions a tendency to use the letter *i* for ē and the letter *e* for ĭ; and since both the intermediate sounds have yielded *e* in most Romance languages, we may expect more instances of *e* for ĭ than of *i* for ē. As a matter of fact, the most common mistake in writing these vowels is the substitution of *e* for ĭ. Typical examples are listed in Table 2.

TABLE 2

admenistrator, CIL 12.674	*Corenthus*, 9.4569
adsedua, 12.2193	*deposeta*, 10.1378
anema, 10.3305, 12.481	*fede*, 12.2089, 2153
aureficinam, 7.265	*Felippus*, 14.1946
bassileca, 4.1779	*Helaritati*, 14.615
baselica, 7.965	*inemitabili*, 10.7586 (*bis*)
bes, 12.481	*ennocens*, 12.2701
Bret(t)annicus, 3.711, 712, 6979	*menus*, 8.9984, etc.
Capetolino, 3.771	*nesi*, 12.2426
carmena, 3.12854	*offecina*, 9.6078.3
castetate, 5.1973	*sales*, 12.2179
condedit, 5.7570	*Salenatoriae*, 14.1571

---

[6] P. Fouché, RLR 63.195–260, minimizes the arguments for a difference in openness between ĕ, ŏ and ē, ō, and holds that the short vowels were chiefly distinguished from the corresponding long ones by a relatively lax articulation. I am not convinced by his reasoning, which is based chiefly upon the relative instability of the short vowels.

TABLE 2—*Continued*

setu, 8.9639	*virgenales,* 12.2384
sebi, 5.1648	*vertute,* 5.6244
trebibos, 9.4204	*dumver, -veratus,* 3.7484, etc.
uteletas, 12.2085	*univera,* 10.7196

The use of *e* for *ĭ* is common in inscriptions in the third person sing. (*facet, vibet*), in the nom. and gen. sing. of the third declension (*civitates,* CIL 9.1128), in the dat.-abl. pl. of the third declension (*victorebus,* 9.5961), and in superlatives (*karessemo, merentessemo,* 2.2997).[7] It will be noticed that these misspellings occur in unaccented syllables as well as in accented syllables; consequently our conclusion that *ĭ* was relatively close to *e* in popular Latin holds also for the unaccented vowels.

116 c. Only less frequent are the instances of *i* for *ē* in inscriptions. Typical examples are those in Table 3.

TABLE 3

adoliscens, CIL 12.1792, 2069	*havite,* 5.1636
agis, 10.1692	*innocis,* 10.4510
Aurilius, 3.2010, etc.	*minsis,* 14.2710, etc.
dibuisti, 14, 2841	*Neclicta,* 12.955
didicavi, 3.3474	*posuirunt,* 3.8729
duodinos, 10.7777	*requiiscit, requiiscet,* 5.6397, etc.
eclisia,[8] 12.2085, etc.	*riges = regis,* 12.2654
Epictisis,[8] 14.1887	*rigna,* 12.975
ficit, 9.3581	*Rhinus,* 4.4905
ficerat, 9.699	*Siricam,*[8] 14.2215
fecirunt, 3.10743	*bix. = vexillarius,* 10.3502
Filix, 4.4511	*vixirunt,* 10.4492[9]
filiciter, 4.6882, 10.6565	

Here again the confusion occurs not only under the accent but also before and after the accent; there is no reason for positing any difference of vowel quality due to presence or absence of accent.

116 d. Undoubtedly some of the spellings with *e* for *ĭ* and *i* for *ē* are due to other causes than a phonetic similarity between the two phonemes. It must be remembered, however, that the argument does not rest upon particular instances, but upon the fact that these misspellings are, with the exception noted in [117], very much more numerous than the converse errors (*i* for *ĕ* and *e* for *ī*). Cf. [123 d].

[7] Further examples in Schuchardt 2.1-69; Grandgent 84 f., and references; Väänänen 33-5.

[8] Perhaps these words reflect the identity of Greek *η* and *ι* in popular speech after about 150 A.D. [28].

[9] Other examples in Schuchardt 1.244-374.

116 e. Aside from Pompeiian graffiti,[10] the inscriptions with *e* for *ĭ* or *i* for *ē* are mostly of the third century or later.[11]   Nevertheless there is no doubt that *ĭ* and *ē* approached each other in early times.   For the open quality of Lat. *i* we have evidence in Greek transcriptions of Latin words and Latin transcriptions of Greek.   During the republic and the early empire Latin *ĭ* was frequently, perhaps at first regularly, represented by Gk. ε.   Among the early instances of this orthography are: Καικελι, CIG 2322 b 30 (probably before 200 B.C.); Ὀφελλιε, 2322 b 86 (probably before 200 B.C.); Λεπεδος, SGDI 2581.122 (189–88 B.C.); κομετιον, Dittenberger, Sylloge³ 646.2 (170 B.C.), IG 9.2.89 a 10 (150– 147 B.C.), IGRRP 4.262.3 (120–95 B.C.); Καπετωλιον, Dittenberger, Sylloge³ 646.33 (170 B.C.), IG 14.986 (first century B.C.); Καμελλια, Gaertringen, Priene 41.3 (136 B.C.); Νεμετωριος, BCH 2.130.37 (120–95 B.C.); Κομπεταλιαστι, BCH 7.13.18 (97–96 B.C.); Δομετιος, IG 9.1.483 (94 B.C.), 2².4144 (probably about 16 B.C.); Τεβεριος, 9.2.483, 2².3243, 3244, 3245, 3246 (these four before 4 A.D.); Δομετιανος, IGRRP 1.862, etc. (first century A.D.); Φλαμενια, IG 2².2337.26 (early empire).[12]   Conversely Gk. ε is represented by Lat. *i* in *Philumina*, CIL 3.14192.16 (a bilingual inscription with Φιλουμένη in the Greek version), 5.2265, 9.1431, etc.; *Philuminus*, 14.3817; *Diaduminus*, 14.3337; *Susomine* (= Σωζομένη), 12.1509; *chizecae* (for Graeco-Latin *chezicē*), 4.1364; *Archilaus*, 10.3699; *Artimisia*, 3.2343 a, 10.5757; *Artimidora*, 14.498.[13] From these facts we infer that Gk. ε and Lat. *ĭ* were similar sounds; that is, Gk. ε was a close *e* and Lat. *ĭ* was an open *i* [29].

116 f. In Oscan-Umbrian as well as in Latin inherited *ē* and *ĭ* approached each other in quality.   In Umbrian this is shown, as in Latin, by frequent use of the character *e* for *ĭ* and of the character *i* for *ē*. In the Oscan alphabet there is a special symbol ⊣, usually transcribed *í*, to denote an open *i* which had developed from an inherited *ē* or *ĭ*.

---

[10] Where *quaeres* for *quaeris*, etc., have (erroneously, I think) been ascribed to Oscan influence by Väänänen 35.

[11] Some scholars assume on scanty evidence that *i* had become [e] by that time; but the consistent distinction between the two sounds in the Peregrinatio Sanctae Silviae is against them.

[12] Other examples in Dittenberger, Hermes 6.130–44, and Eckinger, Die Orthographie lateinischer Wörter in griechischen Inschriften 29 ff.

[13] The words *Cliarcus, Panthia, Thiagene, Tiodorus, Tiudosius, Thiodotos, Thiophanes, Thiophiles,* and *Thrasia* may belong here instead of in the list in [117 a].

Instances of ε for Lat. *i* in papyri are listed by Meinersmann 109, and similar evidence from Latin-Greek lexica of the sixth century A.D. is adduced by Dain, REL 8.101 f.

Table 4 indicates the regular correspondence of the front vowels between Latin and Oscan.

TABLE 4

Latin	est	lēgātīs	quis	īmus
Oscan	est	ligatúís	pís	imad-en

It is not to be assumed that the Italic languages all had the same vowel system; in fact it is clear that in the second century B.C. Oscan had gone farther than either Umbrian or Latin in assimilating ē and ĭ. But, since both Oscan and Umbrian agree with the Romance languages, the late Latin inscriptions, and Greek transcriptions of early Latin in a tendency toward fusion of these two sounds, we may conclude that the tendency existed throughout the history of the Latin language, beginning with Primitive Italic.

116 g. That the quality of e differed according to its quantity is stated by several of the Roman grammarians:

Victorinus 6.33.3 f. K:[14] *O, ut e, geminum vocis sonum pro condicione temporis promit, unde inter nostras vocales η et ω Graecorum ut supervacuae praetermissae sunt.*

Pompeius 5.102.4–13 K:[15] *E aliter longa aliter brevis sonat. ... Ergo quomodo exprimendae sunt istae litterae? Dicit ita Terentianus, "Quotienscumque e longam volumus proferri, vicina sit ad i litteram."[16] Ipse sonus sic debet sonare, quomodo sonat i littera. Quando dicis evitat, vicina debet esse—sic pressa, sic angusta ut vicina sit ad i litteram. Quando vis dicere brevem e, simpliciter sonat.*

Servius, In Donatum 4.421.16–21 K:[17] *Vocales sunt quinque, a e i o u. Ex his duae, e et o, aliter sonant productae, aliter correptae. ... E quando producitur, vicinum est ad sonum i litterae, ut meta; quando autem correptum, vicinum est ad sonum diphthongi [133], ut equus.*

---

[14] 'O, like e, produces two vowel sounds according to the quantity; wherefore η and ω of the Greeks have been omitted from the list of our vowels as superfluous.'

[15] 'Long e has one sound, short e another. ... How then are those letters to be pronounced? Terentianus says: "Whenever we want to produce long e, let it be near to the letter i." The sound itself should sound as the letter i sounds. When you say evitat, it should be near—so compressed, so narrow as to be near the letter i. When you want to pronounce short e, it has an unmixed sound.'

[16] There is no such statement in the extant writings of Terentianus; but the passage just cited from Marius Victorinus, who usually paraphrases Terentianus, is probably based upon the remark that Pompeius quotes.

[17] 'There are five vowels, a e i o u. Two of these, e and o, sound in one way when long, in another when short. ... Similarly when e is long it is near to the sound of the letter i, as meta; but when short it is near to the sound of the diphthong (i.e. ae), as equus.'

These remarks are to some extent a reflection of the fact that Lat. *e* corresponds to Gk. *ε* and *η*, and Lat. *o* to Gk. *o* and *ω*; but they are so definite and so different from any extant passages in Greek that they have some value as evidence. Furthermore one grammarian of the fifth century testifies to the difference between long *i* and short *i*.

Consentius, De Barbarismis et Metaplasmis 16.1–4 Niedermann = 5.394.19–22 K:[18] ⟨*I* littera⟩ medium quiddam inter *e* et *i* habet, ubi in medio sermone est, ut *hominem*. Mihi tamen videtur, quando producta est, vel acutior vel plenior esse, quando brevis est, medium sonum exhibere. ...

The first sentence clearly describes an open *i*, while the second distinguishes long *i* from this.

117 a. There is evidence that short *e* was closer before a vowel than in other positions. Although there are in inscriptions relatively few instances of the letter *i* for *ĕ* final or before a consonant, *i* for *ĕ* in hiatus is not uncommon. Typical instances are listed in Table 5.

TABLE 5

aria, CIL 6.541, etc.	*lentia*, 9.1655
argentiam, 14.35	*liciat*, 9.3437
balnia, 14.914	*nocias*, 10.4053
balinio, 14.2112.2.31	*oliarius*, 9.5307
calciamenta 2.5181.32, 35, 36	*Panthia*, 12.421, etc.
casium, 4.5380.18	*pariat*, 1².582.10
Cerialis, 12.4371	*periat*, 4.1173, etc.
Cliarcus, 14.1880	*piliatum*, 12.4247
commiantium, 5.1863	*Putiolanus*, 4.2152, etc.
iamus, 4.5092, etc.	*Thiagene*, 14.2781
exiat, 10.6707	*Tiodorus*, 5.1683
gallinacio, 12.4377	*Tiodosius*, 10.6936
glaria, 8.2532 B b 9	*Thiodotos*, 2.4970.514
(h)abias, 4.2083, etc.	*Thiophanes*, 14.420
(h)abiat, 4.538	*Thiophiles*, 5.4510
Hordionia, IG 14.1362	*Thrasia*, 10.1786, etc.
horriorum, CIL 6.8680	*baliat*, 4.4874
Labio, 2.4970.257, etc.	*viniarum*, 5.5543[19]

The grammarians censure some of these and several similar forms (Appendix Probi 4.198.2–31 K, Caper 7.106.11 K), and there are

---

[18] '⟨The letter *i*⟩ has a sound intermediate between *e* and *i* when it is in the middle of a word, as *hominem*. To me, nevertheless, it seems to be sharper or (perhaps) fuller when it is long, and when it is short (it seems) to show the intermediate sound.'

[19] Further examples from Pompeii in Väänänen 61–4.

numerous such misspellings in manuscripts.[20] The same tendency appears in Greek transliterations; e.g. ἀρια, CIL 8.12508.15, 39, etc.; Κεριαλις, IG 14.760.5, 1027; λεντιαριοι, 14.2323; Ὀρδιονιον, CIG 3831 a 7; ὀρρια, IG 7.24.11; πειλιον, Ed. Diocl. 8.16; Ποτιολανος, IG 14.1102.8.[21]

117 b. The poets convert ĕ in hiatus, as well as ĭ in hiatus, to [j]. Examples are dissyllabic *eōdem* (Lucilius 3.43 M), *alveō* (Vergil, Aen. 7.33), *aurea* (Ovid, Met. 12.395). Cf. [158].

117 c. In the Romance languages unaccented Lat. ĕ in hiatus develops in the same way as original ĭ in hiatus [118]. One stage of the process must have been consonantal *i* [j], and perhaps that is the way that most of the words in Table 5 should be read. An earlier stage, however, was probably syllabic *i*. Accented Lat. ĕ in hiatus appears as syllabic *i* in a number of Romance words (It. *cria* from *creat*; It. *dio*, Sp. *dios* from *deus*; It. and Sp. *mio* from *meus*).

117 d. With these forms should be compared Ποτιολοι, IG 14.737, 739, 830, 1102.22, 1114; λειων = *leō*, Audollent, Defixionum Tabellae 271.34; *dia* = *dea*, CIL 9.4178; Βοναδιης = *Bonae deae*, IG 14.1449; *mia* CIL 4.3494; *iam* = *eam*, censured by Caper 7.106.11 K; and *fassiolus*, censured in the Appendix Probi 4.198.27 K.[22]

117 e. That the close quality of ĕ in hiatus belonged also to preclassical Latin is made probable by the similar phenomena of Umbrian and Oscan.[23] In the latter language the symbol Ⱶ (transcribed *í*) is regularly employed for inherited ĕ before a vowel as well as for inherited ē and ĭ [116 f].

118. Probably ĭ also was closer when followed by a vowel than when followed by a consonant; for the Romance forms of Latin *diēs* show the normal reflex of Lat. ī rather than of ĭ (It. *di*, OFr *di*, Sp. *dia*, Rum. *zi*). Varro's (RR 1.2.14) citation of a "rustic" form *veham* for *viam* may mean that the urban practice of pronouncing ĭ in hiatus closer than ĭ before a consonant did not hold in the country.

118 a. If ĭ was followed by inherited ī contraction occurred before the time of Plautus, and about the middle of the second century B.C. -ĭī from earlier -*iei* contracted to -ī [121]. Nevertheless the archaic spellings -*iei* and -*ii* were often used for [i·], and so both orthographies,

---

[20] Further examples in Schuchardt 1.424–42.

[21] Similar forms in papyri are listed in Meinersmann 109.

[22] Purely orthographic *dii*, *diis*, *ii*, and *iis* should not be confused with these forms. See Sturtevant, Contraction in the Case Forms of the Latin *io*- and *iā*-stems and of *deus*, *is*, and *īdem*.

[23] See Buck, Gramm. 32.

especially *ii*, came to be used for original long *i*.[24] The common words *ii*, *iis*, *dii*, and *diis* were pronounced [i·, i·s, di·, di·s].

119. Classical Latin had two phonemes written *e*, a short open *e* [ε], more or less like Eng. *e* in *ten* or Fr. *e* in *dette*, and a long close *e* [e·], similar in quality to Fr. *é* in *élevé*, or Germ. *e* in *Beet*, *sehne*. We know of one positional variant of the phoneme *ĕ*, a closer sound appearing before another vowel.

There were also two phonemes written *i*, a short open *i*, possibly somewhat like the *i* of Eng. *pin* (although there is no evidence for the lax articulation characteristic of the latter), and a long close *i*, similar to the *i* of French. There was a positional variant of *ĭ*, which occurred before another vowel; it was closer than ordinary *ĭ*, but in Classical Latin sharply distinguished from *ī* at least in quantity.

EARLY LATIN *ę̄*

120. In the time of Plautus and Terence Latin possessed a fifth front vowel phoneme, namely a long vowel intermediate between *ē* and *i*, which was written sometimes *ei* and sometimes *e*. In our earliest records *ei* represents a diphthong roughly the same as that denoted by early Ionic and Attic ει [21, 23]. In initial syllables this was an inherited *ei* (*deicerent*, CIL 1².581.4), while in medial and final syllables it represented inherited *ei* (*exdeicendum*, *sibei*, 1².581.3 f.), *ai* (*inceideretis*, 1².581.26), or *oi* (*virei* [pl.], 1².581.19).[25] No doubt the change of *ai* and *oi* to *ei* in medial and final syllables was a part of the change of originally unaccented *a* and *o* to *e* in closed syllables.

By the time of Plautus *ei* in all positions had changed to a monophthong which was often written *e* (*devas*, CIL 1².975, *ploirume*, 1².9), although the archaic spelling with *ei* was often employed, as in the forms cited in the last paragraph.[26] About 150 B.C. this monophthong came to be identical with inherited *ī*. Thereafter the three spellings *ei*, *e*, and *i* were employed indiscriminately; but *e*, which was needed for the phonemes *ē* and *ĕ*, presently ceased to be used for earlier *ei* and *ī*.

Since earlier *ei* came to be written *e* before 200 B.C. and then yielded

[24] Sturtevant, Contraction 3–15.

[25] These illustrations are taken from the Senatus Consultum de Bacchanalibus of 186 B.C. At that time *ei* no longer represented a diphthong, but in this document such a spelling is generally good evidence for the former presence of the diphthong.

[26] The evidence for this statement comes from inscriptions. Our manuscripts of Plautus and Terence present the orthography of imperial times [121].

long *i* about 150 B.C., we must conclude that in the meantime the phoneme was a long *e*; but since it was kept quite distinct from original *ē* after 150 B.C., we must suppose that it had a different sound all the time. Since its final result, *ī*, was closer than *ē*, it is a safe inference that it was closer than ordinary *ē* from the time of its development out of the diphthong *ei* until its final amalgamation with *ī*. It is customary nowadays to write this early Latin phoneme *ẹ̄* when any notation is needed. A satisfactory phonetic symbol is [ẹ˙].

121. The texts of Plautus and Terence were extensively modernized by the grammarians and copyists of classical and later times, and in the process the letter *i* was regularly substituted for *ei* and *e* where these represented *ẹ̄*. Nevertheless certain features of early Latin can be understood only by reintroducing that phoneme. The gen. sg. of *fīlius* is regularly *fīlī* in Plautus and Terence, because -*iī* contracted to *ī*, but the nom. pl. was trisyllabic *fīliẹ̄*, since -*iẹ̄* did not contract. About 150 B.C., however, -*iẹ̄* became -*iī*, and this combination promptly contracted; in place of Plautine *grātiẹ̄s* (*gratiis* in our editions), classical Latin has only *grātīs*. On the other hand nom. pl. *deẹ̄* 'gods' contracted to *dẹ̄*, and that is the only form that Plautus and Terence employ. This *dẹ̄*, of course, yielded classical *dī*; but when once *ẹ̄* had become *ī*, the sing. *deus* induced a new pl. *deī* (like *amīcī* beside *amīcus*), and this did not contract.[27]

Varro's (RR 1.2.14) citation of "rustic" *vellam* for *vīllam* indicates that *ẹ̄* maintained itself in some country districts down to the Ciceronian period. Probably it was *ẹ̄* that Cicero heard Cotta pronounce instead of *ī*:

De Orat. 3.12.46:[28] Quare Cotta noster, cuius tu illa lata, Sulpici, non numquam imitaris, ut iota litteram tollas et *e* plenissimum dicas, non mihi oratores antiquos sed messores videtur imitari.

O AND U

122. An almost unanimous tradition assigns to the Latin letters *o* and *u* the value of back vowels, of which *o* represents the more open sound. Loan-words and the remarks of the grammarians cited in [123 g] confirm the conclusion.

[27] Solmsen, IF 4.240–52; Sturtevant, Contraction in the Case Forms of the Latin *io*- and *iā*-stems and of *deus, is,* and *īdem*; Leumann 77 f.

[28] 'Wherefore our friend Cotta (whose broad sounds you sometimes imitate, Sulpicius, so that you remove the letter iota and pronounce a full *e*) seems to me to be imitating, not the early orators, but the reapers.'

123. As there is usually a certain harmony between the front vowels and the back vowels of a language [11], we may expect to find that *ū* and *ō* were respectively closer than the corresponding short vowels, since *ī* and *ē* have been shown to be closer than *ĭ* and *ĕ* respectively [116]. We find, in fact, evidence of the same general character as in the case of the front vowels.

123 a. Table 6 illustrates the development of accented *o* and *u* in the Romance languages. Everywhere, except in Sardinian and Rumanian, *ō* and *ŭ* yielded the same result (the differences observable in French are due to the surrounding sounds). Consequently Vulgar Latin *ō* was a close *o* [o·] and Vulgar Latin *ŭ* was an open *u*, at least in accented syllables. Furthermore *ū*, like *ī*, remains a close sound everywhere, even though in French it has become a front rounded vowel.

TABLE 6

	ŏ	*ō*	*ŭ*		*ū*
Latin	rota	dolorōsus	vōx	gula	nux	mūrus
Italian	ruota	doloroso	voce	gola	noce	muro
French	roue	douloureux	voix	gueule	noix	mur
Spanish	rueda	doloroso	voz	gola		muro
Portuguese	roda	doloroso	voz	gola	noz	muro
Sardinian	roda		boge	bula	nuge	muru
Rumanian	roata		boace	gura	nuc	

123 b. As in the case of the front vowels, the misspellings of inscriptions confirm the evidence of the Romance languages and also justify us in extending our conclusion to the unaccented vowels. Table 7 contains a few typical instances of *o* written for *ŭ*.

TABLE 7

actoarius, CIL 5.1595

Calagorrit(anus), 2.4245

canont, 4.4112

colobar(ia), 2.4592

colomnas, 9.4875

com, 4.3935

comulatis, 10.5349

co(n)iogi, 2.2997; 3.14309

Exoperius, 12.492

Februarius, 12.936

fondabet = fundavit, 12.936

moritor, 3.14190

Patroinus, 9.1278

resorge, 12.2120

ridicola, 4.5360

sob, 12.933

so = sum, 10.2070

trebibos, 9.4204

obique, 4.2288

Verecondus, 8.6070

orna, 12.972

oxor, 3.9585

oxsor, 3.9605[29]

---

[29] Virtually complete epigraphical material in Prinz 15–60, 103–19. This author, however, goes to absurd lengths in an effort to explain away the evidence [123 d].

123 c. The use of *u* for *ō* is most common in Southern Italy and Gaul, where the native languages, Oscan and Gaulish, lacked *ō*. It is nevertheless significant that in both regions Lat. *ō* was confused with *u* rather than with *a*;[30] for if Lat. *ō* had been nearer to Oscan or Gaulish *a* than to *u* (or even as near to it), that fact would have been reflected in these misspellings, unless, to be sure, the fact that both Lat. *ō* and the native *u* involved lip-rounding outweighed other phonetic features. There are besides a few instances of *u* for *ō* from other parts of the Roman world. In Table 8, forms cited from CIL 4, 9, and 10 are likely to reflect Oscan influence, and those from CIL 5 and 12 Gaulish influence.

TABLE 8

cernu CIL 4.6698	*numin[clator]*, 14.4010
Custantina, 9.4660	*Octubris*, 2.2959.13; 3.14893
dolurem, 9.648	*oraturiu*, 14.3898
Flurinus, 12.2086	*Pannunia*, 12.15
flus, 4.5735	*parenturum*, 9.648
lectur, 12.2701	*punere*, 3.9585
maiures, 9.648	*praeturianum*, 12.4355
Mausuleum, 8.9189	*rectur*, 12.338, 1499
mensurum, 9.648	*Victurina*, 9.1373
nepus, 9.648; 10.4523; 12.5336	*uxure*, 5.5416
pronepus, 9.648	

We have besides many ablatives sing. and accusatives pl. of the second declension such as *quartu* and *annus*.[31]

123 d. These orthographic mistakes on inscriptions are significant only because of their uneven distribution; *o* for *ŭ* is by far the most frequent error, next *u* for *ō*, while *o* for *ū* and *u* for *ŏ* are comparatively rare.[32] Prinz undertakes to explain as many as possible of the errors of all four categories as due to Greek, Celtic, or Oscan-Umbrian influence, to analogy, to assimilation to neighboring sounds, etc. He allows himself such latitude in these assumptions that very few examples earlier than the sixth century remain. One may fully agree with his conclusion (p. 73) that Lat. *ō* and *ŭ* were distinct phonemes until the sixth century; but the prevailing direction of the orthographic errors nevertheless indicates a phonetic approach, which led to occasional confusion in various regions and particularly in the speech of certain persons.

123 e. Just as Lat. *ĭ* was represented by Gk. *ε* [116 e], so Lat. *ŭ*

[30] In Gaulish, IE *ō* yielded *ā*.
[31] Virtually complete epigraphical material in Prinz, 60–75, 120–39. Cf. [123 d].
[32] Prinz requires only 24 pages to treat these two groups.

was often represented by Gk. *o* (Μόμμιος, Πόπλιος, Λευκολλος); but since Greek had no short [u], we can infer only that Gk. *o* was more similar than any other Greek short vowel to Lat. *ŭ*.   More significant is the representation of Gk. *o* by Lat. *u* in such words as *ampura*, CIL 4.6710, 6711; *Cleunica*, 2.3451, 3505; *empurium*, 9.10; *Laudice*, 2.147; *Menupilus*, 9.6082.53; *Theudosius*, 9.1365, 1946, 12.5750; *Tiudosio*, 10.6963.[33] Since Gk. *o* was a close *o* [45] and Lat. *ŭ* was an open *u*, they were so similar in quality that confusion between them might be expected.

123 f. Confirmatory evidence is afforded by Umbrian and Oscan. In the Umbrian tablets written in the Latin alphabet,[34] *ŏ* is kept distinct from *u*, while inherited *ō* is written sometimes *o* and sometimes *u*. In Oscan inherited *ŏ* is in general retained, but original *ō* is regularly written *u*.

123 g. The grammarians speak of a difference in quality between *ō* and *ŏ*.   The earliest description is by Terentianus: 6.329.121–34 K.:[35]

> 121 *O* Graiugenum longior altera est figura,
> alter sonus est et nota temporum minori;
> compendi nostri meliora crediderunt,
> vocalibus ut non nisi quinque fungeremur;
> 125 productio longis daret ut tempora bina,
> correptio plus tempore non valeret uno.
> Hinc ῆτα minus scribimus, hinc et ω supremum;
> una quoniam fas habitum est notare forma,
> pro temporibus quae geminum ministret usum.
> 130 Igitur sonitum reddere cum voles minori,
> retrorsus adactam modice teneto linguam,
> rictu neque magno sat erit patere labra.
> At longior alto tragicum sub oris antro
> 134 molita rotundis acuit sonum labellis.[36]

---

[33] Further examples in Schuchardt, 2.92–4.

[34] The Umbrian alphabet has but a single character for *o* and *u*; it was merely a form of the Etruscan alphabet, and the latter language had no use for the letter *o*. On the treatment of inherited *u* and *o* in Oscan-Umbrian, see Buck, Gramm. 36–41.

[35] 'Greek long *o* is one character and there is another sound and letter for the shorter vowel; our fellow-countrymen thought economy better, so that we should employ only five vowels, and length should give long vowels two morae each and shortness should have the value of only one.   Hence we do not write η and ω; for it is considered proper to write with one letter, which shall render double service according to quantity.   Therefore when you want to give sound to short *o*, hold the tongue drawn back moderately, and it will be enough for the lips to be parted a little.   But long *o*, formed in the deep cavern of the mouth, sharpens its tragic sound with rounded lips.'

[36] In the first edition of this book I cited lines 142–5 as Terentianus' description of the vowel *u*, but I am now inclined to think that they refer merely to *u* as the

Victorinus describes the two back vowels as follows:

6.33.3–9 K:[37] *O*, ut *e*, geminum vocis sonum pro condicione temporis promit. ... Igitur qui correptum enuntiat, nec magno hiatu labra reserabit et retrorsum actam linguam tenebit. Longum autem productis labris, rictu tereti, lingua antro oris pendula, sonum tragicum dabit, ... *U* litteram quotiens enuntiamus, productis et coeuntibus labris efferemus.

We are clearly informed that *ō* was pronounced with the lips rounded, and the implication is that there was distinctly less rounding for *ŏ*. *U* was similar to *ō* in the protrusion of the lips; Lat. *u* must have been similar to German and Italian *u* rather than to English *u* as in *full*.

124. At some time before Plautus, inherited *ŏ* became *u* before velar *n* [ŋ], before velar *l* [167], and in final syllables. But if *ŏ* in these positions was preceded by *u*, *v*, or *qu* it survived for a time, probably until after Terence. Not later than 152 B.C. the conjunction *quom* became *cum*; otherwise one cannot understand the spelling *quom* for the preposition *cum* in CIL 1².611 and a number of other republican inscriptions.[38] The earliest epigraphic instance of *u* in an unaccented syllable after *u* or *v* is *suum* (CIL 1².593.32) of 45 B.C.[39] It is probable that this had long been the usual pronunciation; but the archaic spellings -*uo*-, etc. persisted to the end of the republic. In such words as *voltis*, *suom*, *equom*, *quom o* was read as [u] from about 150 B.C. until the spellings *vultis*, *suum*, *ecum*, *cum*, etc. became current.[40]

125. Classical Latin had two phonemes normally written *o*, a short open *o* [ɔ], resembling Germ. *o* in *voll*, and a long close *o* [o·], similar to the vowel of Fr. *peau* or Germ. *Sohn*. There were also two phonemes normally written *u*, a short open *u*, more or less like the vowel of Germ. *dumm*, and a long close *u*, similar to Germ. *u* in *gut*.

THE ALLEGED "INTERMEDIATE" VOWEL

126. The Roman grammarians have a good deal to say about a vowel intermediate between *i* and *u*. This is first mentioned by Quintilian 1.4.8:[41]

---

second member of a diphthong. Apparently his description of the vowel *u* has been lost.

[37] '*O*, like *e*, produces two vowel sounds according to the quantity. ... Therefore one who pronounces short *o* will open the lips slightly and keep the tongue drawn back. But long *o*, with lips protruding and rounded, the tongue low in the mouth, will give a tragic sound. ... When we pronounce *u*, we shall produce it with the lips protruding and coming together.'

[38] Cited by Prinz 45.

[39] Other instances are cited by Prinz 44.

[40] Sturtevant, CP 11.202–7 and references; cf. Prinz 42–50.

[41] 'There is a certain sound intermediate between *u* and *i*; for we do not say *optimum* in the same way as *opimum*.'

Medius est quidam *u* et *i* litterae sonus; non enim sic *optimum* dicimus ut *opimum*.

Elsewhere Quintilian shows that, in spite of the phonetic implications of the passage just quoted, he is really interested in a question of orthography.

1.7.21:[42] Etiam *optimus, maximus* ut mediam *i* litteram, quae veteribus *u* fuerat, acciperent, Gai primum Caesaris inscriptione traditum factum.

126 a. The later passages also that deal with this topic[43] contain a certain amount of phonetic terminology (e.g. *exilis, pinguis, plenus*), but are largely occupied with the variation in spelling in such words as *optimus, maximus, manubiae, libīdō, mancipium, aucupium, alimentum, carnifex.* All the examples they cite and all the others that can be supplied from documentary sources concern a variation between short *u* and short *i*. The former letter is generally preferred in early Latin and *i* tends to supplant it later. Nevertheless *i* is in use in some words from the earliest times, particularly in the neighborhood of front vowels *(ferimus)*, while in others, particularly in the neighborhood of back vowels *(volumus)*, *u* is never displaced.[44]

It is not easy to reconcile the historical facts with the theory, accepted with some hesitation in the first edition of this book, that in the words under discussion there was actually a short front rounded vowel. We have just seen that the orthographical evidence adduced begins as early as Plautus, and so, if we are to regard Quintilian as a reliable witness, we must suppose that an unstable phoneme, short in quantity and confined to unaccented syllables, alternating both with *ŭ* and with *ĭ*, preserved its identity for more than two centuries.

The evidence suggests rather a variation between two distinct phonemes, as in Eng. *roof, room*, etc., pronounced either [ruf, rum] or [rʊf, rʊm].

126 b. Bücheler[45] long ago argued on the basis of a hopelessly corrupt passage in Velius Longus[46] that one of the new letters introduced by the Emperor Claudius, namely Ⱶ, was intended to denote the "inter-

---

[42] 'That *optimus* and *maximus* should take *i* as their middle letter, which for the ancients had been *u*, is said to have been brought about first in the writing of Gaius Caesar.'

[43] Cited by Seelmann 203–5.

[44] For details see the historical grammars or Niedermann, Précis de phonétique historique du latin (1931) 28–37.

[45] De Ti. Claudio Caesare Grammatico (1856) 13–20.

[46] 7.75.12–76.3 K.

mediate" sound.   Bücheler thought that it was the same sound as that
denoted by *y* in words borrowed from the Greek, and that the pedantic
reformer wanted to imitate Greek exactness without introducing a
Greek letter into Latin words.   Bücheler should have seen how un-
favorable to his theory the epigraphical instances of Claudius' letter ⊦
really are; the character occurs only in Greek loan-words, such as
Aeg⊦pti and *N⊦mphius*.   We must suppose that the letter ⊦ was
intended as a substitute for the Greek letter *y* precisely in Greek words;
Claudius cannot be cited as a witness for the "intermediate" sound in
Latin words.[47]

126 c. We may be quite certain, at any rate, that such words as
optimus, *libet*, and *mancipium* did not contain the sound written *y* in
Greek loan-words.   The Romans who introduced Greek aspirates into
Latin words like *pulcher* and *chommodus* [183] would not have missed
such an opportunity to display their learning by writing *optymus*,
lybet, *mancypium*, etc.   Or, if we assume that pedants would always
realize that these words were Latin and should not be written with a
Greek letter, surely honest ignorance would sometimes have introduced
such spellings.   As a matter of fact the few citable forms like *unibyriae*
(CIL 14.418) and *Byrgenio* (14.1064) are late enough so that we may
regard *y* as a graphic variant for *i* [36].

126 d. Furthermore we have excellent testimony that the sound
denoted by *y* was unknown in Latin words.

Quintilian 12.10.27 f.:[48] Latina mihi facundia, ut inventione, dispositione,
consilio, ceteris huius generis artibus similis Graecae ac prorsus discipula eius
videtur, ita circa rationem eloquendi vix habere imitationis locum.   Namque
est ipsis statim sonis durior, quando et iucundissimas ex Graecis litteras[49] non

---

[47] I cannot suggest a plausible emendation of Velius Longus to accord with this
conclusion; but that fact does not make the passage valid evidence.

[48] 'Although Latin eloquence appears to me on a level with the Greek in invention, arrangement, judgment, and the other qualities of that kind, and to be
indeed in all respects its pupil, yet it seems scarcely to have the power of imitation
in the matter of phonetics.   For, first of all, it is harsher in the sounds themselves;
for we do not possess the most euphonious letters of the Greeks, one a consonant
and the other a vowel, than which none of theirs sound more sweetly, and which
we usually borrow, whenever we adopt any of their words.   When this occurs,
our language somehow immediately assumes a more pleasing tone, as for example
in the words *Zephyri* and *zopyra*; for if these words are written in our letters,
they will give something of a dull and barbarous sound.'

[49] The *iucundissimae litterae* which Latin does not possess are *v* and *ς*, which
were added at the end of the Latin alphabet but were never regarded as properly
Latin letters.   On the punctuation at the end of the passage, see Addenda.

habemus, vocalem alteram, alteram consonantem, quibus nullae apud eos dulcius spirant; quas mutuari solemus, quotiens illorum nominibus utimur.   Quod cum contingit, nescio quo modo hilarior protinus renidet oratio, ut in *Zephyris* et *zopyris*.   Quae si nostris litteris scribantur, surdum quiddam et barbarum efficient.

Compare the passages quoted in [127].

It is at any rate perfectly clear that if there was a Latin sound intermediate between ŭ and ĭ, it differed from the sound of Classical Latin *y*. It is furthermore clear that such a sound, if it existed, originated before Plautus.

Y

127. The Latin alphabet originally did not contain the letter *y*. Early loan words from the Greek represented Gk. *v* by Lat. *u*, as is shown by many epigraphical instances, e.g. *Amucos*, (CIL $1^2.548$), *mustae* ($1^2.665$), *Erucinai* ($1^2.2222$).   Some of these words were probably taken from Greek dialects which had normal *u* [u] in place of Attic-Ionic [y], but many of them doubtless came from the Hellenistic dialect, which had [y], although other transcriptions were sometimes used [35 c].

Educated Romans of the late Republic and the early Empire, however, pronounced Greek words in Latin as they did when speaking Greek, and to represent the sound of Hellenistic *v* they borrowed the Greek letter in the form that was current among the cosmopolitan Greeks of that time, i.e. Υ.   They were thoroughly aware that they were using both a Greek sound and a Greek letter, as we learn from frequent references to the matter in the literature.   In addition to the passages quoted below, see the one in [126 d].

Cicero, Or. 160:[50] *Burrum* semper Ennius, numquam *Pyrrhum*; "Vi patefecerunt *Bruges*," non *Phryges*, ipsius antiqui declarant libri.   Non enim Graecam litteram adhibebant, nunc autem etiam duas.   Et cum *Phrygum* et *Phrygibus* dicendum esset, absurdum erat aut etiam in barbaris casibus Graecam litteram adhibere aut recto casu solum Graece loqui; tamen et *Phryges* et *Pyrrhum*[51] aurium causa dicimus.

---

[50] 'Ennius wrote *Burrus*, never *Pyrrhus*; "By force the *Bruges* gained passage," not *Phryges*, declare ancient copies of the poet.   For they did not use the Greek letter, but now we even use two of them.   And when one had to say *Phrygum* and *Phrygibus*, it was absurd either to use a Greek letter even in non-Greek cases (i.e. along with Latin case-endings) or to speak Greek in the nominative case only; still we say *Phryges* and *Pyrrhus* for our ears' sake.'

[51] Or rather *Pyrrhus*; *Phryges* doubtless has short *e*.

Terentius Scaurus 7.25.13–16 K:[52] *Y* litteram supervacuam Latino sermoni putaverunt, quoniam pro illa *u* cederet. Sed cum quaedam in nostrum sermonem Graeca nomina admissa sint, in quibus evidenter sonus huius litterae exprimitur, ut *hyperbaton*, et *hymnus*, et *hyacinthus*, et similia, in eisdem hac littera necessario utimur.

Caper 7.105.17 f. K:[53] *Y* litteram nulla vox nostra adsciscit. Ideo insultabis *gylam* dicentibus.

128. The Romance languages do not present any separate phoneme resulting from Lat. *y*. Perhaps it is most frequently treated in the same way as inherited *u*; *tumba* (Gk. τύμβος) becomes It., Sp., Port. *tomba*, Log. *tumba*, Fr. *tombe*; *lynx* It. *lonze*, and *crypta* It. *grotta*. We may be sure that popular speech always substituted a normal Latin phoneme for the foreign sound. Some late loans in Romance may have taken over Greek *v* in its modern value [i].

129. The history of the letter is understandable only on the assumption that in standard Latin of classical times it indicated the pronunciation of *v* in standard Greek of the same date, namely a sound similar to Fr. *u* or Germ. *ü*, [y]; see [37].

AE[54]

130. Lat. *ae* is traditionally confused with *ĕ* in the pronunciation of modern scholars and the two sounds develop alike in the Romance languages; but the consistent distinction in early and carefully written later inscriptions shows that we have to do with different phonemes. In many words *ae* clearly comes from an Indo-European diphthong (*aedēs* : Gk. αἴθω). Cf. [47, 48].

Our earliest Latin documents show *ai* where classical Latin has *ae*, as in *aide* = *aedem* (CIL 1².9). No doubt the diphthong had at first about the same sound as αι in Greek [47, 48]. The spelling *ae* began to appear about 200 B.C. (*Aetolia*, CIL 1².616—189 B.C.; *aedem*, 581.1—186 B.C.) and became usual before 100 B.C. The change in spelling must have represented a change in pronunciation, but the change cannot have been to *ē* [e·] or [ε·]; the new spelling would have been *e*, since

---

[52] 'They considered *y* superfluous for the Latin language, because *u* was employed for it. But since certain Greek words, in which the sound of this letter is spoken, have been admitted to our speech (as *hyperbaton*, *hymnus*, *hyacinthus*, and the like) we necessarily employ this letter in them.'

[53] 'No Latin word admits the letter *y*. Therefore you will scoff at those who say *gyla*.'

[54] Sturtevant, TAPA 47.107–16. Otherwise Sihler, PAPA 29. xl–xliv.

that letter represented both [e·] and [ɛ], see [119]. The orthography *ae* must reflect merely a more open pronunciation of the second member of the diphthong; the earlier *ai* stood for a diphthong ending in a close *i*, as in It. *mai*, while the later *ae* denoted a diphthong ending in a more open sound approaching a close *e*, somewhat as in Eng. *my* or Germ. *mein*.

That this was actually the pronunciation even at a much later date appears from a passage in Terentius Scaurus.

> 7.16.6–10 K:[55] *A* igitur littera praeposita est *u* et *e* litteris. . . . Et apud antiquos *i* littera pro ea (i.e. *e* littera) scribebatur, ut testantur μεταπλασμοί, in quibus eius syllabarum diductio, ut *pictai vestis* et *aulai medio* pro *pictae* et *aulae*. Sed magis in illis *e* novissima sonat.

130 a. The diphthong *ai* had a similar but quite independent history in Oscan. The character ⊣ (transcribed *í*), which represented the open *i* from inherited *ē* or *ĭ* and also from *ĕ* before another vowel [116 f, 117], was used for the second member of the inherited diphthong *ai*, as in *víaí*, *svaí*. Osc. *aí* must have been similar to Lat. *ae*.

All this is significant for our purposes because of the representation of the Oscan diphthong *aí* by *ae* in the document written in the Latin alphabet (*suae*, *aeteis*, *Bansae*). When the Oscans took over *ae* in this value it must certainly have represented a true diphthong in Latin; for if it had stood for a monophthong or a diphthong scarcely distinguishable from a monophthong,[56] the Oscans would have transcribed their diphthong *aí* by *ai*, as they actually transcribed *úí* by *oi* (*feíhúís* 'muris' : *eizois* 'eis'), although the digraph *oi* was foreign to Latin orthography.

130 b. In the second half of the second century B.C., when *ei* was a common orthographical variant for *ī*, we find such forms as *Caeici* (CIL 1².2270), *Caeician(us)* (1² Nummus 231), *Caeicilius* (1².633), *conquaeisivi* (1².638.11). Surely *aei* must represent a diphthong.

130c. To the same period belongs Lucilius' jest, 1130 M:

> Cecilius ⟨pretor⟩ ne rusticus fiat.

The jest itself proves merely a difference between the rustic and urban pronunciation of the inherited diphthong, but the fact that it could be

---

[55] 'Well then, the letter *a* is prefixed to *u* and *e*. . . . And among the ancients *i* was written for *e*, as is shown by alterations of sound, among them the separation of syllables as *pictaï vestis* and *aulaï medio* for *pictae* and *aulae*. But in those words the final sound is more nearly that of *e*.'

[56] So Lindsay, Short Historical Latin Grammar 13 f., supposes it was pronounced in the age of Cicero.

put over by this difference in spelling indicates that *ae* was not a mere digraph for open *ē*.

130 d. Our knowledge of this rustic *e* is derived largely from the passage in Varro, in which the Lucilian fragment just quoted is preserved.

Varro, LL 7.96:[57] Apud Matium:

Obscaeni interpres funestique om⟨i⟩nis auctor.

Obscaenum dictum ab *scaena*; eam, ut Graeci, et Accius scribit *scena*⟨m⟩. In pluribus verbis *a* ante *e* alii ponunt, alii non; ut quod partim dicunt ⟨*scaeptrum*, partim⟩ *sceptrum*, alii Plauti *Faeneratricem*, alii *Feneratricem*; sic *faenisicia* ac *fenisicia*, ac rustici pappum *Mesium*, non *Maesium*. A quo Lucilius scribit:

Cecilius ⟨*pretor*⟩ ne rusticus fiat.

Quare turpe ideo *obscaenum*, quod nisi in *scaena* palam dici non debet.

In 5.97 of the same treatise Varro refers briefly to the rustic monophthong in place of the diphthong *ae*:[58]

Hircus, quod Sabini *fircus*; quod illic *fedus*, in Latio rure *hedus*, qui in urbe ut in multis *a* addito *haedus*.

In the time of Varro, then, as well as in the time of Lucilius, *e* was a familiar rustic variant for urban *ae*; the two cannot have been pronounced alike.

130 e. Evidence for the diphthongal pronunciation at a slightly later date is provided by Germ. *Kaiser* from OHG *keisar*. Goth. *kaisar* is sometimes cited in this connection, but Goth. *ai* is ambiguous [49].

131. We must now consider more carefully the early dialectic *ē* for urban *ae*, for which we have found some evidence [130 c]. This *ē* was evidently a feature of Sabine as well as of rustic Latin. Epigraphic evidence shows that Faliscan, Volscian, and Umbrian had also simplified inherited *ai* to *ē*, and the same dialects seem, as far as we can judge from the scanty evidence, to have simplified *au* and *ou* to *ō*. Apparently this type of monophthongization spread at an early date

[57] 'In Matius ⟨we read⟩: "Interpreter and sponsor of foul and funereal omen." *Obscaenum* is from *scaena*; this word Accius writes *scena*, as the Greeks do. In a number of words some set *a* before *e*, others do not; for instance, what some pronounce *scaeptrum* and others pronounce *sceptrum*, some the *Faeneratrix* of Plautus and others the *Feneratrix*; just so they say *faenisicia* and *fenisicia*, and the rustics call the (stage) granddaddy *Mesius*, not *Maesius*. From which pronunciation Lucilius writes: "Let's not make *Cecilius* a rustic *pretor*." Wherefore anything foul is *obscaenus* because it should not be mentioned in public except on the *scaena*.'

[58] '*Hircus*, which the Sabines call *fircus*; and what there is *fedus*, in rural Latium is *hedus*, and in the city it is *haedus*, with an added *a* as in many words.'

over nearly all Central Italy west of the Appennines, except for the region of the lower Tiber. This generalization is important for us since it gives us some ground for assuming identical character of the resultant $\bar{e}$ and $\bar{o}$ in the entire area.

The passages quoted from Varro prove that even after Roman Latin had become the norm, country people continued their use of $\bar{e}$ instead of ae. Their usage, supported by that of the districts where Latin supplanted Volscian, Umbrian, Sabine, or Faliscan, introduced a number of words with $\bar{e}$ for ae into the standard Latin of the city of Rome. A clear case is $l\bar{e}vir$ = Skt. $dev\bar{a}$, Gk. δάήρ (IE $daiv\bar{e}r$), whose second vowel is due to the analogical influence of vir 'husband', and whose initial l for d has been thought to indicate Sabine origin. The tradition in favor of $\bar{e}$ is not quite so clear in $s\bar{e}pes$, $praes\bar{e}pes$, $praes\bar{e}pia$, but the monophthong is supported by the Romance languages. Walde, s.v., thinks that $f\bar{e}num$ contains an original monophthong, but Varro's evidence for $faenisicia$ is supported by It. $fieno$, whose vowel would require Lat. ae or $\breve{e}$.[59]

131 a. The rustic $\bar{e}$ from ai was probably an open e [ε·] rather than the equivalent of inherited $\bar{e}$ [e·]. That this was the resultant of inherited ai in Umbrian is certain,[60] and we have found reason [131] to think the change uniform throughout the area affected. The few rustic words with $\bar{e}$ for ae that got into standard Latin were promptly assimilated to the phonemic system of that dialect; they show the same result as inherited $\bar{e}$ in most of the Romance languages. Only in Italian, where the rustic dialects may be expected to exert some influence, and in Rumanian, the language of the latest region to be Romanized, do any of these words show forms that indicate Latin open e. Table 9 contrasts the normal development of $\breve{e}$ and of $\bar{e}$ with that of rustic $\bar{e}$ for ae.

TABLE 9

	Open e	Rustic $\bar{e}$ for ae		Close $\bar{e}$
Latin	$m\breve{e}l$	$s\bar{e}pes$	$f\bar{e}num$	$v\bar{e}rum$
Italian	$miele$	$siepe$	$fieno$	$vero$
French	$miel$	$soif$	$foin$	$voire$ ($<v\bar{e}r\bar{e}$)
Spanish	$miel$		$heno$	$vero$

A similarly inconsistent development has been observed in three or four other words; we must assume that they too spread over the Roman

---

[59] Other examples in Meyer-Lübke, Grammaire des langues romaines 1.255.
[60] Buck, Gramm. 44.

world in a form that urban Latin had adopted from rural speech but had assimilated to its own speech material. The peculiar Italian development indicates that *ē* from *ae* remained [ɛ] in the rural districts where it originated until it was amalgamated with general Vulgar Latin [ɛ] from *e* and *ae*.

131 b. The conflict between rustic *ē* and urban *ae* led to overcorrection[61] in some words, notably *scaena* for *scēna* from Gk. σκηνή. We have seen [130 d] that Varro preferred the pronunciation with the diphthong, and we find *scaena* in a number of inscriptions (CIL 1².593.77, 1214.13) and also *scaenarium* (11.3583), *scaenicis* (2.1663), and *proscaenium* (2.183). The spelling with *ae* is supported also by excellent manuscript authority.[62] No doubt persons who took pains to say *praetor* instead of *prētor* overcorrected *scēna* to *scaena*. In the same way *scēptrum* from Gk. σκῆπτρον was overcorrected to *scaeptrum*.[63] An additional reason for explaining *scaena*, etc., in this way is the similar overcorrection of original *ō* to *au* [136 b].

132. When *ae* became a monophthong elsewhere than in the old Praenestine-Sabine-Umbrian district, it showed affinities with open *ĕ* rather than with close *ē*. Pompeian graffiti of the first century A.D. indicate an extensive confusion of *ĕ* and *ae* (*etati, maeae, haberae*, CIL 4.1684).[64] A few plebeian inscriptions of the city of Rome show that a similar confusion was beginning there also in the first century A.D., e.g. *Clarie* (dat.), CIL 6.5180; *saenatus*, 6.2066. In the second century the confusion became much more extensive in Rome and appeared also in the provinces.[65]

132 a. The Romance languages reflect Lat. *ae* in the same way as

[61] This is a familiar linguistic process whenever one dialect comes to be preferred to another. Rural Americans who are learning to say *writing* in place of their native *writin* are likely to say also *kitching*. Cf. [182].

[62] Sommer 72 and references.

[63] Walde, IF 30.139 fn. 1; Sommer 72. It is impossible to suppose (with Lindsay 42; Claussen, Rom. Forsch. 15.854; Carnoy, Latin d'Espagne 79, and others) that the *ae* of *scaena* and *scaeptrum* was a peculiarly exact way of transcribing Gk. η. Gk. η was no longer an open *e* [30]; and besides we have shown [130] that Lat. *ae* was a diphthong. Peculiarly significant is Varro's remark, quoted in [130 d], that Accius' spelling *scena* is the same as that of the Greeks. If further proof is wanted that *scaena* contains a real diphthong, it is furnished by the form *scaina* (CIL 1².1794).

[64] Other examples in Hammer, Roman. Lautwandlungen 11 ff.

[65] The occasional confusion between *ē* and *ae* was merely graphic; since *ĕ* and *ē* were traditionally written by the same letter, the new writing of *ĕ* was sometimes extended to *ē*.

Lat. *ě*, while Lat. *ē* is kept distinct from both. Typical examples are presented in Table 10.

TABLE 10

	Open *e*	*ae*	Close *ē*
Latin	*měl*	*caelum*	*vērum*
Italian	*miele*	*cielo*	*vero*
French	*miel*	*ciel*	*voire* (< *vērē*)
Spanish	*miel*	*cielo*	*vero*

The confusion of *ae* with *ě* first appears in Rome and in Pompeii (whose pre-Latin speech was Oscan); in neither region was the prehistoric monophthongization of *ai* at home. It now appears that while the earlier monophthongization led to confusion of *ae* and close *ē*, except in a few Italian words, [131 a], the later monophthongization led to confusion of *ae* and open *ě*. It is therefore unlikely that the two processes had any connection.

133. It remains to fix the date when the monophthongization of *ae* made its way into standard Latin. Terentius Scaurus, a contemporary of Hadrian, is unusually explicit in his remarks on *ae*. He says, 7.16.6–10 K (quoted in [130]), that in his day the second member of the diphthong sounded more like *e* than *i*.

The frequency of the confusion between *ae* and *ě* in inscriptions of the second century inclines one to suppose that the newer pronunciation won general approval shortly after the time of Terentius Scaurus, perhaps toward the end of the century.

Various passages in grammarians of the fourth century show clearly that *ae* had become a monophthong in standard Latin of that time. One quotation will be enough.

Marius Victorinus 6.66.28–67.4:[66] Consimili ratione quaeritur *Orpheus* in metro, ut:
Non me carminibus vincat nec Thracius Orpheus,
utrum trisyllabum an disyllabum sit, an idem nomen duplici enuntiatione promatur, aut sine *a* littera, ut *Peleus, Pentheus*, aut cum *a*, ut ita declinetur *Orphaeus* ut *Aristaeus*. Visum est tamen hoc posse discerni, ut illa sine *a* littera Graeca sit enuntiatio, haec Latina quae per diphthongon effertur.

---

[66] 'There is a similar question about *Orpheus* in such a line as:
Non me carminibus vincat nec Thracius Orpheus;
is it a trisyllable or a dissyllable, or is the same noun pronounced in two ways, either without *a*, as *Peleus, Pentheus*, or with *a* so that *Orphaeus* is declined like *Aristaeus*? It has seemed nevertheless that this distinction can be made, so that the pronunciation without *a* shall be Greek, and the one that is expressed by the diphthong shall be Latin.'

Compare with this Servius, In Donatum 4.421.20 f. K (quoted in [116 g]).

134. The change from *ai* to *ae* during the first half of the second century B.C. reflected a change that had taken place in the second member of the diphthong from a close *i* (as in It. *mai*) to a more open sound approaching an *e* (as in Eng. *aisle*). In several dialects of Central Italy *ai* became *ē* in prehistoric times, and this rustic *ē* made its way into urban Latin in a few country words, such as *sēpes* and *fēnum*, and there it became close *ē* like inherited *ē*. The monophthongization of genuine Latin *ae*, on the other hand, led to confusion between *ae* and open *ĕ*. It began in the popular speech of Southern Italy and of the city of Rome during the first century A.D., and made its way into standard Latin probably in the latter part of the second century A.D., certainly by the fourth century.

AU

135. There can be no doubt that Lat. *au*, like Gk. αυ, originally represented a diphthong consisting of an *a*-sound plus an *u*-sound. The correspondence of the two in inherited words [54] harmonizes with this conclusion. That the Greek and Latin diphthongs were similar in historic times is shown by their constant use to represent each other (*Augias, glaucus,* Παυλλος, Κλανδιος). That is still the nature of the diphthong in some of the Romance languages, and various lines of evidence show that the diphthongal pronunciation must have been retained well into the separate history of certain others. Typical instances are presented in Table 11.

TABLE 11

Latin	aurum	nausea	causa	gaudēre	laurus	pausāre
Rumanian	aur				laur	
Veglian	yaur		kausa	gaudar		
West Rhetic		nauscha				
Provençal	aur	nausa	kauza	gauzir	laur	pauzar
Portuguese	ouro		cousa	gouvir	louro	pousar
French	or	noise	chose	jouir		poser
Spanish	oro		cosa	godere		posare
Italian	oro		cosa		loro	posar

The *au* of Rumanian, West Rhetic, and Provençal requires no comment; the Veglian evidence has no significance since here Lat. *ō* has become *au*. Portuguese still shows a diphthong, but has changed its character.

The French change of *au* to *o* must be later than the change of inherited *c* and *g* to *ch* and *j* respectively before *a*; compare *chose* and *jouir* with *charbon* from *carbo* and *jardin* from Germanic *gard-*, as against *côte* from *costa* and *gomme* from *gumma*. The change of *au* to *o* in Italian and Spanish therefore occurred independently after the separation of the various Romance languages from one another.

136. The change of *au* to *ō*, like the change of *ai* to *ē* [131], was characteristic of Umbrian, Volscian, and Faliscan. Since the native Umbrian alphabet had no separate letter for *o*, it is only Umbrian written in the Latin alphabet that can give evidence on the character of this *o*. Whereas inherited *ō* is written sometimes by the Latin letter *o* and sometimes by the Latin letter *u*, *ō* from *au* is written only by the Latin letter *o*. The examples, however, are few, and Buck[67] refrains from drawing the obvious conclusion. In view of the change of *ai* to [ɛ·], it seems extremely probable that *au* became [ɔ·], not only in Umbrian but throughout the area that simplified the diphthongs in this way [131], including parts of rural Latium [11]. As a matter of fact at least one of the Romans ascribed the use of *o* for urban *au* to the *rustici*.

Festus 196.26–31 Lindsay:[68] *Orata*, genus piscis, appellatur a colore auri, quod rustici *orum* dicebant, ut *auriculas oriculas*. Itaque Sergium quoque praedivitem, quod et duobus anulis *aureis* et grandibus uteretur, *Oratam* dicunt esse appellatum.

It seems best to interpret the word *rustici* here as we are compelled to do in Varro LL 7.96 on account of the parallel phrase, *in Latio rure*, in 5.97 (both passages quoted in [130 d]). Brüch,[69] however, makes the word in the Festus passage refer to the Umbrians, Volscians, and Faliscans. He follows von Planta,[70] but with more confidence than his authority, in denying the change of *au* to *o* to the Sabines, on account of two glosses.

136 a. For Praeneste we have from the earliest times on spellings with *o* and with *au* (*Polia*, CIL 1².83—perhaps as early as the seventh century B.C.; *Plotina*, 14.3369; *Plautio*, 1².242—from the same site as

---

[67] Gramm. 46. Brüch, Glotta 26.145, argues from the spelling with *u* in the Umbrian alphabet that it was a close *ō*; but that, of course, was the only possible spelling!

[68] '*Orata*, a kind of fish, is named from its color of gold (*aurum*), which the rustics used to call *orum*, just as they said *oriculae* for *auriculae*. And people say that a certain millionaire Sergius was called *Orata* because he wore two large gold rings.'

[69] Glotta 26.145.

[70] Grammatik der oskisch-umbrischen Dialekte 1.156.

Polia; *alaucus*, 14.3369).[71] Apparently the pronunciation with *ō* instead of *au* was just getting established at Praeneste at the time when writing was introduced, and both spellings were traditionally preserved. Perhaps both pronunciations were to be heard side by side.[72]

136 b. At any rate rustic *ō* for *au* got into urban Latin in a considerable number of words not later than the early part of the first century B.C. Among the best authenticated forms are *ōlla*, *cōda*, *cōdex*, *cōlis*, *cōpō*, *lōtus*, *plōdere*, *plōstrum*.[73] When these words are preserved in Romance their *ō* gives the same result as inherited *ō*. Illustrations are given in Table 12.

TABLE 12

	au	*ō* from *au*		Inherited *ō*
Latin	*aurum*	*cōda*	*dolorōsus*	*vōx*
Rumanian	*aur*	*coadă*		*boace*
Provençal	*aur*	*coza*		*voz*
French	*or*	*queue*	*douloureux*	*voix*
Italian	*oro*	*coda*	*doloroso*	*voce*

It is clear, then, that, just as rustic *ē* for *ae* was assimilated to close *ē* when it was brought to town [131 a], so rustic *ō* for *au* became identical with inherited *ō* in the country words that urban Latin adopted.

136 c. In spite of this naturalization in Rome of a number of rustic words with *ō* for *au*, the substitution of *ō* for *au* certainly had a substandard flavor for some time. Cicero remarks in a letter to Paetus:

Ad Fam. 9.21.1:[74] Verum tamen quid tibi videor in epistulis? nonne plebeio sermone agere tecum?

No doubt he refers in part to such words as *ōlla*, *lōreola*, and *pōllulus*, as Brüch[75] has suggested. There is no reason to doubt the correctness of Lindsay's (41) suggestion that Cicero's enemy changed his name from *Claudius* to *Clōdius* for political reasons; if other members of the gens, both before and after this time, were sometimes called *Clōdius* or *Clōdia*, that does not alter the fact that *Clōdius* was the popular Latin form of *Claudius*.

[71] Other examples in Brüch, Glotta 26.145. Brüch arbitrarily explains the spellings with *o* as due to Volscian influence.

[72] So, apparently, Ernout, Les éléments dialectaux du vocabulaire latin 53.

[73] The evidence has been collected by Brüch, Glotta 26.146–68.

[74] 'But how do I appear in my letters? Don't you think I'm talking to you in the language of the people?'

[75] Glotta 26.159.

Hence the way was clear for overcorrection of inherited $\bar{o}$ to *au*; cf. [131 b] and fn. 61.

Suetonius, Vespasian 22:[76] Et tamen nonnulla eius facetissima extant, in quibus et haec. Mestrium Florum consularem, admonitus ab eo *plaustra* potius quam *plostra* dicenda, postero die *Flaurum* salutavit.

Several scholars have gone to absurd lengths in the search for *au* due to this sort of hyperurbanism, but there are several perfectly clear cases, notably *austium* for *ōstium*, *ausculārī* for *ōsculārī*, *cautēs* for *cōtēs*, *raudus* for *rōdus*, *saurex* for *sōrex*, and *scauria* for σκώρια.[77]

137. The diphthong *au* always remained unchanged in standard Latin; but from prehistoric times central Italy possessed $\bar{o}$, probably [ɔ·], for inherited *au*. Although a few country words with this pronunciation got into the standard language and then changed [ɔ·] to [o·], the use of $\bar{o}$ for *au* was always sub-standard in Latin, and, with the few exceptions already alluded to, it had no effect upon the Romance languages.

OE

138. The diphthong *oe* is usually the representative of Gk. οι (*Oedipus*, *poena*) or of Gk. ῳ (*tragoedus*).   In a few Latin words it results from the contraction of *o* with *e* or *i*, as in *coetus* from **co-itus*, *coepere* from **co-ipere*, and *coepī* from *co-ēpī*. Inherited *oi* if unaccented became $\bar{e}$ and then $\bar{\imath}$ [120, 121], and if accented it became first *oe* and then $\bar{u}$;[78] but in a few words the stage *oe* persisted either on account of phonetic surroundings or as a conservative spelling which afterwards affected the pronunciation (*foedus* 'treaty', *foedus* 'ugly', *foetor*, *moenia*, *amoenus*).

138 a. Our earliest documents show *oi* (*Oinomavus*, CIL 1^2.554; *foideratei*, 581.2), and the change doubtless indicates a more open pronunciation of the final member of the diphthong, as in the case of the change of *ai* to *ae* [130].

138 b. Lat. *oe* yields the same result as $\bar{e}$ in the Romance languages, thus contrasting with *ae*, which coalesces with $\breve{e}$.   Table 14 gives typical examples.

[76] 'And yet some excellent jests of his are still told, among them these. When he had been admonished by the consular Mestrius Florus that he should say *plaustra* rather than *plostra*, the next day he greeted *Florus* as *Flaurus*.'
[77] The matter is treated sanely and exhaustively by Brüch, Glotta 26.145–74.
[78] Sommer 74–8. On inherited initial *woi-*, see Sturtevant, Lang. 10.6–16

TABLE 13

Latin	*mĕl*	*caelum*	*poena*	*vĕrus*	*plēna*
Italian	*miele*	*cielo*	*pena*	*vero*	
French	*miel*	*ciel*	*peine*		*pleine*
Spanish	*miel*	*cielo*	*pena*	*vero*	

Confusion between *oe* and *e* begins in inscriptions of the first century A.D. (*Phebus*, CIL 4.1890; *ceperint*, 2.1964.4.27—81–84 A.D.). We do not know at what date the monophthongal pronunciation got into standard Latin.[79]

EU

139. Aside from its use to represent Gk. ευ, the Latin diphthong *eu* occurs in the interjections *heu* and *heus* and as the product of contraction in *neuter, neutiquam, ceu, neu,* and *seu*.

140. The conjunctions *ceu, neu,* and *seu* come from *cẹve, nẹve,* and *sẹve*,[80] from earlier *ceive, neive,* and *seive*. The short final vowel was lost under certain conditions, whereupon consonantal *u* became the final member of a diphthong and *ẹ* was shortened. Clearly this must have been a diphthong similar to Gk. ευ [57], *e* followed in the same syllable by *u* [eu]. That *neuter*, when dissyllabic, must contain the same diphthong is clear. Although Consentius, De Barbarismis et Metaplasmis 7.12–4 Niedermann = 5.389.28 f. K, calls this dissyllabic pronunciation a barbarism, it has to be admitted in Vergil, Ciris 68:

> Sive est neutra parens, atque hoc in carmine toto.

That the interjection *heu* was similar in sound to *eo* and *eho* in the fifth century A.D. appears from a paragraph in Agroecius' work on homonyms and synonyms.

7.122.11–16 K:[81] *Eo verbum primae personae facit, eo, is, it. Eho adverbium interrogantis est, ut: Eho, Parmenonem nosti? Eo item adverbium loci, ut si dicas: Eo redactus sum. Heu interiectio dolentis est, eu laudantis: Terentius: Eu Phormio. Heus adverbium vocantis, heu respondentis. Eho est interiectio iubentis vel hortantis: Terentius: Eho, puer, curre ad Bacchidem.*

---

[79] There may have been an intermediate stage between *oe* and *ē*, but if so we know nothing about it. The use of *oe* for Gk. υ in *Moesia, lagoena,* and *coloephia* merely shows that υ could not be exactly represented in Latin.

[80] For *ẹ*, see [120, 121].

[81] 'Eo spells a verb of the first person. . . . Eho is an adverb of interrogation. . . . Eo is also an adverb of place . . . Heu is an interjection of grief, and eu of praise . . . Heus is an adverb of calling, heu of replying. Eho is an interjection of ordering or urging. . . .'

141. The use of *eu* in Greek loan words (*Eurōpa, euge*) further indicates its diphthongal value. It is noteworthy, also, that final *-eus* in Greek proper names varies between monosyllabic and dissyllabic value just as *eu* in *neuter* does. Contrast Accius 668 Ribbeck (trimeter):

> Iam hanc úrbem férro vástam fáciet Péleus

with Vergil, Ecl. 8.55:

> Certent et cycnis ululae, sit Tityrus Orpheus.

Compare Marius Victorinus 6.66.28–67.4 (quoted in [133]).

UI[82]

142. The diphthong *ui* occurs occasionally in contractions such as dissyllabic *fluitat* in Lucretius 3.189 and *fluitant* in 4.77. Each form fills the last foot of a dactylic hexameter, and therefore a pronunciation with consonantal *u* and short *i* is as impossible as the ordinary trisyllabic pronunciation of the word. We must run the two short vowels, *ŭ ĭ*, of the normal pronunciation into a single syllable, keeping the stress in its normal position upon the first. The inevitable result is a falling diphthong. In such cases it helps not at all to name the phenomenon synizesis; the only important question is: how is the word pronounced?

143. The same diphthong occurs in the genitives *cuius* and *huius*, the datives *cui* and *huic*, and the interjection *hui*.

The genitives *cuius* and *huius* (pronounced and sometimes written *cuiius, huiius* [160–162]) come from early Lat. **quoiios, *hoiios*, which yielded Plautine *quoiius, huiius*.[83] Beside these forms Plautus and Terence often use syncopated *quois* and *huis*, like *eis* beside *eiius* and *illīs* beside *illīus*.[84] There is no doubt that all these forms, except *illīus* and *illīs*, contained diphthongs, and it is equally sure that classical *cuiius* and *huiius* contained the same falling diphthong that we have found in dissyllabic *fluitat* [137]. See also Terentianus Maurus 6.348.789–96 K (quoted in [144e]).

144 a. The datives *cui* and *huic* come from early Lat. *quoi* and *hoi-ce* through Plautine *quoi* and *huic*. Their history is closely parallel to that of *cuiius* and *huiius* [143]; it would be difficult to assign them a

---

[82] Sturtevant, TAPA 43.57–66 and references.

[83] For the difference in vocalism in Plautus and for later *cuiius*, see Sommer 76, 103, 436.

[84] Our texts regularly spell *quoius, huius, eius,* and *illius,* whether the verse requires one syllable or two. See Sommer 443 f. and references.

different vocalism.   If only for this reason we might safely reject the
opinion of some scholars that they are to be pronounced [kwi·, hwi·k].
There are, however, several other reasons.

144 b. If we pronounce [kwi·], this is the only word in the language in
which consonantal *u* follows *c*.   If it be argued that the dative *cui* was
pronounced like the nom. *quī* [193], it would be impossible to explain the
constant difference in spelling.

144 c. Just as *ui* in *fluitō* is sometimes a diphthong and sometimes
dissyllabic [142], so *cui* and *huic* may be dissyllabic, e.g.:

Seneca, Troades 852 (Sapphic):

> Mittat et donet cuicumque terrae.

Statius, Silvae 1.1.107 (hexameter):

> Laetus huic dono videas dare tura nepotes.

See also Silvae 1.2.135.

144 d. Perhaps the strongest proof comes from prosody; elision is
allowed before *huic*, whose *u* must therefore be a vowel, e.g. Vergil,
Aen. 5.849:

> Ignorare iubes?   Mene huic confidere monstro?

Similarly the short second syllable of *alicui* makes it impossible to take
u as a consonant.   Verses in which this quantity is required are Lucretius 3.932; Sulpicia ap. Tibullum 4.7.2; Ovid, Amores 2.5.41, Ars 2.289,
Tristia 4.7.7; Martial 5.52.3.

144 e. Terentianus Maurus tells us quite explicitly that *u* in *huius* and
huic is not a consonant.

6.348.789–96 K:[85]
> (*H*) sola nec vocalis usum nec tuetur consonae,
> 790   tempus aut ministrat ullum brevibus usquam syllabis;
>   et tamen vim consonantis adimit, una in syllaba[86]
>   praedita est quotiens duabus *u* et *i* vocalibus.
>   *Huius* aut *huic* solemus nam frequenter dicere;
>   *u* digammon esse nunc iam non sinit nec consonam,

---

[85] '*H* alone has the use neither of a vowel nor of a consonant, and does not add
any quantity to short syllables anywhere; and yet it takes away the consonantal
force whenever it is prefixed to the two vowels *u* and *i* in one syllable.   For we
often say *huius* or *huic*; but now *h* no longer permits *u* to be digamma, which it
always must be when without aspiration it is placed before a vowel, as *vigor*,
valens, *vetus*.'

[86] Line 791 must be interpreted according to lines 795 f.; initial *u* before a vowel
is regularly a consonant, but not in the initial group *hui-*.

795   esse quam semper necesse est cum carens spiramine
        ante vocalem locatur, ut *vigor, valens, vetus.*

The other passages in which the Romans discuss the value of *ui* in
cui and *huic* are extremely difficult.   It will be worth while to quote
only four of them.

Quintilian 1.7.26 f.:[87] Nostri praeceptores *servum cervum*que *u* et *o* litteris
scripserunt, quia subiecta sibi vocalis in unum sonum coalescere et confundi
nequiret; nunc *u* gemina scribuntur ea ratione quam reddidi.   Neutro sane modo
vox quam sentimus efficitur.   Nec inutiliter Claudius Aeolicam illam ad hos usus
litteram adiecerat.   Illud nunc melius, quod *cui* tribus quas praeposui litteris
enotamus, in quo pueris nobis ad pinguem sane sonum *q* et *u* et *o* et *i* utebantur,
tantum ut ab illo *qui* distingueretur.

The reason why the spelling *cui* is better than the spelling *seruus* seems
to be that in the latter word the first *u* stands for a consonant, while *u*
in *cui* is a vowel.

Terentianus 6.347.760–77 K:[88]
760   Nec potest et hoc liquere, an *i* putemus consonam,
        longa *cui super* paretur ceu duabus consonis;

---

[87] 'Our teachers wrote *servus* and *cervus* with the letters *u* and *o*, because a
vowel following itself cannot combine and fuse into one sound; now double *u* is
written on the principle which I have stated.   In neither way, to be sure, is the
sound which we hear exactly represented.   Nor was it without advantage that
Claudius introduced the Aeolic letter for such uses.   The following innovation is
much better, that we spell *cui* with the three letters which I have set down, in
which, when we were boys, in order to represent what is, I grant you, a full sound
they spelled *quoi* merely that it might be distinguished from *qui*.'

[88] 'And we cannot settle this question either, whether we should think that *i*
is a consonant and the long syllable *cui* in *cui super* is produced as if by two consonants; for *i* following another vowel is always a vowel, and the case-forms which
follow show that the third letter of the word is a vowel; in fact, if we think now
that *u* has the vowel sound, the following *i* must all the more be considered a
vowel.   Shall we then perhaps say that this is a diphthong consisting of *u* and *i*,
not in such a way that *u* is a Latin letter but rather the diphthong is Greek υι
when they say γυῖα and υἶας?   Then *cui* would have a similar sound and, having
two morae in itself, would not need a consonant, while *cui super* would become
such a phrase as *trans mare*, in that a long vowel renders otiose the accompanying
consonants.   Or should we rather write *cuii* with double *i*, because this seems to
be the sound of the next case, which forms *cuius* like *Troia* and *Maia* with three
vowels?   Then *cui super* would not be helped at all by the neighboring consonant,
because the first syllable of *cuius* has been made long by having a consonant of its
own.   I though I ought to mention these considerations; follow whichever theory
you choose.'

alteram quia consequendo semper *i* vocalis est,
tertiam et casus sequentes esse vocalem docent;
immo si nunc *u* putamus esse vocalis soni,
765 *i* magis vocalis esse iudicanda est subsequens.
Numquid hanc diphthongon ergo ex *u* et *i* sic dicimus,
non ut *u* nunc sit Latina, sed magis Graecum sit *vι*,
γυῖα cum dicunt et *vίas*, tale quid *cui* ut sonet
temporum et per se duorum non requirat consonam,
770 *cui super* sed tale fiat quale dudum *trans mare*,
longa cum reddit vacantes quae simul sunt consonae?
An magis *cuii* nos oportet per duas *i* scribere,
quia sequens casus videtur hoc sonare, qui facit
cuius (ed. pr. *quius*) ut *Troia* atque *Maia* de tribus vocalibus,
775 *cui super* nil ut iuvetur a propinqua consona,
quando *cuius* longa prior est facta, cum sit consonans?
Haec putavi colligenda; tu sequere quod voles.

With these words Terentianus closes his discussion of *ui* in *cui*. He
has not been able to reach a certain conclusion in the more than one
hundred lines devoted to the topic, but he leaves us just these alterna-
tives: either *ui* is a diphthong or *u* is a vowel and *i* is a consonant.
These two solutions of the problem are really one; for all his difficult
verbiage Terentianus merely confirms the conclusion we have already
reached.

Audax 7.329.4 f. K:[89] . . . concurrentibus inter se vocalibus duae syllabae in
unam quasi per diphthongon contrahuntur, ut *cui* . . .

Priscian 2.303.11–4 K:[90] Ergo si *Pompeius* et *Vulteius* trisyllaba sunt in nominativo, necessario in vocativo disyllaba esse debent, quod non potest fieri nisi *i*
loco consonantis accipiatur. Unde illud quoque possumus scire quod bene *cui*
pro monosyllabo accipiunt metrici et *huic*.

Audax seizes the first horn of Terentianus' dilemma, and Priscian the
second.

The notices which the Romans have left on the pronunciation of
cui and *huic* accord with the indications furnished by orthography and
prosody. The words undoubtedly contained the vowel *u* followed in
the same syllable by *i*.

[89] '. . . When two vowels come together, and two syllables are contracted into
one as if by a diphthong, for example, *cui*. . . .'
[90] 'Therefore if *Pompeius* and *Vulteius* are trisyllabic in the nominative, they
must necessarily be dissyllabic in the vocative, which is impossible unless *i* be
taken as a consonant. Wherefore we can understand this too, that the students
of metric do well in taking *cui* and *huic* as monosyllables.'

OI, EI, ETC.

145. The diphthongs *oi* and *ei* occur in classical Latin only as the result of contraction in such words as *proinde, proin, deinde, dein.* That these contained real diphthongs appears from the occasional use of *proin* and *dein* as dissyllables. Similarly we may infer that monosyllabic *dehinc* had a diphthong from its use as a dissyllable in Vergil, Georg. 3.167:

> Cervici subnecte; dehinc, ubi libera colla.

Early Latin *ei* and *quoi, eis*[91] and *quois* (dat. and gen. of *is* and *qui*) are shown to contain diphthongs by their parallelism with *eius* and *quoius* [143, 144 a]. Of the same general character are instances of synizesis, as contractions evidenced by verse are sometimes called; for example, dissyllabic *aureī, aureīs, reice, dehiscas, alveō, eōdem, aurea, Orphea,* and monosyllabic *ain.*

---

[91] *Eis* for *eius* occurs not only in the early dramatists but also in Cicero, Aratea 87.

CHAPTER VI

THE LATIN CONSONANTS

VOICED AND VOICELESS CONSONANTS

146. Although the ancients have nothing to say about any distinction between the consonants in the matter of voicing, certain phonetic changes in Latin, as in Greek [65], separate the consonants into two groups whose distinguishing criterion can be nothing else. The two classes are (1) *b, d, g, v, i, m, n* and (2) *p, t, c, q, f, s*. Members of either class are commonly combined into consonant groups with other members of the same class, but either not at all or only under certain conditions with members of the other class. On the one hand we have such words as *abdō, abnuō, obiectus, obviam, admittō, adiectus, advehō, imbuō, induō, iniectus, invectus, ingerō*, and on the other hand such words as *ecferō, ecquis, rēx, rēctus, urbs, obtineō* (pronounced *urps, optineō* [198 b]), *scrībō, specimen, stō*. While *l* and *r* combine frequently with members of both groups (*obligō, glaber, albus, obruō, gravis, ardeō* but also *plānus, clārus, ultimus, premō, creō, artem*), their assimilative influence induced voicing, at least in preliterary times. Latin once had a voiced *s* [z] before voiced consonants, which was lost with compensatory lengthening before the beginning of the literature (*dīgerō* from **diz-gerō, dīnumerō* from **diz-numerō* beside *dis-tineō, dis-crepō*). But *dīrigō* from **diz-regō, dīligō* from **diz-legō*, etc. show that initial *r* and *l* voiced a preceding *s*. Furthermore Lat. *r* is frequently a later development of intervocalic voiced *s* [z] [185 a]. The Latin nasals may also stand ·before a voiceless consonant (*īnferō, īnserō, interior, imperō, incola*); but they never follow any but a voiced consonant, and their possession of voice in the pre-literary period is evidenced by *dīnumerō, dīmittō*, etc.

147 a. The Romance languages confirm these conclusions for the most part; they have voiced a number of consonants between vowels, but all such changes are obviously secondary. Table 1 illustrates the development of initial mutes.

TABLE 1

Latin	*pellis*	*bellus*	*tālis*	*digitus*	*crēdere*	*grandis*
Italian		*bello*	*tale*	*dito*	*credere*	*grande*
French	*peau*	*beau*	*tel*	*doigt*	*croire*	*grand*
Spanish	*piel*		*tal*	*dedo*	*creer*	*grande*

147 b. Loan-words to and from Greek make available for our purpose the tradition preserved by Modern Greek (Γαιος, Κοιντος, Καπετωλιου, Βασσος, Δομετιος, *catapulta, basis, Daedalus, Agamemnōn*).

Of equal significance are loan words in the Celtic and Germanic languages; such as Welsh *poc* from *pācem* and *bendith* from *benedictio*, Eng. *kitchen* (OE *cycene*) from *coquina*, Goth. *kaisar*, German *Kaiser*, Goth. *Agustus, Qartus, akeit*, etc.

CONSONANTAL V[1]

148. At an early period in the history of the parent language the *u* phoneme (or, if one prefers, the *u/w* phoneme) included a syllabic and a non-syllabic variant. At that time, it is safe to say, the latter was phonetically similar to the former; it was [w] rather than [β] or [v]. Although this single phoneme apparently became two in Primitive Indo-European, it is extremely probable that the non-syllabic one of the pair was still [w], as it is, indeed, in modern English; e.g., *was* : Skt. *vasati* 'dwells'. This Primitive Indo-European phoneme is the source of Lat. *v* in such words as *vōx, vocāre* : Skt. *vacas* 'speech', Gk. ἔπος; *novos* : Skt. *navas* 'new', Gk. νέος; etc.

149. The earliest Italian alphabets took over from the Greeks the letter F (commonly written Ⅎ by Etruscans, Oscans, and Umbrians) and also the digraph FH, by which some of the Greeks wrote their voiceless digamma [w̥], see [77, 78]. The Italians, however, having no such sound as [w̥], employed the digraph to represent their [f], see [188]. At an early date the Romans simplified the digraph to F and gave up the use of F in its Greek value of [w]. Either at this time or earlier they began, unlike their Italian neighbors, to employ the letter V as a consonant in words with inherited [w], see [148]. It is safe to say that this change of orthography would not have occurred if consonantal *u* had not still been very similar to the vowel *u*; it must still have been [w].

150. That the sound remained [w] for some centuries is shown by several early Latin phonetic laws. Consonantal *u* became the second member of the diphthong *au* [135, 137] upon the loss of a following short vowel in *fautor* beside *faveō, lautus* beside *lavō, naufragus* beside *nāvis*. Consonantal *u* was lost by dissimilation before ŏ in non-initial syllables, as in *parum* from *parvom, deorsum* from *dēvorsom. In the numerous words in which consonantal *u* was restored by analogy, it operated in

[1] In this book we usually distinguish between *U* and *V* and between *u* and *v* in the modern fashion; but one must not forget that the Romans made no such distinction.

the same way as vocalic *u* to prevent the change of following *o* to *u* in early Latin, as in *parvos, parvolus* [124].

Unaccented *ru* or *lu*, if followed by a vowel, changed vocalic to consonantal *u*; e.g. *volvō* from **veluō* (Gk. ἐλύω), *solvō* from **se-luō* (Gk. λύω). The change was complete after short vowels at the beginning of the literature (*volvō*, Ennius, Ann. 174 V, *solvō*, Lucilius, 48 M); but after long vowels the comic poets have *lārŭa* (Plautus, Amph. 777), *mīlŭos* (Aul. 316; Terence, Phor. 330), and *pēlŭim* (Laberius 94 R). When *u* in these words became consonantal, at some date later than Terence, it must at first have been [w].

Upon the change of *ŏ* to *ŭ* after *u* or *qu*, at some time after Terence [124], preceding *u* was lost, if consonantal, and preceding *qu* became *c*; hence *bovom* became *boum*, *vīvos* became *vius*, *quom* became *cum*, *quoiios* became *cuiius*, *equos* became *ecus*, etc. Evidently consonantal *u* was still so similar to vocalic *u* that the latter could induce dissimilative loss of the former, and, quite as clearly, consonantal *u* was still similar to the labial element in *qu* [193 d].

Horace's use of *silvae* as a trisyllable (Carm. 1.23.4, Epod. 13.2) may have been an imitation of early Latin *mīlŭos*, etc.; but such a treatment of the sound [β] or [v] would scarcely have been chosen by a poet of Horace's exacting taste.

151. That consonantal *u* between vowels had considerable similarity to the second member of the diphthong *au* is indicated by Cicero's story of the omen which warned Marcus Crassus not to set out on his fatal expedition against the Parthians.

Div. 2.84:[2] Cum M. Crassus exercitum Brundisii imponeret, quidam in portu caricas Cauno advectas vendens *Cauneas* clamitabat. Dicamus, si placet, monitum ab eo Crassum *caveret ne iret*, non fuisse periturum si omini paruisset.

Phaedrus' (126 = Appendix 21) tale of a wayfarer who understood a raven's cry as "Ave, ave," is much less cogent evidence.

152. Quintilian refers to the distinction between vocalic and consonantal *u* as a fine point requiring a trained ear; this would certainly not be true of the difference between [u] and [v].

Quintilian 1.4.6–8:[3] Ne quis igitur tamquam parva fastidiat grammatices elementa, non quia magnae sit operae consonantes a vocalibus discernere ipsasque

---

[2] 'When Marcus Crassus was embarking his army at Brundisium, someone at the harbor who was selling figs imported from Caunus was crying, *"Cauneas"*. We may say, if we please, that Crassus was warned by him, *"Cave ne eas"*, and that he would not have perished if he had obeyed the omen.'

[3] 'Let no man, therefore, look down on the elements of grammar ⟨i.e. the letters of the alphabet⟩ as small matters; not because it requires great labor to

eas in semivocalium numerum mutarumque partiri, sed quia interiora velut sacri
huius adeuntibus apparebit multa rerum subtilitas, quae non modo acuere ingenia
puerilia sed exercere altissimam quoque eruditionem ac scientiam possit.   An
cuiuslibet auris est exigere litterarum sonos?   Non hercule magis quam nervorum.
At grammatici saltem omnes in hanc descendent rerum tenuitatem, desintne
aliquae nobis necessariae litterarum, non cum Graeca scribimus (tum enim ab
iisdem duas mutuamur) sed propriae in Latinis, ut in his *servus* et *vulgus* Aeolicum
digammon desideratur.

153. In the first century before Christ and the first two centuries
after Christ the Germanic languages certainly had both [w] and either
[β] or [v] (written *b*), although scholars are not in full agreement as to
the details.[4]   Consequently the treatment of Latin consonantal *u* in
early Germanic loans is peculiarly valuable evidence.[5]   Latin *vīnum*
was undoubtedly borrowed by the Germans along with the commodity
itself, and we learn from Caesar, BG 1.1, that wine preceded the Roman
arms in this direction.   Hence Gothic *wein* and OE *wīn* are evidence for
Latin [w] of a very early date.   In all probability Lat. *vallum* was
borrowed at the time when the Germans learned to fortify their camps,
and so OE *weall* is also evidence for Latin of the first century A.D. at the
latest.   Goth. *Silbanus* is evidently a later borrowing.

154. A confusion of *b* and *v* in inscriptions begins in the first century
A.D.;[6] e.g. *Berus = Vērus*, CIL 4.4380; *baliat*, 4.4874;[7] *lebare*, 3.7251

---

distinguish consonants from vowels, and to divide the former into the proper
number of semivowels and mutes ⟨cf. [90 a]⟩, but because, to those entering
the recesses, as it were, of this temple, there will appear much subtlety on points,
which may not only sharpen the wits of boys, but may exercise even the deepest
erudition and knowledge.   Is it in the power of every ear to distinguish accurately
the sounds of the letters?   No more, assuredly, than to distinguish the sounds
of musical strings.   But all at least who are grammarians will descend to the
discussion of such fine points as these; whether any necessary letters be wanting
to us, not indeed when we write Greek words, for then we borrow two letters from
the Greeks, but letters that are proper to Latin words, as for example in *servus*
and *vulgus* the Aeolic digamma is needed.'

[4] Prokosch, A Comparative Germanic Grammar 54, 75 f.

[5] On the other hand, since Attic and Hellenistic Greek had no [w] and no [β]
or [v] before the beginning of the Christian era (probably not for a century or
so longer) [95], little can be learned from the various make-shift attempts to
write Latin *v* in Greek letters.   For an elaborate attempt to extract evidence
from this hopeless material, see G. B. Grundy, JPhS 1907.1–56.

[6] In the Lex Iulia Municipalis, CIL 1².593, of 45 B.C., occurs *triumphavit*
for *triumphabit*; but the document is so carelessly written that one may suppose
that the stone cutter substituted a perfect for a future.

[7] For other Pompeian examples and a discussion of the matter, see Väänänen
86–90.

(49 or 50 A.D.); *iuvente = iubente,* 11.137 (1 A.D.?); *vene = bene,* 6.7582 (187 A.D.). This confusion is understandable only on the assumption that consonantal *u* and *b* had become indistinguishable under some circumstances, and some of the Romance languages show that in the end consonantal *u* became [β] or [v] in all positions (Fr. *vin, laver*) while original *b* got this value between vowels (Fr. *avoir*); cf. [199]. This, then, is the pronunciation that we must assume for some part of the population as early as the first century A.D. By the third century the confusion of *v* and *b* was so common that we must assume a value [β] or less probably [v] even in standard Latin.

The older pronunciation must have continued in use for some time, however; Consentius, who is probably to be placed in the fifth century, knew it, although he himself apparently preferred the pronunciation [β] or [v].

Consentius, De Barbarismis et Metaplasmis 17.16 f. Niedermann = 5.395.15 f. K:[8] *V* quoque litteram aliqui exilius ecferunt, ut cum dicunt *veni* putes trisyllabum incipere.

Other evidence shows that *v* in late Latin was not normally [w]. Late Germanic loans in Italian and Gallic Latin show *gu* for *w*, evidently because that was nearer to Germanic [w] than was Lat. *v*. Hence It. *guarire* and *guerra,* Fr. *guerre* beside Goth. *warjan,* OE *werian* 'ward off'; Fr. *guise* beside OE *wīse.*

Priscian gives a remarkable rule for distinguishing between *v* and *b* in spelling:

3.465.12–14 K:[9] . . . omnia nomina a *vi-* syllaba incipientia per *v* scribuntur exceptis *bitumine* et *bili* (quando *fel* significat) et illis quae a *bis* adverbio componuntur, ut *biceps, bipatens, bivium.*

155. It is clear that in classical Latin consonantal *u* was similar to English *w.* The beginnings of a spirant pronunciation led to a confusion with *b* as early as the first century A.D. No doubt the sound at first was a bilabial spirant [β], but it has now yielded a labio-dental [v] in most of the Romance languages. For *qu* and *gu* see [193, 194].

[8] 'Some make the letter *u* too thin, so that when they say *veni* you think a trisyllable is starting.'

[9] '. . . all nouns beginning with *vi-* are written with *v*, except *bitumen* and *bilis* (when it is equivalent to *fel*), and those that are compounds of the adverb *bis*, as *biceps, bipatens, bivium.*'

Consonantal I

156. Consonantal *i*, like consonantal *u* [148], comes from a pre-Indo-European phoneme, which functioned either as a syllabic or as a non-syllabic, and which we may write *i* or *i/y*. Such an automatic variation implies that the non-syllabic variant was at first very similar to the syllabic, hence [j]. Primitive Indo-European *y*, which resulted from the non-syllabic variant of *i/y*, certainly retained this character; in fact it survives to the present day in Eng. *yoke, young*, Germ. *Joch, jung*, Lith. *jùngas, jáunas*, etc. The Latin words corresponding to those just cited are *iugum* and *iuvenis*.

157. That the inherited phoneme, consonantal *i*, was maintained without phonetic alteration in early Latin is indicated by the fact that it was written with the same character as vocalic *i*. In this case the Italians were confronted with the necessity for some innovation when they took over the Greek alphabet, since it had no character for [j] or for any similar sound except [i]. It is nevertheless significant that the Romans, as well as the Oscans, Umbrians, etc., employed the vowel letter *i* for the consonantal *i*.

The only escape from this inference would be to argue that [i] and [j] still constituted a single phoneme but had diverged phonetically. That they were separate phonemes in historical times is clear (cf. *iit, iērunt, adiēns, initium, etiam* with syllabic *i* beside *iam, adiiciō, adiectus* with consonantal *i*), and it is probable that similar conditions prevailed at the time when the alphabet was introduced.

158. Consonantal *i* must still have been [j] at the time (before Plautus) when *et iam, nunc iam*, and *quom iam* became *etĭam, nuncĭam*, and *quonĭam*, and when *coniicio*, etc. changed to *conicio*, etc. (e.g. *conicitis*, Plautus, Asin. 814, with short initial syllable).[10]

There always continued to be some interchange between consonantal and vocalic *i* in the position after a consonant. Poets show such forms as the following with *i* = [j]: *insidiantēs*, Ennius, Ann. 436 V; *fluviōrum*, Vergil, Georg. 1.482; *omnia*, Vergil, Aen. 6.33. Since *i* makes position in the first two of these passages and in many others, it was certainly a full consonant, and there is no reason to doubt that it was identical with the consonantal *i* of other words. The alternative is to endow the Latin language with an additional phoneme just to take care of these

---

[10] More commonly the early dramatists show analogically restored *coniiciō* (or *conieciō?*), etc. See M. W. Mather, Harvard Studies in Classical Philology 6.83–126.

literary passages.[11] We have seen [117 b] that *e* in hiatus sometimes has a parallel treatment in the poets.

The Romance languages show that unaccented *ĭ* (and also unaccented *ĕ*) in hiatus ultimately became consonantal; for the [j] has combined with certain preceding consonants; e.g. It. *grazia*, Fr. *grâce* from *gratia*; It. *giorno*, Fr. *jour* from *diurnus*.   Cf. [196].

159. Greek had no accurate means of transcribing consonantal *i*, and consequently the writing of Latin loan words in Greek cannot furnish conclusive evidence on the pronunciation of the Latin phoneme.   It is noteworthy, however, that while consonantal *u* is represented sometimes by vowel letters (*o*, *ov*, *v*) and sometimes by *β*, consonantal *i* is almost always represented by *ι* or, in a few cases, by *ει* or *η* (Εἰονιος, IG 12.5.143.14; Εἰουλια, 14.1582; μαηουρος, IGRRP 1.1220).   Instances of *ζ* are rare (Ζουλιαι, IG 14.1349; κοζους, 698, 1516, 1910 a, 2192).   The total lack of *γ* for consonantal *i* is remarkable, since *γ* seems to have become a spirant before *β* did, and since it is actually written with *ι* in inscriptions [95].

160. Cicero and Caesar are cited by the grammarians as authority for writing consonantal *i* double when it stands between vowels.

Quintilian 1.4.11:[12] Sciat etiam Ciceroni placuisse *aiio Maiia*mque geminata *i* scribere; quod si est, etiam iungetur ut consonans.

Velius Longus 7.54.16–55.2 K:[13] Et in plerisque Cicero videtur auditu emensus scriptionem, qui et *Aiiacem* et *Maiiam* per duo *i* scribenda existimavit (quidam unum esse animadvertunt, siquidem potest et per unum *i* enuntiari, ut scriptum est).   Unde illud quod pressius et plenius sonet,[14] per duo *i* scribi oportere existi-

---

[11] The meaningless traditional terms *synizesis*, *synaeresis*, etc. merely confuse the issue, although they are still current in discussions of classical prosody and metric.

[12] 'Let ⟨the grammarian⟩ also know that Cicero approved of writing *aiio* and *Maiia* with double *i*; if this is done ⟨the one *i*⟩ will be joined ⟨to the other⟩ as a consonant.'

[13] 'And in many particulars Cicero seems to have referred spelling to the standard of hearing; for he thought that *Aiiax* and *Maiia* should be written with double *i* (certain writers observe that there is one *i*, if it is possible to pronounce with one *i*, as we write).   Wherefore that which would be pronounced more strictly and completely so, he thinks should be written with two *i*'s; so also *Troiia*, and all such words.   Then the doubling increases, and in *coiiicit* we begin to write with three *i*'s, so that the first syllable is *coi-* and the following two *-iicit*.   For, if *iacit* is another word ⟨i.e., if we compare *iacit*⟩, *a* is substituted for *i* to carry the force of the vowel, while the first *i* remains, which has the force of a consonant.'

[14] I have taken the translation of this clause from C. Murley, CJ 16.316.

mat; sic et *Troiiam* et siqua talia sunt.   Inde crescit geminatio, et incipit per
tria *i* scribi *coiiicit*, ut prima syllaba sit *coi-*, sequentes duae *-iicit*.   Nam si est
aliud *iacit*, pro *i a* substituitur, ut vim vocalis obtineat, manente priore *i*, quae
consonantis vicem implebat.

Priscian 2.14.5–14 K:[15] . . . antiqui solebant geminare eandem *i* litteram et
maiius, peiius, eiius scribere, quod non aliter pronuntiari posset quam cum superiore syllaba prior *i*, cum sequente altera proferretur, ut *pei-ius, ei-ius, mai-ius*;
nam quamvis sit consonans, in eadem syllaba geminata iungi non posset; ergo
non aliter quam *tellus, mannus* proferri debuit.   Unde *Pompeii* quoque genetivum per tria *i* scribebant, quorum duo superiora loco consonantium accipiebant,
ut si dicas *Pompelli*; nam tribus *i* iunctis qualis possit syllaba pronuntiari?   Quod
Caesari doctissimo artis grammaticae placitum a Victore quoque in Arte Grammatica de syllabis comprobatur.

161. There are numerous instances of this orthography in inscriptions
(e.g. CIL 2.1964.1.41, 60, 2.10, 11, 28, 43, 45, 3.3, 4.26, 33, 5.6.13, 17,
22, 24, 43) and in manuscripts.   That it was really a phonetic spelling
is shown by the fact that the preceding syllable is always long (*maiior*
beside *măgis*; *cuiius* from *quoiios*, although it is only short *o* that becomes
u in unaccented syllables; *Troiia* from Gk Τροία).[16]

162. There are some special reasons for believing that long intervocalic
i was [j·].

162 a. In *Troiia, Maiia, Aiiax* the original Greek had diphthongs
(Τροία, Μαία, Αἶας); and these could not in the first place have been
represented by any Latin phoneme but the corresponding diphthongs
oi and *ai*.   The reason why *oi* and *ai* in these words did not develop
into *oe* and *ae* (cf. *poena, Haemus, Aegyptus, Maeander*) was that they
early fell into line with native words such as *aiiō, eiius*, etc., and had
their prevocalic [j] lengthened.   Thereafter their development was
parallel with that of the native words.   We may be sure, however, that
if this had involved any serious distortion of the Greek these words also
would have been changed in classical times to something like *Troea,
*Maea, and *Aeax.

---

[15] ‘. . . the ancients used to double the same letter *i* and write *maiius, peiius,
eiius*, which could not be pronounced unless the first *i* were spoken with the
former syllable and the second with the following syllable, *pei-ius, ei-ius, mai-ius*;
for, although a consonant, it could not be doubled in the same syllable; therefore
it had to be pronounced in the same way as *tellus* and *mannus*.   Whence they
also wrote the genitive *Pompeii* with three *i*'s, the first two of which they understood as consonants, as if one should say *Pompelli*; for what kind of a syllable
could be pronounced with three *i*'s together?   This opinion of Caesar, who was
learned in grammatical science, was approved by Victor also in the chapter on
syllables in his Ars Grammatica.'

[16] On *i* for *ii* and *iii* in standard orthography, see Kent, TAPA 43.35–56.

162 b. There is an obvious parallelism between the genitives *cuiius* (from *quoiios*) and *huiius* (from **hoiios*), and the datives *cui* (from *quoi*) and *huic* (from **hoice*)—a parallelism that still persisted in the time of Terentianus Maurus, as one sees from his discussion in 6.348.772–6 (quoted in [144 e]). Since, therefore, we must pronounce *cui* and *huic* with diphthongs [143, 144], we must pronounce *cuiius* and *huiius* with diphthongs, which amounts to prescribing [kuj·us, huj·us].

163. The misspellings of late inscriptions and also the Romance languages show that consonantal *i* came to be identical in sound with *g* before *e* and *i*, with *ge* and *gi* in hiatus [191 e], and, in popular but never in standard Latin, with *de* and *di* in hiatus [196 a]. Whether this sound was [j] or some sort of an affricate does not concern us at present.

164. At any rate it is quite clear that in early and classical Latin consonantal *i* was similar to Eng. *y* in *yet* and *yoke*, namely [j]. Between vowels consonantal *i* was long; it formed a diphthong with the preceding vowel, but was prolonged to begin the next syllable.

L

165. A consistent tradition assigns to Lat. *l* the value of a lateral consonant, that is, of a sound formed with the oral passage closed in the median line by the tongue against the roof of the mouth but open at the sides. This tradition is confirmed by the corresponding sound in cognates in most of the related languages (e.g. *lūx*, *lūceo* beside Gk. λευκός 'white', Ir. *loche* 'lightning', Goth. *liuhaþ*, Germ. *Licht*, Eng. *light*, OCS *luča* 'beam of light' and by loan words (e.g. *Lacōnia*, *lychnus*, Λουκιος, Παλατιος, Eng. *wall*).

166. Our ancient authorities describe an *l* produced with the tongue against the upper gum. Whether the closure was as far back as the alveolar ridge may be questioned; Lat. *l* may have been similar to the Fr. and It. *l* or, on the other hand, to the Eng. *l*.

> Terentianus 6.332.230–4 K:[17]
> 230   Adversa palati supera premendo parte
>   obstansque sono quem ciet ipsa lingua nitens
>   validum penitus nescio quid sonare cogit,
>   quo littera ad aures veniat secunda nostras,
>   ex ordine fulgens cui dat locum synopsis.

---

[17] 'By pressing the opposite parts of the palate with its upper surface and vigorously opposing the sound of which it is itself the cause, the tongue produces a powerful sound within the mouth whereby may come to our ears the brilliant letter, to which our list assigns second place.'

One might take this to apply rather to the velarized *l* which formed one variant of the Latin *l* phoneme [167]; but Marius Victorinus gives us a briefer paraphrase of Terentianus, which makes the front closure clear.

Victorinus 6.34.10 f. K:[18] Sequetur *l* quae validum nescio quid, partem palati qua primordium dentibus superis est lingua trudente, diducto ore personabit.

Martianus Capella 3.261:[19] *L* lingua palatoque dulcescit.

167. There are several proofs that Latin had also a back (velar) *l* [ł].[20]

167 a. This was the value in early Latin of *l* final or before another consonant (except a second *l*) or, in non-initial syllables, before any vowel except *i*. For before *l* in these positions *ĕ* and unaccented *ă* became *ŏ*; and then *ŏ*, whether of this origin or of any other, became *ŭ*, unless *u* or *v* preceded[21] (*facul, facultas* but *facilis*; *Siculus* but *Sicilia* from Σικελός and Σικελία; *spatula* from σπατάλη; *multa* from *molta*; but *volt, volgus, parvolus*). At some date later than Terence the latter change extended to *ŏ* after *u* and *v* (*vult, vulgus, parvulus*), and this is evidence for the continued existence of [ł].

167 b. The Roman grammarians record a difference in the sound of *l* according to its surroundings.

Priscian 2.29.8–12 K:[22] *L* triplicem, ut Plinio videtur, sonum habet: exilem quando geminatur secundo loco posita, ut *ille, Metellus*; plenum quando finit nomina vel syllabas et quando aliquam habet ante se in eadem syllaba consonantem, ut *sol, silva, flavus, clarus*; medium in aliis, ut *lectum, lectus*.

It is clear that Pliny means velar *l* by his *plenus sonus*, but if so, it is strange that he does not include *l* before the vowels *e*, *o*, *u*; for we have just seen that early Latin sound changes require us to group *l* in this

[18] 'Next will come *l*, which, with the tongue pressing the part of the palate where the roots of the upper teeth are, will send a powerful sound through the open mouth.'

[19] '*L* with tongue and palate grows sweet.'

[20] By this is meant a lateral consonant with closure between the central part of the tongue and the back part of the palate. See [169]. On Lat. velar *l*, see H. Osthoff, TAPA 24.50–65.

[21] The change last mentioned did not affect *ŏ* of an initial syllable if *l* was followed by a back vowel (*solūtus, columna, solum, color*).

[22] '*L* has a triple sound, as Pliny thinks: thin when it stands second in double *ll*, as *ille, Metellus*; full at the end of a word or a syllable and when it has a consonant before it in the same syllable, as *sol, silva, flavus, clarus*; intermediate in other words, as *lectum, lectus*.'

position with final *l* and *l* before a consonant. We must, apparently, suppose that *l* before vowels had ceased to have velar character by Pliny's time. As to Pliny's *sonus exilis*, see [168].

Consentius 5.394.29–36 K:[23] Romana lingua emendationem habet in hoc quoque distinctione. Nam alicubi pinguius, alicubi debet exilius proferri; pinguius cum vel *b* sequitur, ut in *albo*, vel *c*, ut in *pulchro*, vel *f*, ut in *adelfis*, vel *g*, ut in *alga*, vel *m*, ut in *pulmone*, vel *p*, ut in *scalpro*; exilius autem proferenda est, ubicumque ab ea verbum incipit, ut in *lepore*, *lana*, *lupo*, vel ubi in eodem verbo et prior syllaba in hac finitur et sequens ab ea incipit, ut *ille* et *Allia*.

Evidently Consentius calls *pinguis* what Pliny called *plenus*; and if we argue again *ex silentio*, it would seem that *l* had lost its velar character when final or after another consonant in the same syllable.

167 c. At any rate it is only *l* before a consonant that the Romance languages change to *u* (Fr. *autre*, Port. *outro*, Sp. *otro*—earlier **autro*— from *alter*).[24] There are traces of the change in late Latin (κανκυλατορι for *calculatori*, Ed. Diocl. 7.6.7; *cauculus* in manuscripts).

168. One might be inclined to interpret Pliny's *sonus exilis* (ap. Priscian 2.29.8 f., quoted in [167 b]) as 'palatalized *l*'; and, in fact, it has recently been suggested[25] that the Spanish palatal *ll* [λ] from Lat. *ll* (e.g. *villa* [βίλα] from Lat. *vīlla*) represents a survival of the palatal color from Pliny's time to the present day. But It. *villa*, Fr. *ville*, etc., which have no palatal color, make it probable that the Spanish palatalization is relatively late. Equally difficult for the theory is the fact that Pliny does not list *li* in hiatus (It. *figlia*, Fr. *fille* from Lat. *fīlia*) as containing the *sonus exilis*, although the Romance evidence for palatal color is in this case much stronger. The evidence cited for a palatal *l* in Latin by Herbig[26] and Altheim[26] is not convincing. As long as the obscure phrase stands so nearly by itself, it would be rash to claim that we understand what Pliny meant by *sonus exilis*.

---

[23] 'The Roman tongue has a correction to make in this matter also by way of distinction. For in some places the sound should be thicker, in others thinner; thicker when *b* follows, as in *albus*, or *c*, as in *pulcher*, or *f*, as in *adelfi*, or *g*, as in *alga*, or *m*, as in *pulmo*, or *p*, as in *scalprum*; but it should have a thinner pronunciation wherever a word begins with it, as in *lepus*, *lana*, *lupus*, or where in the same word the preceding syllable ends with this letter and the following begins with it, as *ille* and *Allia*.'

[24] On the Romance development of Lat. *l*, see most recently, W. Meyer-Lübke, Berichte der sächsischen Akademie, Phil.-hist. Klasse 86.2.1–83 (1934).

[25] Ettmayer, Zeitschrift für romanische Philologie 30.653 f.; cf. Meyer-Lübke, loc. cit. 31–43.

[26] Glotta 5.249–53; 20.160 f.

169. Classical Latin had in most words a dental *l* similar to Fr. *l* or an alveolar *l* more or less similar to Eng. *l* in *let, seller*. Latin had also a back *l* [ɫ] whose precise nature is unknown; it may have been similar to Eng. *l* in *silk, elk, bulk*, etc. Perhaps a safer comparison would be with Russian or Polish [ɫ]. The rather scanty evidence suggests a gradual spread of front *l* at the expense of back *l* during the known history of the Latin language.

R

170. In most of the Romance languages *r* is a trilled tongue-tip *r*. The inference as to Latin *r* is confirmed by a similar inference, based upon other modern Indo-European dialects, for *r* in the parent speech. The correspondence of Latin *r* with Gk. ρ in loan words (*Argos, Alexander*, Μαρκος, Τιβεριος) is scarcely significant, since neither language provided an alternative transcription.

171. The nature of Lat. *r* is definitely fixed by the numerous and unusually explicit characterizations of the sound by the Romans themselves.

Lucilius 9.377 f. M:[27]
> *R non multum abest hoc cacosyntheton atque canina*
> *si lingua dico, "nihil ad me".*

Persius 1.109:[28] *Sonat hic de nare canina.*

Terentianus 6.332.238 f. K:[29]
> *Vibrat tremulis ictibus aridum sonorem*
> *has quae sequitur littera.*

Victorinus 6.34.15 f. K:[30] *Sequetur r, quae vibrato †vocis palatum† linguae fastigio fragorem tremulis ictibus reddit.*

Martianus Capella 3.261:[31] *R spiritum lingua crispante corraditur.*

---

[27] 'This cacophonous *r* isn't much different from saying in dog's language, "It's nothing to me".'

[28] 'Hereupon the dog's letter sounds through the nose.' This is Persius' way of saying: "A sound is heard like a dog's snarl."

[29] 'The next letter ⟨*r*⟩ shakes out a dry sound with rapid blows.'

[30] 'Next will come *r*, which by vibrating the tip of the tongue ... gives a thunderous noise with rapid blows.'

[31] '*R* is scraped forth while the tongue puts breath into tremulous motion.'

Ovid, Fast. 5.481, and Augustine, De Dialectica 32.2 = Principia Dialecticae 6 (reprinted by GS 239), use the adjective *asper* of the sound of *r*, contrasting it with *lenis*, used of the letter *l*.

172. Lat. *r* was, throughout the history of the language, a trilled tongue-tip *r* [r], similar to *r* in Italian, in rural French and German, or in Scotch and Irish English.

M

173. The ancient descriptions, supported by the tradition of scholars and by the Romance languages, leave no doubt that Lat. *m* was a bilabial nasal.

Terentianus 6.332.235 K:[32]
  At tertia clauso quasi mugit intus ore.

Victorinus 6.34.12 f. K:[33] *M* impressis invicem labiis mugitum quendam intra oris specum attractis naribus dabit.

Martianus Capella 3.261:[34] *M* labris imprimitur.

174 a. Final syllables ending in *m* are treated in Latin verse as if they ended in a long vowel; they are normally elided before initial vowels (*multum ille et* in the third line of the Aeneid is scanned as three long syllables), but before an initial consonant they are treated as long (e.g. the final syllable of *Ītaliam* before *fātō* in the second line of the Aeneid). That this peculiarity was not confined to verse is shown by stereotyped phrases in which final *m* is lost either alone (*circuire*, CIL 2.3420, etc.; *cura ago*, 6.6144 a—first century A.D., etc.; *queadmodum*, 2.5439.4.2.14, 18, etc.; *datuiri*, etc., late future infinitive passive), or along with the preceding vowel (*animadvertō, cūragō, vēneō*). Significant in this connection is the frequent omission of final *m* in early inscriptions (e.g. *duonoro optimo fuise viro*, CIL 1².9) and again in late plebeian inscriptions. In the Romance languages final *m* is lost except in a few monosyllables such as Fr. *rien* from *rem*.

174 b. The grammarians have a good deal to say about final *m*.

Quintilian 9.4.40:[35] Atqui eadem illa littera, quotiens ultima est et vocalem verbi sequentis ita contingit ut in eam transire possit, etiamsi scribitur, tamen

---

[32] 'The third letter ⟨m⟩ may be said to moo within the closed mouth.'

[33] 'With the lips pressed together *m* will sound like the mooing of cattle within the cavern of the mouth and the nostrils as well.'

[34] '*M* is spoken with tight closed lips.'

[35] 'But the same letter *m*, when it ends a word and is in contact with an initial vowel of the next word so that it may coalesce with it, is written but scarcely

parum exprimitur, ut *multum ille* et *quantum erat*; adeo ut paene cuiusdam novae litterae sonum reddat.   Neque enim eximitur sed obscuratur et tantum aliqua inter duas vocales velut nota est ne ipsae coeant.

The last sentence in this passage seems to say that Quintilian read the Vergilian phrases *multum ille* and *quantum erat* without complete loss of the final *-um*.[36]   More important for our present purpose is the fact that Quintilian has difficulty in deciding whether *m* is pronounced or not; it is clear that final *m*, at least before a vowel, indicated some feature of speech which Quintilian could hear, but which was different from the sound of *m* in other positions.   The same phenomenon, no doubt, is described by Velius Longus and Priscian, although they do not confine it to the position before an initial vowel.

Velius Longus 7.54.13–15 K:[37] Nam quibusdam litteris deficimus, quas tamen sonus enuntiationis arcessit, ut cum dicimus *virtutem* et *virum fortem consulem Scipionem*, pervenisse fere ad aures peregrinam litteram invenies.

Here it is noteworthy that the "almost foreign letter" occurs before initial consonants.[38]

Priscian 2.29.15 f. K:[39] *M* obscurum in extremitate dictionum sonat, ut *templum*, apertum in principia, ut *magnus*, mediocre in mediis, ut *umbra*.

174 c. This feature of pronunciation that the grammarians hear but cannot describe is probably a nasalization of the vowel preceding the final *m*.   That such a vowel should be elided under the same conditions as other vowels is not strange, and neither is it strange that it should be a long vowel when not elided.

174 d. In the first edition of this book I concluded that final *m* before an initial consonant had not nasalized and lengthened a preceding vowel, since such words as *quom*, *suom*, *servom*, and *equom* suffered the change to *u*, a change to which only short *o* was subject.   Probably,

---

pronounced, as *multum ille* and *quantum erat*; so that it gives the sound almost of a new letter.   For it is not omitted but obscured and is merely a kind of a mark between two vowels to prevent them from combining.'

[36] Sturtevant and Kent, TAPA 46.145–7.

[37] 'For we lack certain letters which pronunciation nevertheless demands; for example, when we say *virtutem* and *virum fortem consulem Scipionem*, you will find that what is virtually a foreign letter has come to the ears.'

[38] It was certainly wrong to punctuate *virum, fortem, consulem, Scipionem* in the first edition of this book (p. 83), and to assume that Velius Longus was speaking here of final *m* before an initial vowel.

[39] '*M* has a dull sound at the end of words, as in *templum*; a clear sound at the beginning, as in *magnus*; an intermediate sound in the interior, as in *umbra*.'

however, the change applied to open *o* whether this was short (as before final *s*) or long and nasalized, as it was before a written final *m*. Positive evidence for nasalization of a vowel before final *m* and an initial consonant of the next word is presented by the omission of final *m* in this position in early and late inscriptions and by Velius Longus' treatment of the phrase *virum fortem consulem Scipionem*.[40]

175. Latin *m* in most positions was a bilabial nasal similar to English, French, and German *m*. Final *m* was merely a mark of nasalization of the preceding vowel. Such a nasalized final vowel might be elided under the same circumstances as any other final vowel.

N

176. Lat. *n* corresponds to the dental nasal of the related languages in cognate words (*novus* : Gk. νέος, Skt. *navas*, Ir. *núe*, Goth. *niujis*, OCS *novъ*), and numerous loan words show the same correspondence (*narcissus*, *dynastes*, Νερων, 'Ιουνιος). More cogent is the evidence of the Romance languages, which regularly show a dental *n* from Lat. *n* (*novus* : It. *nuovo*, Sp. *nuevo*, Fr. *neuf*; *contrā* : It., Sp. *contra*, Fr. *contre*).

There is also a brief but perfectly clear ancient description of the tongue position in the production of the sound.[41]

Martianus Capella 3.261:[42] *N lingua dentibus appulsa conlidit.*

177 a. Before *s*, *n* was about to disappear at the beginning of our records. The early inscriptions especially show such forms as *cosol* and *cesor*, and that the pronunciation *cosul* was current in classical times is shown by the spelling of Latin words in Greek inscriptions and papyri (e.g. Κλημης, καστρησιος), and also by explicit testimony, e.g.:

Velius Longus 7.78.21–79.2 K:[43] Sequenda est vero non numquam elegantia eruditorum virorum, qui quasdam litteras lenitatis causa omiserunt, sicut Cicero qui *foresia* et *Megalesia* et *hortesia* sine *n* littera dicebat.

---

[40] Cf. Safarewicz, Actes du troisième congrès international de linguistes 176–9, Eos 35.133–8, Munera Philologica L. Ćwiliúski Oblata 304–11; M. Leumann, Glotta 27.67 f.

[41] Terentianus, 6.332.361 f. K, and Victorinus, 6.34.13 f. K, prescribe contact with the palate, and this might suggest that the passages refer to velar *n*. But cf. Gellius 19.14.7, quoted in [178 a].

[42] 'The tongue placed against the teeth makes the contact for *n*.'

[43] 'Sometimes one should imitate the good taste of learned men, who have omitted certain letters for euphony, as Cicero who liked to say *foresia*, *Megalesia*, and *hortesia* without the letter *n*.'

The moribund sound continued to be written in standard orthography for some centuries, and no doubt spelling pronunciations were common. Furthermore analogy tended to reintroduce the sound in some words, as we learn from Cassiodorus' excerpts from Papirian:

7.160.12–15 K:[44] *Formosus* sine *n* secunda syllaba scribendum est, ut *arenosus, frondosus, aquosus, herbosus.* Participia vero habent *n*, ut *tonsus, tunsus, mensus, pensus.* Antiquorum nulla observantia fuit, cum *n* an sine *n* scriberent; illi enim *tosus, tusus, prasus* plerumque scribebant.

Nevertheless there is no trace of Lat. *n* before *s* in the inherited words of the Romance languages. In popular Latin certainly, and probably in most words in standard pronunciation, there was no consonantal *n* before *s*.

177 b. Since we have clear evidence that original short vowels were lengthened before early Lat. *ns*, both in words in which the *n* was in classical times written and in those in which it was not written, it has been inferred that *n* before *s* nasalized a preceding vowel and ceased to be pronounced as a consonant. This would furnish a convenient explanation of the fluctuating spelling and the strange discussions of whether or not *n* in this position should be pronounced.

If *n* before *s* dropped with nasalization of the preceding vowel, the result must have differed in some way from the nasalized vowels that resulted from final *m* [174]; for we never have *m* written for *n* in words like *ēnsis* or *n* for *m* in words like *ignem.* A further difficulty with the theory is that while the lengthening of short vowels occurs also before *nf*, there is no tendency in pre-classical or classical times to omit the *n* in writing this group.

178 a. The Romans recognized the existence of a velar *n* (the *n* of Eng. *ink*), i.e. [ŋ], in such words as *anguis.*

Gellius 19.14.7:[45] Item ex eodem libro ⟨Nigidi Figuli⟩ verba haec sunt: "Inter litteram *n* et *g* est alia vis, ut in nomine *anguis* et *angari* et *ancorae* et *increpat* et *incurrit* et *ingenuus.* In omnibus his non verum *n* sed adulterinum ponitur. Nam *n* non esse lingua indicio est; nam si ea littera esset, lingua palatum tangeret."

---

[44] 'One should write *formosus* without *n* in the second syllable, as *arenosus, frondosus, aquosus, herbosus.* But participles have *n*, as *tonsus, tunsus, mensus, pensus.* The ancients had no rule whether to write with *n* or without *n*; for they generally wrote *tosus, tusus, prasus.*'

[45] 'In the same book ⟨Nigidius Figulus⟩ says: "Between *n* and *g* there is another sound, as in *anguis, angari, ancorae, increpat, incurrit, ingenuus.* In all these there is written not a genuine but a false *n*. For the tongue gives evidence that it is not *n*; for if it were that letter the tongue would touch the palate." '

Varro ap. Priscian 2.30.15–21 K = GS 201.6–8:[46] Ut Ion scribit, quinta vice-
sima est littera quam vocant *agma*, cuius forma nulla est et vox communis est
Graecis et Latinis, ut *aggulus, aggens, agguilla, iggerunt.* In eiusmodi Graeci
et Accius noster bina *g* scribunt, alii *n* et *g*, quod in hoc veritatem videre facile
non est. Similiter *agceps, agcora.*

178 b. There are several reasons for thinking that *gn* was pronounced
[ŋn]:[46a] (1) *Pn* and *bn* became *mn* (*somnus* : Skt. *svapnas*, ON *swefn*;
amnuit for *abnuit*, CGL 4.308), and *dn* became *nn* (*annuō* for *adnuō*).
A parallel development of *cn* and *gn* would yield [ŋn], whereas we find
gn written as in *īlignus* : *īlex*, *dignus* : *decet*, and *cognōscō* : γιγνώσκω.
(2) Before velar *n* [ŋ] *ĕ* became *ĭ* (*tinguō* : τέγγω; *quīnque* : πέντε has
secondary length of *ī* after *quīntus* from *quīnctus*), and the same change
appears in *dignus* : *decet*, *lignum* : *lego*, *īlignus* : *īlex*, *signum* : *īnsece.*
(3) The nasal pronunciation of *g* is indicated by such epigraphical forms
as *congnatus* (CIL 6.14931; 10.1220, 2758, 3408), *dingnissime* (14.1386),
ingnes (4.3121), *ingnominiae* (1².593.120 f.), *singnifer* (6.3637), *sinnu* =
signum (9.2893), *mana* = *magna* (6.14672.12), *Pelinam* (9.3314),
aprunae (Ed. Diocl. 4.43). Greek inscriptions sometimes show Ναιος
for *Gnaeus*, e.g., IG 3.1436. (4) The nasal pronunciation of *g* explains the loss of prefixal *n* in *ignārus, ignāvus, ignōbilis, ignōminia,
ignōscō, cognātus, cognōscō*, etc.

The grammarians' failure to mention this use of *g*, though strange,
is perhaps explained by the fact that the Greek grammarians say
nothing of the similar phenomenon in Greek [71].

179. In most positions Lat. *n* was a dental *n* like initial or intervocalic *n* in French. It was not an alveolar, as in English. Before *s*,
n was lost, but it was frequently restored, especially in writing; it is
not quite certain that vowels before *ns* or *nf* were nasalized.

Latin had also a velar nasal [ŋ] before *c, q*, or *g* and also before *n* in
the group written *gn*. On account of the group [ŋn], it is necessary to
consider [ŋ] a separate phoneme.

H

180. Lat. *h* in native words usually comes from Indo-European *ĝh*,
as does Oscan *h*; and it is probable that an intermediate stage was a

[46] 'As Ion writes, there is a twenty-fifth letter which they call *agma*, for which
there is no character, but whose sound is common to the Greeks and the Latins,
as in *aggulus, aggens, agguila, iggerunt.* In such words the Greeks and Accius
write double *g*, others *n* and *g*, because in this matter it is not easy to see the
truth. Similarly *agceps, agcora.*'
[46a] See Addenda.

spirant more or less like the German *ach*-sound [x]. The letter *h* comes from Greek η (heta), whose earliest value must have been [x], as we have seen [79]. One might, therefore, allege a certain plausibility for the theory that *h* was [x] in early Latin.[47]

From the time of our earliest documents, however, Lat. *h* was an unstable sound. It had already been lost between like vowels and after consonants[48] (*bīmus* from **bi-himus*; *nēmō* from **ne-hemō*; *diribeō* from *dis* + *habeō*), and in other positions it was preserved only by certain classes, in general the higher social strata, and even among them the schoolmasters soon found it necessary to reinforce tradition. In spite of everything they could do, a certain amount of uncertainty is to be found in our documents. The rustic word *ānser* (Skt. *haṃsas*, Eng. *goose*) and the vulgar words *liēn* (Skt. *plīhā*) and *meiō* (Skt. *mehati*) are not surprising. But unhistorical *h* in such words as *humerus* (Gk. ὦμος) *ahēnus* (*aes*, Skt. *ayas*, Goth. *aiz*) must be due to the overcorrection that is to be expected when standard usage differs from the native habit of the masses. This conclusion is supported by the fact that, although the pronunciation and writing of *h* was a recognized mark of social prestige, the Pompeian graffiti, our earliest extensive body of popular writing, often omit this letter.

180 a. Clear evidence that *h* was a weak sound is presented by its regular lack of prosodic effect at all periods; it does not prevent elision and it does not unite with another consonant to make position. The constant identification of *h* with the Attic and Hellenistic rough breathing by the Roman grammarians points in the same direction, but we must remember that there was no other Greek sound with which *h* could possibly have been identified. The use of *ch*, *ph*, and *th* to represent the Greek aspirates is somewhat stronger evidence for the character of *h* as mere aspiration, although here again there was no alternative.

Furthermore the Romans refer to the sound of *h* as *aspiratio* (e.g., Cicero, Or. 160; Quintilian 1.5.19—both quoted in [183]) or as *spiritus* (e.g. Gellius 2.3.1—quoted in [183]; Martianus Capella 3.261—quoted in [111]). If it were [x] we might expect some discussion of the articulation, such as is preserved for *f* [188 a].

180 b. The proper use of *h* came to be in classical times a mark of culture, and correctness in this matter was cultivated. The sound was persistently indicated in standard orthography, and it has even been reintroduced into the spelling of some modern Romance words (Fr. *herbe, homme*, Sp. *haber, hombre*). In popular Latin *h* seems to have

---

[47] So Birt, Der Hiat bei Plautus und die lateinische Aspiration, Marburg, 1901.

[48] In compounds like *perhibeō* the *h* has been restored by analogy.

been completely lost in Pompeii in the first century A.D., and not much later everywhere in the empire. The Romance languages contain no trace of it except in the scholastic orthography just mentioned.

181 a. Since Latin had no aspirated mutes it was inevitable that *p*, *t*, and *c* should be substituted for *φ*, *θ*, and *χ* in loan words. This was clearly the normal pronunciation of such words in popular Latin at all periods, and of the educated as well except for two or three centuries beginning shortly before 100 B.C. In a few early loans (whether direct from the Greek or through Etruscan mediation does not concern us here) the non-aspirate spelling and, no doubt, pronunciation was invariable at all periods (e.g. *puniceus, tus, calx*).

181 b. During the classical period, however, many Romans knew Greek very well, and they undertook to pronounce Greek words accurately even when they used them in a Latin context. This is the reason why the more exact transcription of Gk. *φ*, *θ*, and *χ* by *ph*, *th*, and *ch* came into use at this time, and was applied even to many Greek words that had already come to be used in Latin. This correspondence was established as the standard orthography, and so the copyists (or perhaps redactors like Varro) have introduced such anachronistic forms as *chlamys, Philippeus*, and *Thēbae* into the text of Plautus and Terence. This introduction of *h* after a consonant, in spite of the simplification of such groups in prehistoric Latin [180], was facilitated by the fact that analogy had already restored some such groups in compounds like *perhibeō, inhaereō, inhūmānus, abhorreō, abhinc, adhortor, adhūc.* Since Greek loan words were very numerous in classical Latin the new sounds had to be worked into the phonemic structure of the language, and it follows from the way in which Catullus, Cicero, Quintilian, and Gellius (quotations in [183]) combine their treatment of *h* after *c*, *p*, and *t* with that of *h* in other positions, that written *h* was a phonemic unit. The standard Latin phonemic system differed from the Greek at this point.

This is the reason why the Latin poets alliterate *c*, *p*, and *t* with *ch*, *ph*, and *th*, as in Horace, Carm. 1.7.3 f.:

> Moenia vel Baccho Thebas vel Apolline Delphos
> insignis aut Thessala Tempe;

and in Vergil, Aen. 1.714:

> Phoenissa et pariter puero donisque movetur.[49]

---

[49] Professor Alice F. Braunlich kindly investigated this matter for me, and found in Vergil's Aeneid, Horace's Odes, and Propertius about twice as many places where alliteration of *p* in *ph* with *p* in other positions is apparent as places where one might assume alliteration of *ph* with *f*, if that were conceivable.

182. Hence the proper use of *h* in Greek loan words that originally had *φ*, *θ*, and *χ* fell in with and reinforced the more or less artificial retention of *h* initial and between vowels in genuine Latin words [180 b]. Since this usage, in both classes of words, was a peculiarity of the upper classes, it was inevitable that climbers and also born aristocrats of defective education should attempt to acquire it, and, as always happens in such cases, their zeal outstripped their knowledge; they introduced *h* into Greek words that had no right to it and even into Latin words in the position after *c*, *p*, and *t*.[50]

183. The record of the rise and fall of *h* as a mark of social distinction is as follows:

Catullus 84:[51]

> *Chommoda* dicebat, si quando *commoda* vellet
> dicere, et *insidias* Arrius *hinsidias*,
> et tum mirifice sperabat se esse locutum,
> cum quantum poterat dixerat *hinsidias*.
> Credo, sic mater, sic liber avonculus eius,
> sic maternus avos dixerat atque avia.
> Hoc misso in Syriam requierant omnibus aures;
> audibant eadem haec leniter et leviter,
> nec sibi postilla metuebant talia verba,
> cum subito adfertur nuntius horribilis,
> *Ionios* fluctus, postquam illuc Arrius isset,
> iam non *Ionios* esse, sed *Hionios*.

Cicero, Or. 160:[52] Quin ego ipse, cum scirem ita maiores locutos esse, ut nusquam nisi in vocali aspiratione uterentur, loquebar sic ut *pulcros, Cetegos,*

---

[50] Wilhelm Schulze's (KZ 33.386 fn. 1 = Kleine Schriften 425) objection to this explanation of Lat. *pulcher*, etc., although accepted by Sommer 200 and Leumann 131 f., is quite without point. I have tried to show (JAOS 44.38–53) that just such overcorrection is of the very essence of phonetic law; but in this case the process did not go so far. It is surprising that three such scholars as those just named should have failed to see how typical the assumed Latin development really is, particularly in view of the relatively full record that has been preserved.

[51] 'Arrius said *chommoda* whenever he meant *commoda*, and *hinsidiae* for *insidiae*, and he hoped he had spoken unusually well when he had said *hinsidiae* with all his might. I dare say that is the way his mother and that free-born uncle of his and his mother's father and mother used to talk. After he had been sent to Syria everybody's ears had a rest; they heard those same mistakes in mild and gentle form, and they were not afraid of such words thereafter, when suddenly comes frightful news: the Ionian waves, since Arrius arrived there, are no longer Ionian, but Hionian.'

[52] 'Since I knew that our ancestors spoke so as to aspirate no sound but a vowel, I used to speak so as to say *pulcer, Cetegi, triumpi, Cartago*; finally after

triumpos, Cartaginem dicerem; aliquando idque sero, convicio aurium cum extorta mihi veritas esset, usum loquendi populo concessi, scientiam mihi reservavi. *Orcivios* tamen et *Matones, Otones, Caepiones, sepulcra, coronas, lacrimas* dicimus, quia per aurium iudicium licet.

Quintilian 1.5.19–21:[53] Illa vero non nisi aure exiguntur quae fiunt per sonos; quamquam per aspirationem, sive adiicitur vitiose sive detrahitur, apud nos potest quaeri an in scripto sit vitium, si *h* littera est, non nota. Cuius quidem ratio mutata cum temporibus est saepius. Parcissime veteres usi etiam in vocalibus, cum *aedos ircos*que[54] dicebant; diu deinde servatum ne consonantibus aspirarent, ut in *Graccis* et in *triumpis*. Erupit brevi tempore nimius usus, ut *choronae, chenturiones, praechones* adhuc quibusdam inscriptionibus maneant, qua de re Catulli nobile epigramma est. Inde durat ad nos usque *vehementer* et *comprehendere* et *mihi*; nam *mehe* quoque pro *me* apud antiquos tragoediarum praecipue scriptores in veteribus libris invenimus.

Quintilian implies that the words cited in the final sentence were pronounced without aspiration, as is to be expected between like vowels [180]. No doubt the form *mehe* that he cites from early tragedians was the dative (*mehe* for *mehẹ̄* from *mehei* [120, 121]).

Gellius 2.3.1–4:[55] *H* litteram sive illam spiritum magis quam litteram dici oportet, inserebant eam veteres nostri plerisque vocibus verborum firmandis

---

a long time, when the truth had been wrested from me by the clamor in my ears, I surrendered to the public in my habit of speech, and kept my knowledge for myself. Nevertheless I say *Orcivii, Matones, Otones, Caepiones, sepulcra, coronae, lacrimae,* because the criterion of hearing permits it.'

[53] 'Those faults which are committed in pronunciation are judged only by the ear; though as to the aspiration, whether it be added or retrenched, in variation from common practice, it may be a question with us whether it be a fault in writing; if *h* indeed be a letter, and not merely a mark. The treatment of this sound has often changed with time. The ancients used it very sparingly even before vowels, as they said *aedi* and *irci*; and it was long afterwards withheld from conjunction with consonants, as in *Gracci* and *triumpi*. But suddenly an excessive use of it became prevalent, so that *choronae, chenturiones, praechones* are still to be seen in certain inscriptions; on which practice there is a well-known epigram of Catullus. Hence there remain even to our times *vehementer, comprehendere,* and *mihi*, indeed among the ancient writers, especially those of tragedy, we find also in old copies *mehe* for *me*.'

[54] These are dialectic forms; if Quintilian found them in genuine Roman documents, they must have been, like *ānser*, loans from the country [180].

[55] 'Whether *h* should be called a letter, or a breathing rather than a letter, the ancient Romans inserted it in many words to establish and strengthen them, so that their sound should be fresher and more vigorous; and they seem to have done this from study of the Attic dialect and according to this precedent. It is well known that the Attic Greeks pronounced ἰχθύς, ἵππος, and likewise many other words with aspiration of the first letter contrary to the practice of the

roborandisque, ut sonus earum esset viridior vegetiorque; atque id videntur fecisse studio et exemplo linguae Atticae. Satis notum est Atticos ἰχθύν et ἵππον et multa itidem alia contra morem gentium Graeciae ceterarum inspirantis primae litterae dixisse. Sic *lachrumas*, sic *sepulchrum*, sic *ahenum*, sic *vehemens*, sic *incohare*, sic *helluari*, sic *halucinari*, sic *honera*, sic *honustum* dixerunt. In his enim verbis omnibus litterae seu spiritus istius nulla ratio visa est, nisi ut firmitas et vigor vocis quasi quibusdam nervis additis intenderetur.

184. Latin *h*, both initial and intervocalic and also after consonants, was mere aspiration, similar to Eng. *h*, i.e. [h]. Its use was early confined to the upper classes, and, since the schoolmasters never ceased to prescribe its use, it is impossible to say when it was given up by them.

S

185. The tradition of scholars and the popular tradition embodied in the Romance languages unanimously make Lat. *s* a sibilant. The ancient descriptions of the sound are in agreement with this evidence, and they enable us to define the sound much more closely.

> Terentianus 6.332.239–43 K:[56]
>> Mox duae supremae ⟨s et x⟩
> 240 vicina quidem sibila dentibus repressis
>> miscere videntur; tamen ictus ut priori
>> et promptus in ore est agiturque pone dentes,
>> sic levis et unum ciet auribus susurrum.

Marius Victorinus 6.34.16–18 K:[57] Dehinc duae supremae, *s* et *x*, iure iungentur. Nam vicino inter se sonore attracto sibilant rictu, ita tamen, si prioris ictus pone dentes excitatus ad medium lenis agitetur, sequentis autem ...

Martianus Capella 3.261:[58] *S* sibilum facit dentibus verberatis.

---

other nations of Greece. Thus the ancients said *lachrumae, sepulchrum, ahenus, vehemens, incohare, helluari, halucinari, honera, honustus.* In all these words, in fact, there seems to have been no reason for that letter or breathing, except that the firmness and strength of the sound should be increased as by the addition of what may be called sinews.'

[56] 'Then the final letters ⟨in the list, i.e. *s* and *x*⟩ are seen to cause a similar hissing against the teeth; still, just as for the former ⟨i.e. *s*⟩ the contact in the mouth is immediate ⟨whereas for *x* it is preceded by the sound of *c*; cf. lines 244–6, quoted in [201]⟩ and it is formed behind the teeth, so it is smooth and brings to the ears an unchanging whisper.'

[57] 'Then the final ⟨letters in the list⟩, *s* and *x*, will properly be joined. For with similar sound they hiss through a contracted opening; provided, nevertheless, that while the impulse of the former begins behind the teeth and, a soft sound, is ...' The rest I do not understand.

[58] '*S* makes a hiss by lashing the teeth.'

Cledonius 5.28.1 f. K:[59] *S* ... sibilus magis est quam consonans.

The words *sibilō*, *exsibilō*, and *sibilus* properly denote a hissing, and so they suggest a voiceless *s*, as in Eng. *sit, hiss* or Fr. *sel, fosse*.

185 a. That the sound was really voiceless, as the word *sībilus* implies, is quite certain, cf. [146]. In prehistoric Latin the Italic voiced sibilant between vowels became *r* (Lat. *erō* : Osc. *ezum*; *dir-imō* : *distineō*), and the voiced sibilant before another voiced consonant was lost (*dī-numerō, dī-ripiō, dī-vidō, dī-gerō*); the *s* that remained must have been voiceless at that time. A voiced consonant that came to stand before *s* was unvoiced in *nūpsī* : *nūbō, maximum* : *magis, rēxī* : *regō*, while the *bs* of *plebs, urbs, abs, obsequor*, etc. was pronounced [ps], [198 b]. The labial mute that developed between *m* and *s* was *p* (*sūmpsī, hiemps*), in spite of the fact that *m* was a voiced sound [146].

185 b. During the Roman period Greek had both a voiced and a voiceless dental sibilant (ς and σ) [86, 89, 99 d, 100], and σ was regularly used to represent Lat. *s* (Συλλας, Σουλπικιος, Καισαρ). Gothic of the fourth century A.D. also possessed both *s* and *z*, and consistently used *s* for Lat. *s* (*kubitus, kaisar, sakkus, sigljo = sigillum, suljo = solea*).[60]

185 c. Intervocalic *s* is generally voiceless in South Italian and Rumanian; the voicing of intervocalic *s* in French and some other Romance languages must therefore have begun in the separate history of those languages.

186. In early Latin inscriptions final *s* after a short vowel is frequently omitted, and in the early poets final *s* often fails to make position. Since final *s* does prevent elision in verse it is safe to say that its loss was limited to the position before consonants. The matter is mentioned by several authors.

Cicero, Or. 161:[61] Quin etiam, quod iam subrusticum videtur, olim autem politius, eorum verborum, quorum eaedem erant postremae duae litterae quae sunt in *optumus*, postremam litteram detrahebant, nisi vocalis insequebatur.

---

[59] '*S* ... is a hiss rather than a consonant.'

[60] J. C. Jones, CR 7.6 f.

[61] 'In fact, from those words whose last two letters were the same as in *optimus* they used to take away the last letter unless a vowel followed, a pronunciation which now seems rather boorish but was once the more fashionable. And so that stumbling block in versification which our modern poets try to avoid did not exist. For we said, *Qui est omnibu' princeps*, not *omnibus princeps*, and *Vita illa dignu' locoque*, not *dignus*.'

Ita non erat ea offensio in versibus quam nunc fugiunt poetae novi. Sic enim loquebamur:

"Qui est omnibu' princeps"

non *omnibus princeps*, et:

"Vita illa dignu' locoque"

non *dignus*.

Quintilian 9.4.38:[62] Quae fuit causa et Servio, ut dixi, subtrahendae *s* litterae quotiens ultima esset aliaque consonante susciperetur; quod reprehendit Luranius, Messala defendit. Nam neque Lucilium putant uti eadem ultima, cum dicit "Aeserninu' fuit" et "dignu' locoque"; et Cicero in *Oratore* plures antiquorum tradit sic locutos.

Opinions differ as to whether early Latin final *s* after a short vowel and before a consonant was lost or somehow reduced,[63] but there seems to be no sufficient reason to doubt Cicero's word. Before Cicero's time the analogical reintroduction of final *s* before a consonant had begun, and during his lifetime it was completed, not only in the literary language, but also in popular speech; in the Pompeian graffiti, full as they are of mistakes, final *s* is usually written.   It is only in late inscriptions of certain parts of the Roman world that we see the beginnings of the loss of final *s* which characterizes modern Italian and Rumanian.

187. Latin *s* was a voiceless sibilant, similar to *s* in English, German, or French. The tendency to voice *s* in certain positions that is seen in French and some other Romance languages seems not to have been a feature of Latin.

F

188 a. The Romans describe *f* quite clearly as a labio-dental spirant.

Quintilian 12.10.29:[64] Nam et illa quae est sexta nostrarum paene non humana voce, vel omnino non voce potius, inter discrimina dentium efflanda est.

---

[62] 'And this, as I have said, was Servius' reason for taking away *s* whenever it was final and followed by another consonant; which practice Luranius blames and Messala defends. For they think that Lucilius does not retain final *s* when he says *Aeserninu' fuit* and *dignu' locoque*; and Cicero in his Orator records that the majority of the ancients spoke thus.'

[63] See Carola Proskauer, Das auslautende *s* auf den lateinischen Inschriften, Strassburg, 1910; Leumann 175 f. and references.

[64] 'For that one also which is the sixth of our letters, of a sound scarcely human, or rather with no sound at all, has to be blown through the interstices of the teeth.'

Terentianus 6.332.227–9 K:[65]
> Imum superis dentibus adprimens labellum,
> spiramine leni, velut hirta Graia vites,
> hanc ore sonabis.

Marius Victorinus 6.34.9 f. K:[66] *F* litteram imum labium superis imprimentes dentibus, reflexa ad palati fastigium lingua, leni spiramine proferemus.

Martianus Capella 3.261:[67] *F* dentes ⟨faciunt⟩ labrum inferius deprimentes.

Although Quintilian's description lacks the physiological detail of the later ones, it is applicable only to a labio-dental *f*; a bilabial *f* does not involve blowing between the teeth.

188 b. Nevertheless the development of Lat. *f* from IE *bh* in a majority of its occurrences suggests that the Primitive Italic sound may have been a bilabial *f*, and there is no reason why this sound may not have survived into early Latin.[68]   Hence there may be significance in the early assimilations *im fronte* (CIL 1^2.1420), *comfluont* (1^2.584.13), etc., as contrasted with constant *in fronte*, *confluo*, etc. in later inscriptions.   Since Lat. *m* was at all times normally bilabial [175], it is unlikely that it stands here for a labio-dental *m*; that sound would rather have been written *n*, as, in fact, labio-dental *m* before *f* is actually written in Spanish.

188 c. Classical Lat. *f* was undoubtedly a labio-dental voiceless spirant [f], similar to English *f*.   In early times, however, the sound may have been a bilabial spirant [φ].

CLASSIFICATION OF THE MUTES

189 a. In classifying the letters, the Roman grammarians list nine mutes (*b, c, d, g, h, k, p, q, t*), although some of them are doubtful about *h*, which certainly does not properly belong in the list [180–4]. Both *qu* and *gu* were separate phonemes [193, 194], and *k* early dropped out of use [190].   We have seen [146] that of the remaining six *c, t*, and *p* were voiceless, *g, d*, and *b* voiced.

Another distinction also is implied by their development in Romance. Although, under varying conditions in the various languages, voiceless

[65] 'Pressing the lower lip against the upper teeth you will sound this letter with a gentle breath, as if avoiding the Greek rough mutes.'

[66] 'Putting the lower lip against the upper teeth, with the tongue withdrawn toward the high point of the palate, we shall pronounce *f* with a gentle breath.'

[67] 'The teeth holding down the lower lip ⟨form⟩ *f*.'

[68] See most recently E. Hermann, Gött. Nachr. 1919.249.

mutes have been voiced, and voiced mutes (whether inherited or developed) have become spirants or have been lost, still the old distinction has been very largely maintained; and today the voiceless mutes are regularly pronounced with a more vigorous articulation (fortes) than the voiced mutes (lenes). There is a limited amount of evidence that this distinction also existed in antiquity.[69]

Terentianus 6.331.186–98 K:[70]

> *B* littera vel *p* quasi syllabae videntur
> iunguntque sonos de gemina sede profectos;
> nam muta iubet portio comprimi labella,
> vocalis at intus locus exitum ministrat.
> 190 Compressio porro est in utraque dissonora;
> nam prima per oras etiam labella figit,
> velut intus agatur sonus; ast altera contra
> pellit sonitum de mediis foras labellis.
> Utrumque latus dentibus applicare linguam
> 195 *c* pressius urget; dein hinc et hinc remittit,
> quo vocis adhaerens sonus explicetur ore.
> *G* porro retrorsum coit et sonum prioris
> obtusius ipsi prope sufficit palato.

Victorinus 6.33.15–24 K:[71] ... *b* et *p* litterae coniunctione vocalium quasi syllabae (nam muta portio penitus latet; neque enim labiis hiscere ullumve

---

[69] The evidence drawn in the first edition of this book from early Greek loanwords has to be given up, since these words were probably not taken directly from Greek [94 fn. 89].

[70] 'The letters *b* and *p* almost seem syllables and they unite sounds coming from two sources; for the mute portion demands that the lips be pressed together, whereas the vocalic portion within provides an exit. The closure of the two, however, differs in sound; for the former brings the lips together along their edges as if the sound were produced between(?); the second, however, drives the sound out from the middle of the lips.

'*C* strives to press both sides of the tongue more closely against the teeth, and then relaxes the pressure on both sides so that the sound of the following vowel may be produced in the mouth. *G*, on the other hand, causes a closure farther back and produces the sound of the former letter, somewhat dulled, near the very roof of the mouth.'

[71] '... *b* and *p* in connection with vowels form syllables, as it were; for their mute portion is imperceptible, in fact their impulse is not strong enough to open the lips or to produce any action of the voice unless the vowels give a passage and open the mouth. They are produced by dissimilar action of the mouth; for the first results when the sound is driven out from the middle of the lips, the second, when the mouth is tightly closed and the impact of the voice is almost held in.

'*C* and *g*, as well as the above mentioned letters, are very close together in sound, but differ in the effort and energy of the mouth. For *c*, pressing the back-

meatum vocis exprimere nisus valet, nisi vocales exitum dederint atque ora reserarint) dispari inter se oris officio exprimuntur.   Nam prima exploso mediis labiis sono, sequens compresso ore velut introrsum attracto vocis ictu explicatur. *C* etiam et *g*, ut supra scriptae, sono proximae, oris molimine nisuque dissentiunt. Nam *c* reducta introrsum lingua hinc atque hinc molares urgens haerentem intra os sonum vocis excludit; *g* vim prioris pari linguae habitu palato suggerens lenius reddit.

Terentianus ascribes an imperfect lip-closure to *b*, which implies a lenis if not a spirant, while the vigorous phraseology of line 193 suggests that *p* was a fortis.   He also makes *g* a duller sound than *c*, while the latter has a relatively close (*pressius*) articulation.   Marius Victorinus' paraphrase of Terentianus' treatment confuses the descriptions of *p* and *b*, but his statement about *c* and *g* is quite explicit; they differ *oris molimine nisuque*.   The descriptions of *d* and *t* [195] do not help much in this connection.

Although the evidence is not as abundant as we should like, it is very probable that the voiceless mutes were fortes and the voiced lenes.

189 b. Tradition unanimously makes *q* and *k* and also *c* and *g* before back vowels and consonants velar mutes.   Furthermore the descriptions of *b* and *p* quoted in [189 a] show that they are labial mutes, while passages quoted below in [195] show just as clearly that *d* and *t* are either dentals or alveolars.   We must therefore expect to find *c* and *g* velars or palatals, and, although the descriptions of these sounds quoted in [189 a] are none too clear, they nevertheless bear out the conclusion.

C, K, AND G

190. It is clear that Lat. *k* and *c* are different graphic representations of the same phoneme.   In some early inscriptions *k* tends to be used before *a*, *q* before *o* and *u*, and *c* before *e* and *i* and before consonants. This system, which is found also in some early Etruscan inscriptions, is recorded by some of the grammarians, e.g.:

Donatus 4.368.7–9 K:[72] ... supervacuae quibusdam *k* et *q*; qui nesciunt quotiens *a* sequitur *k* litteram praeponendam esse, non *c*, quotiens *u* sequitur, per *q*, non per *c*, scribendam.

---

drawn tongue on both sides against the molars, and shutting the sound of the vowel within the mouth ⟨then⟩ forces it out; *g*, with the same position of the tongue, makes the sound of the preceding letter weaker by lifting it up to the roof of the mouth.'

[72] '... *k* and *q* seem superfluous to certain writers, who do not know that whenever *a* follows, *k* should precede, not *c*, and whenever *u* follows we should write *q*, not *c*.'

In standard orthography k was completely crowded out by c, except in a few abbreviations, and it is perfectly clear that this development occurred because both letters represented the same phoneme, cf. [193 a].

As to the approximate character of c and g before consonants and back vowels there has never been any doubt. Scholarly tradition is unanimous, and, in general, so is the evidence of the Romance languages, to the effect that they were back palatal or velar mutes. Completely in harmony with tradition are the loan words, such as καλανδαι, κομετιον, Μαρκος, *Calacte* (for Καλὴ 'Ακτή), Goth. *kaisar*, Germ. *Kalk*.

191. Before e and i both c and g have been variously modified in the Romance languages. Table 2 includes typical examples.

TABLE 2

Latin		*centum*	*circus*	*circellus*		*gēns*	*gingīva*
Sardinian	[k]	*kentu*	*kirku*			*gente*	*zinzia*
Dalmatian	[k]			*kercellu*			
Rumanian	[tš]		*cerc*	*cercel*	[dž]		*gingie*
Italian	[tš]	*cento*	*cerco*		[dž]	*gente*	*gengiva*
French	[s]	*cent*			[ž]	*gent*	*gencive*
Spanish	[θ]	*ciento*	*cerco*	*zarcillo*	[j]	*yente*	*encia*
Portuguese	[s]	*cento*	*cerco*		[ž]	*gente*	*gengiva*

Since Lat. c before e and i remains a mute [k] in central Sardinian and Dalmatian, it is certain that there was no general Latin change of that articulation. Besides, the nature of the palatalization differs in the several Romance languages. For a discussion of the palatalization of g, see [191 e].

191 a. That c was actually a mute throughout the classical period is shown by the following evidence. (1) The earlier grammarians nowhere speak of a difference in the sound of c. How strong this testimony of silence really is, as far as standard Latin is concerned, appears when we remember the recognition of velar n [178 a] and of velar l, although this was not a separate phoneme [167 b], and the clear notices of [tsj] for ti in hiatus [196 b]. (2) In Umbrian k before e and i was assibilated in some way and a special character for the sound existed in the native alphabet. When Umbrian was written in Latin letters c was used for k before consonants and back vowels, and s (with or without a diacritic over it) for the sibilant that had developed out of k before e and i; evidently Latin c could not naturally be used for the sound. (3) Latin inscriptions show the letter k for c before front vowels as well as in other positions (*Keri*, CIL 1².445; *Dekem⟨bres⟩*, 1².1038; *Mukianus Markellino*, 5.3555; *pake*, 10.7173). (4) Among the words that in Cicero's time tended to change mutes into aspirates in imitation of Greek loan words were *pulcer* and *Orcīvius*, and Quintilian records *chenturiōnēs* [182, 183]. It is improbable that the Greek aspirated mutes would induce aspiration after an affricate or sibilant. (5) Varro couples *anceps* with *ancora* as a word containing the velar nasal [178 a]. Therefore *c* must also have been a velar or at least a palatal sound before *e*. (6) Latin loan words in Greek are constantly written with κ for *c* (Κικερων), never with ξ, ζ, or τσ, as we might expect if *c* before *e* and *i* had become an affricate. (7) Corroborative evidence is furnished by Goth. *lukarn* from *lucerna*, Germ. *Kiste* and *Keller* from *cista* and *cellārium*, etc. Although, as Mikkola[73] points out, they merely prove that Germanic *k* was more nearly equivalent to Lat. *c* before *e* and *i* than any other Germanic phoneme was, the fact remains that [č] or [ts] would probably have been heard as [s] or a consonant group containing [s], rather than as [k].

191 b. In many languages, as in English, *k* before front vowels is pronounced further forward in the mouth than when it is followed by other sounds. Some such difference may plausibly be assumed for Lat. *c* as the first stage in the development which has resulted in It. *cento*, Fr. *cent*, etc.

There is, however, no valid evidence that the differentiation had gone far in classical times. The confusion between *ce* and *cie* in inscriptions (*circiensibus*, CIL 1².593.64—45 B.C.; *munificientiam*, 8.32; *facet*, 12.915—first or second century A.D.; *deces*, 12.2086—558 A.D.) has sometimes been alleged as evidence for a considerable degree of palatalization, but such confusion is scarcely more frequent or significant than the variation between *e* and *ie* after other consonants.[74]

191 c. The Romance developments of Lat. *ce* and *ci* (cf. Table 2 [191]) show that sooner or later a glide between *c* and a front vowel actually developed. In time *c* plus the glide yielded an affricate similar to Eng. *ch* in *church* [tš] in a part of the Romance territory and an affricate similar to Germ. *z* in *Zahn* [ts] in another part. The epigraphical evidence of this change is not abundant enough to inspire confidence until the sixth century. The isolated *Pitzinnina* (ICUR

---

[73] Mémoires de la société néo-philologique 7.261.

[74] It has been held by some, e.g. Guarnerio, Archivio glottologico italiano, Suppl. 4.34–7, that *c* before *e* and *i* was palatal or even prepalatal; but the evidence cited is altogether inconclusive. See Giovanni Campus, Atti della accademia di Torino 54.271–84, 366–76.

404) of 392 A.D. may possibly represent a personal idiosyncracy of pronunciation; it can scarcely have more significance than that.[75]

191 d. There is less evidence on the nature of *g* before *e* and *i* in the classical period, but what there is indicates that it was a mute. (1) The earlier grammarians never suggest a difference from *g* in other positions. (2) Varro cites *ingenuus* and *ingerunt* as examples of the velar nasal [178 a]. (3) Latin loan words in Greek always represent *g* by γ regardless of the following sound; we do not find ξ, ζ, or ι for *g* before front vowels. This argument, however, has little weight in view of the relatively early spirant pronunciation of γ [95]. (4) The confusion with *i* mentioned in [191 e] does not occur in classical times, and that is strong evidence that *g* was not at that time similar to consonantal *i*.

We may safely assume that the pronunciation of *g* conformed to that of *c* [191 b] in the classical period. It was a mute in all positions, but it was probably articulated somewhat further forward in case it was followed by *e* or *i*.

191 e. In most of the Romance languages *g* before *e* and *i* has yielded the same result as consonantal *i*. Table 3 presents typical instances.

TABLE 3

Latin	*gēns*	*gingīva*	*iungere*	*iacere*
Italian	*gente*	*gengiva*	*giungere*	*giacere*
French	*gent*	*gencive*	*joindre*	*gésir*
Spanish	*yente*	*encia*	*uncir*	*yacer*
Portuguese	*gente*	*gengiva*	*jungir*	*jazer*

The two sounds begin to be confused in inscriptions about 500 A.D.; examples are: *Gerosale*, CIL 12.649 (end of the fifth century); *Gianuaria*, 11.4335 (503 A.D.); *geiuna*, 12.2193 (527 A.D.); *Genoarias*, 12.934 (529 A.D.); *Gennara*, ICUR 1036 (530–3 A.D.); *trienta*, CIL 13.5359; *Gen(uarius)*, 5.1717; *Magias*, 10.4545; *congigi*, 9.2892. The few literary indications of an earlier date for the confusion, even if authentic, can scarcely establish more than a local development. By 500 A.D., however, *g* before *e* and *i* had become [j], at least in Italy and Gaul. From this sound have developed the various consonants exhibited by the Romance languages [191, Table 2; 191 e, Table 3].

[75] It has been thought that the frequent epigraphical *ci* for *ti* in hiatus from the second century on indicated an earlier change of *c* before *i* in hiatus than in other positions. Carnoy, TAPA 47.146 f., explains this orthography as a reaction against the assibilation of *t* before *i* in hiatus [196 b]. At any rate it cannot indicate assibilation of *ci* plus vowel or any real confusion between *ci* and *ti* in that position; the two are still distinct in Italian.

192. Lat. *c* was a voiceless velar mute, probably fortis, similar to Fr. *c* or *qu* in such words as *cache, comme, pacte, que, cinq,* i.e. [k].

Lat. *g* was a voiced velar mute, probably lenis, similar to French *g* or *gu* in such words as *gant, gout, grâce, guerre,* i.e. [g].

Before front vowels both *c* and *g* were probably articulated somewhat further forward, but there is no reason to suppose that the difference was important.

QU AND GU[76]

193 a. We have seen [190] that standard Latin orthography eliminated *k* because it was not phonemically different from *c*. The digraph *qu*, however, was permanently retained, in spite of a rather widespread grammatical theory that the letter *q* was superfluous.[77] This is good reason for believing that *qu* was not merely [kw], which would surely have been written *cu*.

193 b. What the difference was is made clear by certain remarks of the grammarians.

Velius Longus 7.58.17–20 K:[78] ... *u* litteram digamma esse interdum non tantum in his debemus animadvertere in quibus sonat cum aliqua adspiratione, ut in *valente* et *vitulo* et *primitivo* et *genetivo*, sed etiam in his ⟨in⟩ quibus ⟨cum q⟩ confusa haec littera est, ⟨ut⟩ in eo quod est *quis*.

Significant for us is the information that in *quis u* is run together or merged with *q* and that it lacks a part of the sound to be heard in consonantal *u* initial and between vowels.

Marius Victorinus 6.34.1–3 K (in contrasting *q* with either *c* or *k*—opinions differ as to which):[79] Quarum utramque exprimi faucibus, alteram distento, alteram producto rictu manifestum est.

This amounts to saying that the lip-rounding for *u* is synchronous with the closure for the mute. Furthermore Donatus, 4.367.16–18 K, says that *u* is neither vowel nor consonant when it stands after *q*; and

---

[76] Sturtevant, Lang. 15.221–3.

[77] Quintilian 1.4.9; Marius Victorinus 6.8.16, 33.28–30 K; Ps.-Sergius 4.520.24–6 K = GS 200.11–13.

[78] '... we must note that the letter *u* is sometimes digamma in these words in which it is spoken with some breath, as in *valens, vitulus, primitivus,* and *genetivus*, but also in these ⟨in⟩ which this letter is run together ⟨with q, as⟩ in *quis*.'

[79] 'It is clear that each of them is produced in the throat, one with the lips open wide, the other with the lip-opening protruded.'

Pompeius, 5.104.16–25 K, adds that in *quidem u* is merely *pars litterae praecedentis*.

193 c. The descriptions just cited are confirmed by the fact that *qu* does not make position; the initial syllable of such words as *aqua* and *equos* is regularly short.[80]   Furthermore *m* does not become [ŋ] before *q* as it does before *c*.   Contrast *quemquam, quamquam, quīcumque, umquam, numquam* with *hunc* and *hōrunc*.   This can scarcely be explained except by assuming that *qu* had a labial affection from its very beginning.

193 d. Lat. *qu* was a voiceless velar mute accompanied by lip-rounding.   While the lip-rounding may have been continued after the explosion of the mute, it evidently did not last long enough to have any appreciable effect upon rhythmic quantity.

194. The Romans have not left us any descriptions of the sound of *gu*. Since it always follows a nasal consonant, no evidence upon its length can be got from verse.   Neither does the process of composition ever bring *m* to stand before *gu*.   The chief reason for supposing that the digraph stands for a voiced velar mute with synchronous lip-rounding is the parallelism with *qu*.   Perhaps some additional evidence can be got from the fact that after consonantal *u* had become [β] [154], new Germanic loan words in Latin substituted *gu* for *w* (It. *guisa*, Fr. *guise* : Germ. *Weise*, Eng. *wise*).   Since we never find *qu* employed in this way it is fair to assume that *gu* was nearer the Germanic [w] than *qu* was.   This would be true if *gu* and *qu* differed chiefly in the presence or absence of voice, but scarcely if *gu* was a consonant group and *qu* was not.

D AND T

195. Tradition makes Lat. *d* and *t* dental mutes, and, although the ancient descriptions are in part obscure, they at least show the general position in which the sounds were articulated.

Terentianus 6.331.199–203 K:[81]

             At portio dentes quotiens suprema linguae
200   pulsaverit imos modiceque curva summos,
             tunc *d* sonitum perficit explicatque vocem;
             t, qua superis dentibus intima est origo,
             summa satis est ad sonitum ferire lingua.

---

[80] The very few instances in which such a syllable counts as long in verse are statistically negligible, however they can be explained.

[81] 'But whenever the upper part of the tongue strikes the tips of the ⟨upper⟩ teeth and, with moderate curvature, the base of the teeth, it produces the sound of *d* and gives passage to the following vowel; for the sound of *t*, it is enough to

Victorinus 6.33.24–8 K:[82] *D* autem et *t*, quibus, ut ita dixerim, vocis vicinitas quaedam est, linguae sublatione ac positione distinguuntur. Nam cum summos atque imos coniunctim dentes suprema sui parte pulsaverit, *d* litteram exprimit. Quotiens autem sublimata partem qua superis dentibus est origo contigerit, *t* sonore vocis explicabit.

Martianus Capella 3.261:[83] *D* appulsu linguae circa superiores dentes innascitur. ... *T* appulsu linguae dentibus impulsis extunditur.

Whether one translate *dentes imos* and *dentes summos* by 'lower teeth' and 'upper teeth'[84] or by 'tips of the teeth' and 'base of the teeth', the description of *d* by Terentianus and Victorinus can apply only to a dental such as Fr. *d*, not at all to an alveolar such as Eng. *d*, in which the tongue does not touch the teeth. The descriptions of *t*, on the other hand, emphasize the alveolar contact but do not exclude the possibility of contact also between the tip of the tongue and the teeth. If we assume that in both *d* and *t* the tip of the tongue touched the teeth and the surface of the tongue was in contact with the upper gum so as to form the actual barrier to the breath stream (as is the case in French), then the more energetic articulation of *t* [189] explains the greater importance that the grammarians attach to the gum in the production of that sound.

196 a. In Vulgar Latin *di* and *de* before vowels came to have the same sound as consonantal *i* (It. *giorno*, Fr. *jour* from *diurnus*; Sardinian *rayu*, It. *raggio*, Sp. *rayo* from *radius*). The confusion appears in misspellings in Latin inscriptions (*Aiutor*, CIL 8.8637—527 A.D.?; 14.871; *aiutrici*, 10.2184; *codiugi*, 10.2559; *Madias*, ICUR 172—364 A.D.). The pronunciation [j] for *di* and *de* was never standard; and the change did not occur at all after *r* and *n*.

196 b. Somewhat later intervocalic *ti* and *te*, and also intervocalic *di* and *de* in words in which these had escaped the change described in [196 a] changed their *i* or *e* to [sj] or [zj]. This pronunciation was standard and consequently it is discussed by the grammarians.

---

strike with the surface of the tongue where the upper teeth have their inmost roots.'

[82] 'But *d* and *t*, which, so to speak, are neighboring sounds, are distinguished by the elevation and position of the tongue. For when it strikes at the same time the tips and the base of the teeth with its upper part, it produces the letter *d*. But whenever it is elevated and touches the place where the roots of the upper teeth are, it will produce *t* with the assistance of the following vowel.'

[83] '*D* is formed by applying the tongue about the upper teeth. ... *T* is forced out by pushing the tongue against the teeth.'

[84] So Seelmann 301 f.; Lindsay 82.

Servius 4.445.8–12 K:[85] Iotacismi sunt quotiens post *ti* vel *di* syllabam sequitur vocalis, et plerumque supra dictae syllabae in sibilum transeunt, tunc scilicet quando medium locum tenent, ut *meridies*.   Quando autem primum locum tenent etiam sic positae sicut dicuntur ita etiam sonandae sunt, ut *dies, tiaras*.

Servius, In Georg. 2.126:[86] *Media*: *di* sine sibilo proferenda est; Graecum enim nomen est, et *Media* provincia est.

Papirianus ap. Cassiodorum 7.216.8 f. K:[87] *Iustitia* cum scribitur, tertia syllaba sic sonat quasi constet ex tribus litteris, *t, z*, et *i*, cum habeat duas, *t* et *i*.

196 c. Of the many spellings in Latin inscriptions that illustrate this change, the earliest seems to be *Marsia⟨nenses⟩*, CIL 15.2612 of the third century A.D.[88]   Other examples are *tersio*, CIL 12.2081 (540 A.D.); *Marsias*, 2094 (579 A.D.); *preziosa*, 8.13854; *Aequisia*, 9.4158; *Laurentzio*, 3.12396.   The same stage of development is seen in a Latin loan word in Gothic, *kawtsjo* from *cautiō*.   A later stage shows loss of the *i*, as *Vincentza*, CIL 8.16208; *Terensus*, 9927; *Marsalis*, 9942; *Marsas*, 9751 (442 A.D.); *Crescensa*, 21540.   The change of *ti* to *ts* and of *di* to *dz* led to confusion with *z*, on which see [204].   The effects of this change appear in such Romance forms as It. *giustezza*, Fr. *justesse*, Sp. *justeza* from *iustitia*; It. *piazza*, Fr. *place* from *platea*; It. *orzo*, Fr. *orge*, Rum. *orz* from *hordeum*.

196 d. Since *di* and *ti* before consonants were not affected, we must assume that an intermediate stage was the consonantization of *i* [158]; the chronological stages were [tia], [tja], [tsja], [tsa].   The final stage never got into standard Latin.   On the contrary the influence of classical poetry, which required an extra syllable, led to the pronunciation [tsia] in scholastic Latin.   The German pronunciation of Latin, which was borrowed from France in medieval times, preserves [justitsia] etc., while in the French pronunciation of Latin [ts] has become [s], e.g. [žystisia], cf. Fr. [žystis].

197. Lat. *d* and *t* were dental mutes similar to Fr. *d* and *t* respec-

[85] 'Iotacism occurs whenever a vowel follows *ti* or *di*, and very frequently the above mentioned syllables pass over into a sibilant, that is, when they are medial, as *meridies*. But when they are initial, even in the position before a vowel, they are to be sounded just as they are spelled, as *dies, tiaras*.'

[86] '*Media*: *di* is to be pronounced without a sibilant; for it is a Greek noun, and *Media* is a province.'

[87] 'When we write *iustitia*, the third syllable sounds as if it consisted of the three letters *t, z*, and *i*, although it has two, *t* and *i*.'

[88] *Martses*, CIL 1².2.5.8 f., is dialectic. *Crescentsian⟨us⟩*, 14.246 (140 A.D.) is based upon reports of an inscription now lost. *Vincentzus*, Audollent 253, may belong to the second century, but that is uncertain.

tively. At some time in the third century (or possibly in the second) A.D. medial *di* and *de*, *ti* and *te* before a vowel developed a sibilant [s] or [z] after the mute. Somewhat later the vowel disappeared from the group.

B AND P

198 a. That *b* and *p* were labials appears from the passages cited in [189] and from the following:

Terentius Scaurus 7.14.3 f. K:[89] *B* cum *p* et *m* consentit, quoniam origo earum non sine labore coniuncto ore respondet.

Martianus Capella 3.261:[90] *B* labris per spiritus impetum reclusis edicamus. ... *P* labris spiritus erumpit.

Martianus Capella clearly defines mutes rather than spirants in both cases. As to *p* both scholarly tradition and the Romance languages agree with him, and so do they as to initial *b* also, with the exception of Spanish and a few other dialects.

198 b. Among the cases in which we know that the Romans used an analogical instead of a phonetic spelling are the digraphs *bs* and *bt*, which were regularly pronounced *ps* and *pt*.

Quintilian 1.7.7:[91] Quaeri solet in scribendo praepositiones sonum quem iunctae efficiunt an quem separatae observare conveniat, ut cum dico *obtinuit*; secundam enim *b* litteram ratio poscit, aures magis audiunt *p*.

Terentius Scaurus 7.27.11–17 K:[92] Non carent quaestione etiam *plebs* et *urbs* et *Pelops*, quae Varro ita distinguit ut per *b* et *s* ea nominativo casu putet esse scribenda quae eandem litteram genetivo singulari reddant, ut *plebs plebis*,

---

[89] '*B* harmonizes with *p* and *m*, since their origin corresponds, the mouth being energetically closed.'

[90] 'With the lips forced open by the impulse of the breath, let us utter *b*. ... The breath causes *p* to burst from the lips.'

[91] 'In regard to the writing of prepositions, it is often inquired whether it is proper to observe the sound which they have in composition or when separate, as when I say *obtinuit*; for analogy demands *b* as the second letter, but the ears hear rather *p*.'

[92] '*Plebs*, *urbs*, and *Pelops* are also subject to dispute; Varro distinguishes them in such a way that he thinks that those words should be written with *bs* in the nominative which have the same letter in the genitive singular, as *plebs plebis*, *urbs urbis*, but those with *ps* which in the genitive of the same number end similarly in *pis*, as *Pelops Pelopis*. But to me it seems that both classes should be written with *ps*, since of these consists the letter *ψ*, which, as I have said, becomes either *bis* or *pis* in the genitive.'

urbs urbis, ea vero per *p* et *s* quae similiter genetivo eiusdem numeri in *pis* ex-currant, ut *Pelops Pelopis*. Sed nobis utrumque per *ps* videtur esse scribendum, quoniam ex his ψ littera constet quam genetivo diximus aut in *bis* aut in *pis* exire.

Velius Longus 7.61.5–9 K:[93] De qua scriptione illud quaeritur, utrum per *p* an per *b* et *s* debeat scribi, quoniam ea quae apud nos ψ litteram sonant putant plerique per *p* et *s* scribenda, quoniam et Graeci pronuntiaverunt ψ litteram constare ἐκ τοῦ π καὶ σ. Sed qui originem verborum propriam respiciunt per *b* scribunt.

The orthography *ps, pt* is common in inscriptions and manuscripts.

199. Even in ancient times *b* must have had a spirant pronunciation under some circumstances. Some examples of confusion between *b* and *v*, beginning with the first century A.D., were given in [154]. For further instances, see Parodi, Romania 27.177–96. Late grammarians devoted much attention to orthographic rules for the use of *b* or *v* in particular words. We even have a treatise by one Adamantius or perhaps Martyrius, entitled De *B* Muta et *V* Vocali (7.165–99 K). The Romance languages show that it was between vowels that *b* became a spirant in Vulgar Latin in general. While most of the lan-guages still retain *b* as a mute in other positions, we regularly meet such forms as It. *dovere*, Sardinian *devere*, Fr. *devoir* from *dēbēre*; Rum. *avea*, It. *avere*, Fr. *avoir* from *habēre*.

We must conclude, therefore, that as early as the first century A.D. both *v* and intervocalic *b* had become a bilabial spirant [β] or, less probably, a labio-dental [v], in the popular speech of some places in Italy, notably Pompeii. The usage spread gradually throughout Vulgar Latin.

200. In classical times standard Latin *b* and *p* were bilabial mutes similar to Fr. *b* and *p* respectively. Intervocalic *b* became [β] in Vulgar Latin. The beginnings of the process are as early as the first century A.D. This pronunciation was never recognized by the schools, but the concern of the grammarians with orthographic rules about *b* and *v* suggests that it made great inroads into the speech of the upper classes.

X

201. To establish the traditional pronunciation of *x* as *c* plus *s*, we need only quote the ancient descriptions of the sound.

[93] 'In regard to this writing there is the following question, whether one should write *ps* or *bs*, since many writers think that those Latin words which have the sound of the letter ψ should be written with *ps*, since even the Greeks have declared that ψ consists of π and σ. But those who have regard to the origin of words write with *b*.'

Terentianus 6.332.244–6 K:[94]

    Mixtura secundae (sc. *x*) geminum parat sonorem,

245 quia *c* simul et quae prior est (sc. *s*) iugando nisum

    retrorsus adactam solidant premuntque vocem.[95]

Victorinus 6.34.19 f. K:[96] ⟨*x*⟩ per coniunctionem *c* et *s*, quarum et locum implet et vim exprimit, ut sensu aurium ducemur, efficitur.

Martianus Capella 3.261:[97] *X* quicquid *c* et *s* formavit exsibilat.

Diomedes 1.425.34 f. K:[98] *X* littera composita, quam ideo duplicem dicimus quoniam constat ex *c* et *s* litteris.

201 a. Of the abundant confirmatory evidence we may cite these items. (1) The morphology of the language shows the composite nature of *x* in such words as *rēx, rēxī, dux, dīxī*. (2) Inscriptions often present redundant spellings such as *vicxit* or *vixsit*, and occasionally they have analytic spellings like *vicsit* (CIL 2.551) and *ucsor* (3.597). (3) *X* corresponds with Gk. ξ in loan words ('Ρηξ, *Naxos*).

201 b. The Romance change of *x* to *ss* (It. *lessi* from *lēxī*) or to *s* before or after a consonant appears on late inscriptions and is censured by late grammarians. This pronunciation was sub-standard and the reaction against it led to overcorrections (e.g. *milex* for *miles*).

Z

202. Whether or not the letter *z* was included in the original Latin alphabet, it does not occur in our earliest documents. It was adopted for use in Greek loan words at about the same time as *y* [127] and the more accurate spellings *ch*, *th*, and *ph* for χ, θ, and φ [181 b]. Since it was, of course, Hellenistic Greek that educated Romans of the late second century B.C. and later were familiar with, they must have pronounced such Greek words as *zōna, lachanizō, citharizō* with the sound of Hellenistic ζ, namely [z] [99 d].

202 a. There is no doubt that in the Oscan Tabula Bantina, which is written in Latin letters, *z* stands for the voiced sibilant [z]. It corre-

---

[94] 'A combination produces the double sound of *x*, because *c* and *s* by uniting their functions, check the voice, strengthen it, and compress it.'

[95] I can understand line 246 only as a description of the mute component. I suspect that the required description of the sibilant element has been lost. Or does *premunt* mean 'press out'?

[96] '⟨*x*⟩ is formed by the combination of *c* and *s*, whose place it takes and whose force it represents, as we shall be convinced by hearing.'

[97] '*X* hisses out what *c* and *s* have formed.'

[98] '*X* is a composite letter, which we call double because it consists of *c* and *s*.'

sponds to written *s* between vowels of the native alphabet (*eiseís* =
eizeis, *eísak* = *eizac*, gen. pl. ending -*asúm* = -*azum*), while in other
positions Lat. *s* of this document represents *s* of the native alphabet
(*senateís* = Bantian *senateis*, *estud* = Bantian *estud*, *pís* = Bantian
pis). Therefore *z* must be a sibilant, but not identical with *s*. In
Umbrian and Latin original *s* between vowels has become *r*; evidently
in Oscan the same change had progressed only as far as [z]. If the
Tabula Bantina can be assigned to the latter part of the second century
B.C.,[99] its use of *z* may be based upon Latin models. Otherwise we
must suppose that the Romans and the Bantians borrowed the letter
independently from Hellenistic Greek. In either case the demonstrable
value of Bantian *z* confirms our inference as to the value of Latin *z*.

203. After *di* and *de* before a vowel became [dz] [196 b, c], *z* was sometimes written in their place (*Azabenicus*, CIL 8.10337, 10338, 10362;
Zadumene, 9.4326; *zeta* = *diaeta*, 8.9433, 9910; *z⟨es⟩*, 5.1665; *zebus*,
14.1137; *Zodorus*, 8.9139, 9742, 14.2325; *Ziomedis*, 8.10839; *Dzoni*,
5.6215; *Zonysati*, 5.1647; *Zonisius*, 8.7933; *Kalenzonis*, 8.9114; *oze*,
8.8424 Add.) The reverse confusion appears in *baptidiata* = *baptizata*,
ICUR 805 (459 A.D.). Since Italian still employs *z* in the value [dz]
(*orzo*, *mezzo*), it is scarcely possible that we should read in any other
way the Latin words just cited. Probably the pronunciation [dz] for
Gk. ζ [99 b] survived long enough somewhere (perhaps among some of
the Italian Greeks) to furnish a model for this Latin orthography.

204. We have seen [99 c] that in early Crete ζ was used in the value
of [ts]. This is also the value of *z* in the native Oscan and Umbrian
alphabets; quite possibly the source of this is to be sought in some
Italian Greek dialect that used ζ = [ts]; but it may be a modification of
the more common value of ζ = [dz]. Papirianus (quoted in [196 b])
indicates the sound of the third syllable of *iūstitia* by the letters *t*, *z*,
and *i*; the only plausible reason for his writing *z* instead of *s* here would
be that he knew the spelling *iustizia*. At any rate Italian still employs *z*
in the value [ts] in such words as *grazie*. In all probability the letter
has been so used in Italy at least since the beginnings of Oscan and
Umbrian writing. Cf. [196 c].

205. The normal value of Lat. *z* at all periods after its first introduction was approximately that of Eng. *z* in *zone* or Fr. *z*, namely [z].
In certain relatively unusual spellings of imperial times it stood for
[dz] or [ts].

---

[99] Conway, The Italic Dialects 1.23; Buck, Gramm. 235.

CHAPTER VII

THE LATIN ACCENT

206. Although the character of the Latin accent has long been a highly controversial question,[1] that is not due to any lack of evidence. The difficulty has been rather that a large amount of evidence indicates that the accent was stress, while the Romans themselves say that it was pitch. Scholars have usually assumed, quite mistakenly, that both could not be true of one and the same system of accentuation.[2]

207 a. The Latin vowel system is characterized by a considerable amount of loss of short vowels. In some instances this is immediately apparent from the existence in the language of the longer and the shorter forms side by side (*calidus* : *caldus*, *balineae* : *balneae*, *porrigō* : *porgō*). More often a comparison of related forms shows what has happened (*avis* : *auceps*, *iuvenis* : *iūnior*, *opifex* : *officīna*, *animālia* : *animal*, *rege* : *dūc*, *cecidī* : *reccidī*).[3] The loss occurred in original final syllables (*dīce* > *dīc*, **agros* > **agrs* > *ager*, **mentis* > *mēns*); in penultimate syllables (*īnfrā* beside *īnferus*, *valdē* beside *validus*, *raucus* beside *ravis*); in antepenultimate syllables (**ūnodecem* > *undecim*, **sēmicaput* > *sinciput*, **repeperī* > *repperī*); and in monosyllabic enclitics (*neque* > *nec*). The only clear limitation upon the process is that it never appears in initial syllables of full words. This is true whether we make the assumption suggested in [209 a] or not.

Such loss of vowels is known to occur in the unaccented syllables in languages that have a strong stress accent, and it is not known to occur under any other circumstances. Until an authentic parallel in a language without strong stress can be cited, we must conclude that in the

---

[1] Abbott, CP 2.444 f.; Leumann, 183-9.

[2] Of course such an assumption has usually not been put into words; in fact the coexistence of stress and pitch has been taken for granted by some of the very scholars who have held that the Latin accent must be predominantly one or the other.

I first published my contention that both kinds of evidence must be accepted in TAPA 42.45-52.

[3] For details, see A. Götze, IF 41.78-149; Niedermann 47-53.

prehistoric period, when most of the syncope took place, Latin had a relatively strong stress on the initial syllable.[4]

207 b. The short vowels which escaped syncope, and which did not stand in an initial syllable, were subjected to very extensive alterations, commonly called "weakening", in the preliterary period. It will be enough for our present purpose to illustrate this process. Thus *a* before two consonants became *e* (*praefectus, artifex, biennis*); *a* before a single consonant except *r* became *i* (*praeficiō, artificis, cecidī*) or *u* (*occupō, contubernalis*); *o* before two consonants and in final syllables became *u* (*onus, onustus* from **onos, euntis* : ἰόντος); *o* before single consonants, except *r*, became *i* (*novitās* from *novo-tās) or *u* (*dēnuō* from *dē novōd).[5] Again we have a clear indication of stress on initial syllables in prehistoric Latin.

207 c. The prehistoric initial stress that we are thus compelled to assume was inherited from Primitive Italic. Oscan and Umbrian display even more syncope than Latin, and here again it affects all syllables except the first.[6] While a considerable part of the losses must be independent, since they differ in the several languages, it is likely that the process began in Primitive Italic. At any rate the initial stress of all the descendent languages at the beginning implies initial stress in the parent language also. It is therefore not surprising that the earliest Greek loan words in Latin show syncope or vowel weakening (*balneum, balineum* from βαλανεῖον; *Tarentum* from (acc.) Τάραντα; *Hecuba* from Ἑκάβη).

On the other hand these two groups of phenomena were less extensive in the time of the earliest Latin inscriptions than they are in the literature. In fact the weakening of *o* to *u* in final syllables seems to have occurred late in the third century B.C., and if, as seems probable, the change of *o* to *u* in medial syllables before two consonants was a part of the same process, we have evidence that the initial stress prevailed almost to the time of Plautus; for the latter change often affected penultimate syllables (*onustus, leguntur*).

---

[4] The claim that it was not stress but some other kind of "netteté" of the initial syllable that caused early Latin syncope, would not deserve mention if it had not been held by such distinguished scholars as L. Havet and A. Meillet. When a serious attempt is made to define this mysterious "netteté", the phraseology, as far as it can be understood at all, is such as might be applied to stress (e.g. Juret, Manuel de phonétique latine 249).

[5] For more illustrations and for details of the changes, see Niedermann 28–42.

[6] Buck, Gramm. 57–61.

208. The prehistoric initial stress was succeeded by an accent falling normally on penult or antepenult. We must determine separately for three different periods, the time of Plautus and Terence [209], the period of the classical and postclassical literature until about 300 A.D. [210], and the period after about 300 A.D. [211], whether or not this historical accent included an important element of stress. We are not primarily concerned with changes in the position of the accent, although several such can be pointed out, and although we may be sure that, if we had full evidence, it would appear that there was no sharp break between the prehistoric and the historic system. Some important work upon the position of the accent in specific Plautine words and phrases has recently been done[7] and more remains to be done; but this matter falls outside the scope of our inquiry, except as far as it affects the data upon which our argument rests.

209 a. We have seen [207 a, b] that syncope is largely due to the prehistoric initial stress. Nevertheless there are some instances that are probably to be ascribed to the historical accent on penult or antepenult. The mere fact that a syncopated form appears late in our records while the original longer form is citable from early Latin authors is not evidence of late syncope; the coexistence of syncopated and unsyncopated forms side by side is demonstrable in some words (*caldus* : *calidus*; *balneae* : *balineae*) and probable in a great many others.

In case a vowel shortened by the iambic law [209 c] is lost by syncope we must assume that it is due to the historical accent. Probable instances of this kind are *calfacere* and *olfacere*, since they are probably parallel formations to *pūtē-facere*, *per-frīgē-facere*, etc. Similar is *maldīxit* (CIL 4.2445).

If we make the phonetically plausible assumption that syncope was confined to the syllable immediately following the accent, the historical accent must be responsible for such forms as *audā́cter* from *audā́citer*, *sinístra* from *sinístera*, *nostrā́s* from *nostrā́tis*, *Arpīnā́s* from *Arpīnā́tis*, *illī́c* from *illī́ce*, *posthā́c* from *posthā́ce*, *tantṓn* from *tantṓne*, *fūmā́t* from *fūmā́vit*. The grammarians prescribe accent on the ultima for all the forms in this list that have suffered syncope of the original ultimate vowel, and that is strong additional evidence that the penult was accented at the time when the syncope took place.

[7] Eduard Fraenkel, Iktus und Akzent im lateinischen Sprechvers, Berlin, 1928; H. Drexler, Glotta 13.42–64, and Plautinische Akzentstudien, 3 vols., Breslau, 1932–3. Cf. Sturtevant, AJP 50.95–9; W Kroll, Glotta 19.271–6; M. Leumann, Glotta 23.128–31.

Some of these syncopated forms occur in Plautus and all of them may have originated as early as that. They furnish evidence for early Latin accentuation rather than for the accent of the classical period.

209 b. Early Germanic and Celtic verse is characterized by extensive alliteration, whereas Greek and the earliest Indic verse makes scarcely any use of that device. It is probable that this difference is connected with the fact that the early Germanic and Celtic languages had initial stress, while Greek and Sanskrit did not.

Early Latin verse goes in this respect with Germanic and Celtic verse; cf. Ennius Ann. 109 V:

O Tite tute Tati tibi tanta tyranne tulisti.

It is perhaps open to question whether this feature of early Latin was a survival from the time of the prehistoric initial stress or whether it was still favored by the accent of Ennius' own time. Not all of the words in the above line had initial accent when this was composed, and the alliteration is quite independent of the verse structure.

209 c. The iambic shortening of numerous long syllables in Plautus and Terence is proof of a strong stress accent at that time. The facts may be summarized briefly as follows: an iambic sequence of syllables tended to become pyrrhic if the accent rested upon the short syllable or upon the syllable following the iambus. Hence arose such forms as *egŏ* beside *egō* (Gk. ἐγώ), *mihĭ* beside *mihī*, *modŏ* 'only' beside abl. *modō*, *avĕ*, *valĕ*, *cavĕ* (but *monē*, etc.), *benĕ*, *malĕ* (but *rēctē*, etc.).[8] That

---

[8] For a convenient account of the iambic law, see Lindsay, The Captivi of Plautus, 30–40. Sommer 128, Kritische Erläuterungen 40, holds that the shortening cannot be "die primäre lautphysiologische *ratio* des Processes," because a syllable long by position could never be short in pronunciation. A sufficient answer is that such words as *velint*, *adest*, *senex* are frequently scanned as pyrrhics, and nothing is more certain than that Plautus and Terence were here following actual pronunciation. Such syllables are often shortened by the stress accent of modern English. In Tennyson's

Kíssing his vóws upón it líke a kníght,

the syllable *his* is short.

[I have learned from experience that many excellent scholars are puzzled by the citation of English verse as evidence for quantity. I can say here merely that, in my opinion, rhythm without quantity is impossible; unless approximately the quantitative relations here indicated are observed, this line of Tennyson ceases to be verse.]

iambic shortening was due to the historic rather than the prehistoric accent is shown by the fact that such words as *amīcus* never shorten their penult while such forms as *amĭcitia* are in order.[9] In fact shortening of an initial syllable is not infrequent; e.g. *tibi ĕvénit* (Merc. 774), *béne ĕvēnisse* (Poen. 1078), *quíd ăbstulistī* (Aul. 645), *tibi ŏbtémperem* (Most. 896), *age ăbdúce* (Stich. 418).[10]

209 d. Many scholars have held that the Roman dramatists constructed their verses, especially those in dialogue meters, so as to make the metrical ictus[11] coincide, as far as possible, with the accent of ordinary speech. In particular it has been observed that such ictuses as *genéra, pectóra, cōnsilía, ingentíbus* are very rarely demanded by the senarii and septenarii of Plautus and Terence. The few exceptions are in such words as *hicíne, hoccíne, sīcíne,* which probably had accented penult in everyday usage, and in phrases which seem to have required or at least permitted such an accentuation (e.g. *nescío quis* [209 f]). No one has satisfactorily explained the avoidance of ictuses on short penults of polysyllables except on the ground that such a syllable bore the weakest stress of the word.

209 e. The prevailing harmony of ictus and accent in the dramatists has by some scholars, however, been ascribed to the undoubted fact that the laws governing the position of the Latin accent tend to make it coincide with the ictus of iambic and trochaic verse. I have tried to determine statistically whether this feature of the language can account for the observed harmony.[12] I first measured the tendency of the structure of the language and of the verse to produce harmony by recording the incidence of the ictus upon all possible combinations of syllables in a number of verses. For example, in about 530 lines of Plautus and Terence the syllable groups of the rhythm —◡ occur 1894 times with ictus on the ultima, 2468 times with the ictus on the penult. Therefore the structure of dramatic verse tends to produce

[9] I have argued, CP 14.243, that such shortenings are to be recognized more frequently than the editors usually do.

[10] It has been thought necessary to admit that iambic shortening often affected also syllables accented by the historic system, but it is now clear that the short second syllables of *volŭptás mea, eŏdém diē,* and similar phrases were not accented. See Sturtevant, AJP 50.97, and reference.

[11] From the demonstration [209 d–210 e] that the Romans tried to place the ictus on accented syllables it follows that both accent and ictus involved stress; for there is no other feature that they can have had in common. See also Sturtevant, AJP 44.319–38.

[12] Sturtevant, CP 14.234–44.

harmony of ictus and accent in Latin words of this type 56.6 per cent of the time. In actual practice, however, words of the rhythmic type —‿ have ictus on the penult in 84.5 per cent of all occurrences. Table 1 presents the comparison for the six commonest rhythmic types.

TABLE 1[12a]

	‿◡̆	‿̄◡̆	◡̆◡̆‿	‿̄◡̆◡̆	◡̆‿̄◡̆	—‿̄◡̆
syllable groups	29%	57%	48.5%	74%	70%	53.5%
words	38.5	84.5	80.9	98.3	90.5	63.8
difference	9.5	27.5	32.4	24.3	20.5	10.3

The first line of Table 1 measures the tendency of the verse structure to place the ictus upon an accented syllable. Our arbitrarily isolated syllable groups are not words, and so the poets did not pay any attention to them, but still, if they had been words, there would have been harmony of accent and ictus in the proportions indicated by the first line of the table. The second line of the table measures the poets' treatment of actual words. The third line shows the improvement of harmony which the poets were able to make over the tendency of the verse.

The rarer words of four and five syllables show similar results, with some exceptions that can easily be explained. It is clear that the poets attained far more harmony of ictus and accent than would have resulted from the structure of the verse and the position of the word accent.

209 f. But some may ask how they could have been content with the 72 per cent of harmony that a rough calculation seems to indicate,[12b] if lack of harmony really involved stressing Latin words on the wrong syllable. The answer is in part that the rules given us for the accentuation of Latin words apply primarily to words in isolation; in connected discourse the accentuation was somewhat different. Everyone knows

---

[12a] In CP 14.238 I published separate percentages for Plautus and Terence; Table 1 gives in each case the average of the two. The results are slightly inaccurate, since the statistics upon which the original percentages were based are not precisely comparable, but those statistics are no longer available, and consequently no other way of simplifying the table is possible, short of counting all over again. The amount of inaccuracy involved is illustrated by the one case where the original figures have been preserved; the 56.6 cited four lines above results from actual calculation, while the 57 percent in the first line of the table is the mean between the 58 percent for Plautus and the 56 percent for Terence reported in CP 14.238. The figures in Table 1 are essentially correct.

[12b] This calculation is based upon the figures published in CP 14.236 and 238.

of the shift of accent when an enclitic was appended to a word (*virúmque, mulierísque*); and it is well recognized that there was much more of this sort of thing, at least in Plautus and Terence, than our ancient authorities have recorded. Plautus regularly places certain common phrases in such a way that we can infer their ordinary accentuation—usually an accentuation that would result from applying the three-syllable law to the phrases as a whole (e.g. *voluptás mea, patér mi, volŏ scíre, apúd me, vaé miseró mihi, quí lubet, nescío quis, operám dās*). It is even held, with some show of reason,[13] that ictuses such as *in meâ nāvĭ, tuós servos, novám nŭptam, méus patér* represent the normal accentuation.

Without going as far as that, we may at least be sure that there was much more harmony of ictus and accent than the statistics summarized in [209 e] indicate. What those figures show is (1) that there was abundant foundation in usage for the mechanical rules of word accent even as early as Plautus and Terence, and (2) that the poets tried to place the verse ictus on the accented syllables.

209 g. Equally cogent evidence for stress accent is furnished by Ennius' treatment of the hexameter, but, for convenience, we postpone the discussion of this to [210 a, b].

210. As far as I can see the only compelling evidence for stress accent in Latin of the period from 150 B.C. to about 300 A.D. is furnished by the tendency to identify the accent with the metrical ictus.[14] This evidence, however, leaves no room for reasonable doubt.

210 a. To compose dactylic hexameters in Latin with a high percentage of harmony between accent and ictus was quite impossible on account of the fact that about 20 per cent of the words in passages of Latin prose selected at random are words which can be got into a hexameter line only with the ictus on an unaccented syllable (*amant, animōs, ingenium*, etc.). To make matters worse, monosyllables, which would have facilitated getting the accents into the desired places, were disfavored in serious poetry.[15] Under these circumstances the Romans seem to have made no serious effort to secure harmony in the hexameter as a whole. They observed, however, that the structure of the last two feet favored harmony if a few simple precautions were taken, namely (1) to avoid final monosyllables, which normally put the sixth ictus on an ultima, (2) to relegate to the early part of the verse words in which harmony is impossible, and (3) to substitute for them

---

[13] See the literature cited in [208 fn. 7].
[14] As to syncope, see [209 a].
[15] Sturtevant, The Classical Weekly 15.73–6.

words requiring harmony. It has long been known that the poets, particularly after Ennius, did the first of these three things, and I have shown[16] that they did the other two also. The result was that Ennius secured harmony of accent and ictus in 92.8 per cent of the words in the fifth and sixth feet.[17]

210 b. Ennius, to be sure, was a contemporary of Plautus, and his efforts to secure harmony of accent and ictus in the last two feet of the hexameter are evidence for the stress accent of the early period. I have shown,[17] however, that the later poets improved upon Ennius' technique in no uncertain way. Table 2, based upon a study of selected passages from thirteen poets, shows the proportion of all words in the fifth and sixth feet that show harmony.[18]

TABLE 2

Ennius	92.8	Ovid	99.6
Lucilius	95.9	Lucan	99.6
Catullus	98.6	Persius	98.1
Lucretius	97.7	Juvenal	97.7
Cicero	98.6	Statius	99.7
Vergil	99.5	Silius	99.7
Horace	95		

In view of the demonstration [210 a] that even Ennius deliberately sought harmony in these feet, it clearly involved considerable manipulation to make so large an increase over his proportion of harmony as is shown by Vergil and all his successors except the satirists (who were evidently influenced by Lucilius and Horace). The inevitable conclusion is that it was still very desirable to put accented syllables under the ictus in the last two feet of the hexameter.

210 c. Important confirmation comes from the fact that Catullus tried with considerable success to secure harmony in the fourth foot also;[19] he increases Ennius' 39 per cent to 67 per cent. Similarly Ovid tried to improve the smoothness of the first part of the line by increasing the proportion of harmony in the first foot from Ennius' 67.8 per cent to 80.7 per cent. Such large statistical differences cannot be dismissed as fortuitous.

[16] Sturtevant, CP 14.373–85, especially 378.

[17] Sturtevant, TAPA 54.51–73, especially 55–7.

[18] Objection has been made to my statistics on the ground that I assumed accentuation of Greek loan words by the Latin rule. I am still inclined to think that my procedure was sound, but in any case the changes involved would be slight and would affect all the poets in about the same degree.

[19] Sturtevant, TAPA 54.58 f., 67.

210 d. The second verse of the elegiac couplet[20] presented an even more difficult problem; all words that exclude harmony in the hexameter do so here, and besides the third and sixth ictuses must fall on final syllables. Apparently Catullus, the earliest author who has left us such verses, did not try to do anything about it. Propertius, however, noticed that the considerable proportion of harmony that naturally occurred under the fourth and fifth ictuses could be greatly increased. Table 3, based upon selected passages from seven poets, shows the proportion of all words in the fourth and fifth feet that have harmony.

TABLE 3

Catullus	37.9	Ovid	99.2
Propertius	87.1	Consolatio ad Liviam	99.2
Tibullus	90.5	Martial	88
Lygdamus	93.1		

The changes from Catullus' practice are even more impressive than those from Ennius' practice in the hexameter, as given in Table 2. There can be no doubt that the poets were trying to secure an effect that seemed to them important.[21]

210 e. A sharp contrast has often been drawn between the versification of the extant literature and the popular verses of which we have some few examples, quoted by the authors or preserved in inscriptions. A thoroughgoing study of these is needed to determine just how far they depart from standard versification, and how much attention they pay to accent. We must content ourselves with citing three verses which Aulus Gellius 15.4 enables us to assign to 43 B.C.

> Concurrite omnes, augures, haruspices.
> Portentum inusitatem conflatumst recens:
> nam mulas qui fricabat consul factus est.

Here we have nearly perfect harmony of accent and ictus.

210 f. In discussing the position of the accent the Romans frequently

---

[20] Sturtevant, TAPA 55.73–89, especially 76.

[21] Other kinds of Latin verse need to be studied from this point of view. It may be predicted with some confidence that Horace's boast (Carm. 3.30.10–14) that he was the first to "compose Aeolic verse according to Italic measures" will be found to refer to some accommodation of ictus and accent. Certain it is that Horace introduced some changes into the Sapphics which produce a perfectly regular succession of accents, and that his successors adopted the innovations without exception. See now Sturtevant, TAPA 70.

cite verses in which the ictus rests upon the syllable that is stated to be accented.

Varro 218.8–10 GS:[22] Mutant accentus adiunctis vocibus *-que*, *-ve*, *-ne* ..., ut *Latiúmque augescere vultis* et *stimulóve meum cor* apud Accium in Pelopidis.

Gellius 7.7.2 f:[23] Is ⟨i.e. Annianus poeta⟩ *affatim* ut *admodum* prima acuta, non media, pronuntiabat atque ita veteres locutos censebat. Itaque se audiente Probum grammaticum hos versus Plauti Cistellaria legisse dicit:
    pótine tú homo fácimus fácere strénuum—áliorum áffatim est ...

Gellius goes on to cite Terence, Phorm. 88, as evidence for the accentuation *éxadversum* and Caecilius, Triumphus frag. 228 R, as evidence for *ádprobus*.

Furthermore Quintilian actually tells us that the meter can change the accent of a word!

1.5.28:[24] Evenit ut metri quoque condicio mutet accentum, ut *pecudes pictaeque volucres*; nam *volucres* media acuta legam ...

These and similar passages have a meaning only on the assumption that the position of the ictus may be evidence for the position of the accent. And this amounts almost to a statement on the part of our authors that accent is stress.

211 a. For the period after 300 A.D. we have contemporary evidence for identifying accent and stress. It will suffice to quote one passage.

Servius 4.426.16–20 K:[25] Accentus in ea syllaba est quae plus sonat. Quam rem deprehendimus si fingamus nos aliquem longe positum clamare. Invenimus enim naturali ratione illam syllabam plus sonare quae retinet accentum, atque usque eodem nisum vocis adscendere.

---

[22] 'Accents change when the words *-que*, *-ve*, and *-ne* are added ... , as *Latiúmque augescere vultis* (Ennius Ann. 466 V) and *stimulóve meum cor* in Accius' Pelopidae (512 R).'

[23] 'Annianus pronounced *affatim* like *admodum* with the first syllable acute, not the middle, and he thought the ancients spoke thus. And he says that in his hearing the grammarian Probus read these verses (231 f.) in the Cistellaria of Plautus as follows:
    pótine tú homo fácinus fácere strénuum?—áliorum áffatim est ...'

[24] 'It happens also that the demands of the meter change the accent, as *pecudes pictaeque volucres* (Vergil, Aen. 4.525); for I shall read *volucres* with the middle syllable acute. . .'

[25] 'The accent is on that syllable which has more sound. This we discover if we imagine that we are calling to someone at a distance. For we find that the syllable that has the accent naturally has more sound, and that the energy of the voice increases up to the same point.'

The striking thing about this and the similar passages in late grammarians is the contrast to the earlier descriptions of accent, some of which are quoted below [212].

211 b. There seems to have been a fresh wave of syncope in late Vulgar Latin (It. *città*, Fr. *cité*, Sp. *ciudad* from *cīvitās*; Sardinian *iša*, Fr. *île*, Prov. *iscla*, Catalan *illa* from *īnsula*).

These two items might plausibly be interpreted to mean that there was an increase in the stress of accented syllables in late Latin, and that may very well have been the case. It cannot be said, however, that the evidence proves more than that the stress of earlier Latin was maintained.

211 c. The accent has continued generally in the same place from our earliest documents to the present day, although the ancient rules of accent do not apply at all to any Romance language. Since the accent everywhere involves more or less stress at present, this is evidence for the continuance of stress through the late Latin period.

212. Until about 300 A.D. all of the numerous descriptions of Latin accent that we possess use terms that apply primarily to musical pitch. It will be enough to quote three of the earlier passages.

Gellius 13.26.1–3:[26] P. Nigidi verba sunt ex Commentariorum Grammaticorum vicesimo quarto, hominis in disciplinis doctrinarum omnium praecellentis: "Deinde," inquit, "voculatio qui poterit servari si non sciemus in nominibus, ut *Valeri*, utrum interrogandi sint an vocandi? Nam interrogandi secunda syllaba superiore tonost quam prima, deinde novissima deicitur; at in casu vocandi summo tonost prima, deinde gradatim descendunt." Sic quidem Nigidius dici praecipit. Sed si quis nunc Valerium appellans in casu vocandi secundum id praeceptum Nigidi acuerit primam, non aberit quin rideatur. *Summum* autem *tonum* προσῳδίαν acutam dicit, et, quem *accentum* nos dicimus, *voculationem* appellat, et *casum interrogandi* eum dicit quem nos *genetivum* dicimus.

---

[26] 'Here is a quotation from the twenty-fourth book of the Commentarii Grammatici of Nigidius Figulus, who excels in the learning of all sciences. He says: "How can modulation be preserved if we do not know in regard to such nouns as *Valeri* whether they are in the case of interrogation or in the case of calling? For the second syllable of the case of interrogation is of higher tone than the first, and the last falls; but in the case of calling the first syllable is of highest tone, and then they gradually fall." So Nigidius directs one to speak. But if anyone nowadays in calling Valerius should put the acute on the first syllable in the vocative case according to the precept of Nigidius, he would not fail to be laughed at. Furthermore, he calls acute accent highest tone, and what we call accent he calls modulation, and what we call the genitive case he calls the case of interrogation.'

Cicero, Or. 56–8:[27] Volet igitur ille qui eloquentiae principatum petet et contenta voce atrociter dicere et summissa leniter et inclinata videri gravis et inflexa miserabilis; mira est enim quaedam natura vocis, cuius quidem e tribus omnino sonis, inflexo, acuto, gravi, tanta sit et tam suavis varietas perfecta in cantibus. Est autem etiam in dicendo quidam cantus obscurior, non hic e Phrygia et Caria rhetorum epilogus paene canticum, sed ille quem significat Demosthenes et Aeschines, cum alter alteri obicit vocis flexiones. . . . In quo illud etiam notandum mihi videtur ad studium persequendae suavitatis in vocibus; ipsa enim natura, quasi modularetur hominum orationem, in omni verbo posuit acutam vocem nec una plus nec a postrema syllaba citra tertiam; quo magis naturam ducem ad aurium voluptatem sequatur industria.

Varro ap. Ps.-Sergium 4.525.24–526.1 = 210.10–16 GS:[28] Scire oportet vocem sicut omne corpus tris habere distantias, altitudinem, crassitudinem, longitudinem. . . . Ab altitudine discernit accentus, cum pars verbi aut in grave deprimitur aut sublimatur in acutum.

213. As already stated [206], the existence of evidence for both stress [207–11] and pitch [212] in the Latin accent need occasion no difficulty. Nevertheless we must notice briefly an attempt to explain away the difficulty that some have assumed.

Abbott[29] maintained that, while the accent was chiefly stress in early and late Latin and in Vulgar Latin of all periods, nevertheless during the classical period the upper classes spoke with a pitch accent borrowed from Greek. Aside from harmonizing the supposedly inconsistent evidence for both pitch and stress, this doctrine was recommended as accounting for the retention of long unaccented vowels in classical Latin and for the frequent clash of accent and ictus in classical verse.

[27] 'Therefore a candidate for honors in oratory will desire to speak threatening words in a tense voice, and gentle words in an even tone, to be impressive with a low tone, and to arouse pity with a wavering tone; for wondrous is the power of the voice, since from its three sounds, circumflex, acute, and grave, such charming variety has been perfected in song. And in speech too there is a less obvious melody, not this final paragraph of the teachers of oratory from Phrygia and Caria, which is almost a song, but that to which Demosthenes and Aeschines refer when they reproach each other with modulation of tone. . . . On this point, in our desire to attain an agreeable voice, I think we should observe that Nature herself, as if she were setting men's speech to music, has put an acute accent in every word, and not more than one, and not farther from the last syllable than the antepenult; wherefore our effort should all the more follow Nature as its guide toward what is pleasant to the ears.'

[28] 'One should understand that the voice, like every body, has three dimensions, height, thickness, and length. . . . The distinction in height is caused by accent, when a part of a word is lowered to the grave or elevated to the acute.'

[29] CP 2.444–60. Cf. Kent, TAPA 51.19–29.

The answer to the latter of these supplementary arguments has been provided [209 d–210 d].[30]   As to the first it is only necessary to point out that while a stress accent does frequently lead to shortening of long accented vowels, it does not necessarily do so.   In fact, the vowel quantities are in general the same in Plautus, Terence, and Ennius as in the classical authors, and yet, according to Abbott's theory, the early Latin accent was chiefly stress.

It is quite possible, as Buck[31] suggests, that familiarity with Greek did induce educated Romans to emphasize the pitch element in their Latin accent.   That would help to explain why the authors before 300 A.D. have nothing to say about stress; but their silence on this point scarcely needs explanation.   Their Greek teachers described accent as pitch, and the description was evidently true of Latin accent; it is not strange that a plus in the Latin accent remained unnoticed.

214. The evidence compels us to conclude that in the period of the classical and postclassical literature the Latin accent involved both stress and high pitch upon the same syllables.   For stress we have abundant evidence also for both the preclassical and the latest periods; but we learn directly of the Latin pitch only for the period from about 100 B.C. to about 300 A.D.   It is probable, however, that it existed both earlier and later.   In fact, it is not unlikely that the considerable element of pitch in the modern Italian accent is a direct inheritance from Latin.

---

[30] Perhaps it is worth while to add that even if Abbott's theory were acceptable as an explanation of clash in Vergil, we should be more than ever puzzled by the existence of clash in Ennius.

[31] Comparative Grammar of Greek and Latin 167.

INDEX OF ANCIENT AUTHORS

PASSAGES QUOTED OR DISCUSSED

References are to paragraphs

190

ADDENDA

126 d. Most editors of Quintilian print a comma instead of a period at the close of the passage cited, but E. Adelaide Hahn will presently publish in Language a demonstration that a full pause must be assumed.

178 b. That *gm* was not pronounced [ŋm] is indicated by the unchanged *e* of such words as *segmen, segmentum, tegmen.*